Victorian Heroines

Victorian Heroines
Representations of Femininity in Nineteenth-century Literature and Art

Kimberley Reynolds
and
Nicola Humble

🏃 **HARVESTER
WHEATSHEAF**

New York   London   Toronto   Sydney   Tokyo   Singapore

First published 1993 by
Harvester Wheatsheaf,
Campus 400, Maylands Avenue,
Hemel Hempstead,
Hertfordshire, HP2 7EZ
A division of
Simon & Schuster International Group

Typeset in 10/12pt Bembo
by Keyboard Services, Luton

Printed and bound in Great Britain by
BPCC Wheatons Ltd, Exeter

British Library Cataloguing in Publication Data

A catalogue record for this book is available from
the British Library

ISBN 0 7108 1301 5
ISBN 0 7108 1302 3 (pbk)

1 2 3 4 5   97 96 95 94 93

For Peter, Polly and Joshua

K.R.

For my parents Patricia and Brian, and my
sisters Julia and Rachel

N.H.

Contents

List of illustrations

Acknowledgements

This book was largely conceived several years ago when I was a graduate student at the University of Sussex. I owe thanks to the many people there who helped and encouraged me at that time, especially Cora Kaplan, Geoff Hempstead, and the library staff. As always, Paul Yates read the work as it developed and gave me advice, encouragement and ideas. Since my final days at Sussex, a number of friends and colleagues have contributed to its development, not least those with whom I worked during a brief but arduous spell at what was then Ealing College of Higher Education. It was they who 'directed' my interests towards autobiography. Subsequently colleagues at the Roehampton Institute have been stimulating and helpful. I would particularly like to thank Cathy Wells-Cole for reading the manuscript, and Sarah Turvey and Ann Brook for knowing when I needed time. Special thanks are due to Nicki Humble, a tireless, sensitive, and cheerful friend, collaborator and colleague. Without her contributions this book would have been much longer in the writing and undoubtedly less fun. For her kind and unflappable support, many thanks. My editor, Jackie Jones, is perhaps the person who has waited longest and most patiently for this manuscript to be completed. As always, her tolerance and editorial acumen have been invaluable. Finally, my family have lived with my bad temper and obsession with Victorian heroines for a long time and have all contributed in different ways to this book. My husband, Peter Reynolds, has made it possible for me to work, think and write. More importantly, he knows when it's time to stop.

K.R.

I would like to thank Kim Reynolds for inviting me to share the writing of this book with her, and for her patience, generosity and sense of fun, which have made the collaboration such a rewarding experience. Most of my share of the book was written during the period of my tutorship at the

University of Exeter, where I was greatly helped by the support and interest of my colleagues. I would particularly like to thank Karen Edwards, Inga Bryden and Jo McDonagh, whose practical and emotional assistance in the final difficult stages made all the difference. Several friends and colleagues read and commented on parts of the book, providing stimulating and productive insights: Cathy Wells-Cole, James Davidson and Sarah Turvey were especially generous with their time and attention. The staff of the Bodleian Library, of the University of Exeter Library, and of Project Pallas at Exeter were generous with their time and expertise. Finally, I am very grateful to my family for their sympathy and support, now as always.

N.H.

We would both like to thank Gill Frith for her detailed, imaginative, and constructive comments on the manuscript.

The authors and publisher gratefully acknowledge the following for permission to reproduce the works of art in this book:

Russell-Cotes Art Gallery and Museum (Bournemouth) for *Midsummer* by Albert Moore; The Mass Gallery, London/Bridgeman Art Library, London for *Flaming June* by Frederick Lord Leighton (plate and cover illustration); The Royal Collection (Windsor Castle) for *Cyrus Liberating the Family of Astyses* by Benjamin West; *Thetis* and *Paolo and Francesca* by G. F. Watts reproduced by permission of the Trustees of the Watts Gallery; J. S. Maas and Co. for *Venus Disrobing* by Frederick Lord Leighton; The National Gallery of Canada (Ottawa) for *Acatea, Nymph of the Shore* by Frederick Lord Leighton; Owen Edgar Gallery (London) for *Playthings* by Ernest Normand; Manchester City Art Gallery for *Hylas and the Nymphs* by J. W. Waterhouse, and the Board of Trustees of the National Museums and Galleries of Merseyside (The Lady Lever Gallery, Port Sunlight) for *In the Tepidarium* by Sir Lawrence Alma-Tadema.

Introduction: All dipt in angel instincts

Victorian heroines and the feminine ideal, or, ideal no more

> No angel, but a dearer being, all dipt
> In angel instincts, breathing Paradise,
> Interpreter between gods and men,
> Who look'd all native to her place, and yet
> On tiptoe seem'd to touch upon a sphere
> Too gross to tread, and all male minds perforce
> Sway'd to her from their orbits as they moved,
> And girdled her with music.
>
> (*The Princess* (1847–50), pt VII, 11. 301–12)

> We seem to have arrived at this point – that the most interesting class of womanhood is woman at her lowest degradation . . . and painters, preachers, and sentimentalists have kept the excitement at fever pitch.
>
> (*The Saturday Review*, 1860)[1]

Angel or fallen woman? – these quotations represent the tendency to think about Victorian images of women in terms of pairs of opposites. This practice, which began in the Victorian period, has been well documented and repeatedly explored over recent decades; especially by feminist critics.[2] This divided thinking characterised the Victorians' public discourses about female sexuality, and continues to dominate our own understanding of the relationship between women and sex in the nineteenth century. Indeed, the sense of being torn between two incompatible positions typifies much twentieth-century feminist criticism: although often uneasy about Victorian images of women, women continue to be influenced by and attracted to them. Stimulated in particular by the work of Michel Foucault, feminists have made many fruitful readings of a wide range of Victorian images which explore the relationship between femininity and sexuality. Time and again the contradictory nature of this relationship has been brought to the fore. The complexity and prolificacy of the discourses surrounding female sexuality amply support Foucault's thesis that traditional images of Victorian Britain as refusing to acknowledge sexuality have been mistaken. However, almost without exception, interest has none the less been focused on the repressive nature of Victorian attitudes to female sexuality. Feminists are frequently worried about the male-dominated conditions in which Victorian representations of womanhood were generated, disseminated, and received, and accordingly may feel compelled to read 'against the grain' in order to expose male fear and hostility toward women.[3] Such readings would recognise the ambivalence towards women contained in both of the extracts above. For instance, the mother described in Tennyson's poem is celebrated through a lexis which simultaneously elevates her (she is on tiptoe, breathing Paradise), debases her (she is no angel) and constrains her (she is protected, but also controlled by the musical girdle).

Thought provoking and diverse as feminist readings of Victorian representations of femininity have been, they inevitably focus on the dichotomy represented by these quotations. It is assumed that public rhetoric surrounding attitudes to femininity represents private experience: Victorian woman is either the sexually passive and angelic wife, sister, and/or mother, or she is the sexually charged and demonic mad-woman-in-the-attic. The Victorian temper is described as 'unyieldingly dualistic', capable only of understanding sexuality in terms of polarities.[4] Thus Bram Dijkstra's study of *fin-de-siècle* images of women thinks always of pairs of opposites, with public opinion swinging from one extreme to the other:

> It was inevitable that the unyieldingly dualistic requirement of the mid-century – which held that woman must be incessantly all-giving, and that she must be the embodiment of altruism to balance the economic necessity of the egotistic ambitions of the male – should lead to its opposite: the myth of the completely self-sufficient and hence completely egotistical woman, whose only wish was to gaze in the mirror and spend herself in autoerotic self-contemplation.[5]

The limitations on contemporary understanding of the relationship between Victorian femininity and sexuality occasioned by the widespread acceptance of this dyadic model, with its uncompromising separation of good women and sex, lies at the heart of this study of Victorian heroines. Indeed, common sense suggests that the Victorians' angelic feminine ideal is entirely suspect. Think how difficult it is to be equable and constructive in our own day, with effective birth control, greater understanding of sexual drives and needs, relatively advanced gynaecological care, a wide range of convenient products designed to make menstruation more comfortable, and medical advances which make pregnancy safer. Our understanding of the effects of hormones on women's moods and behaviour, our more relaxed styles of dress, and our wide range of women's products, services, and equal opportunities legislation have immeasurably improved the lot of women today. By contrast, multiple pregnancies (not to mention post-natal complications) must have left many Victorian women feeling permanently exhausted and dispirited. Under such conditions even the perkiest and most shiny of haloes must occasionally have become saggy and dull. Where is the reality, the personal discourse, in the representations of women who are the heroines of Victorian literature? One of our tasks has been to suggest answers to this question, and in the process, to recover the aspects of female experience which were banned in the only model of femininity which was officially approved.

In calling this book *Victorian Heroines* we have potentially created a rod for our own backs, for both terms are problematic and often contested. Our use of the word 'heroines' is simple and specific. Our concern is primarily with the women at the centre of Victorian literature, and to a lesser extent with some of the men and women who created them. In each case, the women we discuss serve as possible role models for women readers and writers seeking to understand their position in society and to explore alternatives. In this sense, and not because they conform to any stereotypical notion of the beautiful, passive, love-objects of romantic fiction, they are heroines.[6]

The more difficult question is, 'Why *Victorian* heroines rather than the less loaded "nineteenth-century"?' Writing in 1957, Walter Houghton addressed precisely this problem in the introduction to *The Victorian Frame of Mind*:

> it is now smart to say that of course there was no such thing as Victorianism. But the literature of those years, while indicating shifts and changes of outlook and showing that there are clear distinctions between the frame of mind at the start and close of this period, nevertheless so constantly reveals the presence of the same fundamental attitudes in every decade and in every group . . . that I cannot doubt that there was a common culture for which the term Victorianism . . . is appropriate.[7]

While there are problems with Houghton's justification, not least for feminists, its focus on dominant, frequently articulated preoccupations, nevertheless his notion of a 'common culture' is useful in constructing a context in which to place the Victorian heroine. Specifically, his emphasis on literature as part of the process for shaping this collective identity, and his implicit expectation that readers would know what Victorianism means, accord with our approach. We also felt that looking at literature produced throughout Victoria's reign (rather than choosing to look at the so-called 'Early', 'Middle' or 'Late' phases) was important; particularly for a study which is concerned with understanding how femininity was constructed and represented in the last century. In the popular consciousness 'Victorian' means during the time that Victoria was Queen, and not 1832 to 1870 (dates often given as the quintessentially Victorian period), or any other pair of dates during her time as monarch. Another reason for choosing to write about 'Victorian' heroines was that important studies such as those by Foucault (trans. 1979) and Steven Marcus (1964) also use the word 'Victorian' to describe not only a historical moment, but also a cultural consciousness.[8] Foucault's work in particular has contributed to a re-evaluation of our understanding of the relationship between the Victorians and sex, and to exclude the *fin de siècle* would seriously limit the range of our discussion.

Clearly the years of Victoria's reign (1837–1901) do not represent a uniquely homogeneous moment in history – far from it. To begin with, Victoria's was a very long reign, and one which saw major changes in social policy (her ascendancy was ushered in by the passing of the Reform Bill of 1832 which was fundamental to the process of making British society more democratic), economic relationships (both domestic and foreign), scientific and philosophical epistomologies, communications, transportation; indeed, the very sense of what it was like to live in the world was felt to be constantly changing. Not only did life feel as if it were changing, but there was also tremendous diversity of actual material conditions for those living in Victorian Britain. Beyond the obvious contrasts of urban and rural, rich and poor, male and female, employer and employee, there were also huge disparities in income, geography, education, expectations, opportunities, and ways of life between those who are often yoked together under the same label. Perhaps supremely, the experience of being middle class (the group which most concerns us in this study) varied tremendously, from those who were at the very bottom of the category (for instance, clerks and minor officials), to the well-to-do (managers, masters, and gentry).

For women, the Victorian period was anything but consistent. It began by inventing the fetishistic cult of the domestic angel and ended with the 'angels' in bloomers, in offices, in higher education, and driving motorcars. At the beginning of Victoria's reign women had very few legal rights over their bodies, their property or their children. Largely through the activities of the suffrage movement (which came to the public's attention in 1866, when John Stuart Mill presented Parliament with the first female suffrage petition) legislation was passed which improved conditions for women, the most important single reform being the Married Woman's Property Act of 1882. This gave women a degree of financial independence – crucial for all other kinds of independence, as Virginia Woolf was soon to argue in *A Room of One's Own* (1929).

Despite these changes, the word 'Victorian' carries with it very definite images, associations and overtones.[9] While Lytton Strachey and his generation are often blamed for the simplistic and frequently derogatory associations between Victorianism and prudery, repression, hypocrisy, smug confidence, and uncompromising patriarchy, it is worth remembering that the description 'Victorian' was used very early in Victoria's reign.[10] Its use throughout the Victorian period is symptomatic of the general movement to create a sense of coherence precisely in response to widespread change and diversity. The study of ideology has taught us that it is useful to emphasise familiar public signs, symbols and a collective sense of social continuity when a society is undergoing a period of profound transformation. The superficial continuity such emphasis provides promotes reform rather than revolution, and this was undoubtedly the objective of those with power in the last century. Certainly, in the early years of Victoria's reign the examples of the American and French revolutions were never far from any public figure's consciousness, and considerable effort was put into creating a new, more stable and democratic society as a consequence. But the drive to promote the self-image of Victorian society as stable, peaceful, prosperous and middle-class did not come only from those in authority. Looking at the writing of those in opposition to established authority as well as those who desired to maintain the status quo, anxiety about the nature and pace of change is unmistakable. Writing shortly before Victoria ascended the throne, John Stuart Mill observed that the sense of being in an age of transition 'forces itself upon the most inobservant'.[11] In the year after the queen's coronation, Thomas Arnold (then headmaster of Rugby) noted a new 'atmosphere of unrest and paradox hanging around many of our ablest young men'.[12] According to Houghton,

> Though the Victorians never ceased to look forward to a new period of firm convictions and established beliefs, they had to live in the meantime between two worlds, one dead or dying, one struggling but powerless to be born, in an age of doubt.[13]

One of the most familiar psychological strategies for dealing with doubt
and uncertainty is to set up boundaries and establish certainties. A clear
manifestation of this tendency is the Victorian obsession with collection
and classification. While the Victorian legacy produced by this obsession is
enormous, and reveals fine qualities such as curiosity and commitment, its
many products also suggest strongly the need for at least the illusion of
control. This need seems to have diminished briefly towards the end of the
Victorian period, as can be seen in the public toleration of the Aesthetes
and Decadents, and the changing attitude to the 'flickering and
inconsistent' nature of life celebrated by their mentor, Walter Pater.[14]
However, we suggest that this change was not a spontaneous, short-lived
phenomenon, but a reaction which had been growing through increasing
dissatisfaction with the problems caused by carrying over the habits and
security of classification into the realms of the personal, emotional and
sexual.

The obsessive nature of the Victorian need to categorise and contain
as many aspects of their lives as possible is nowhere more clear, and
nowhere more unsatisfactory, than in its application to the sexual. This
categorisation culminated in an ideology which espoused the division
of experience and activity into separate spheres for men and women;
further divisions of women into the two, mutually exclusive, categories of
'pure' and 'impure', and sex into 'licit' and 'illicit'. The amount of time
and attention given to promoting and legitimating the doctrine of separate spheres of influence and codes of morality for men and women
implies a fear that sexuality was in need of control, and statistics suggest a
variety of reasons why this may have been the case. There is an obvious
and well-established link between the Victorian ideology of the bourgeois
family and the rise of industrial capitalism.[15] One aspect of this
relationship lay in a general increase in wealth and property in the middle
classes. Under a patriarchal social system like that which prevailed in
Victorian Britain, increased prosperity is likely to lead to increased
regulation of female sexuality; since property was passed on by the father,
paternity could not be in doubt. Thus wifely infidelity was more a threat
to the economic stability of society than to its morality, a fact which
throws an even more jaundiced light on the many images of 'erring'
women being cast off from the family home at this time. The need to
regulate a girl's sexuality was held to be most acute in the 'dangerous'
years of puberty, and the narrative strategies for reconciling the need for
surveillance (in order to ensure purity) with the need to recover the young
wife's sexuality (to promote a successful marriage) provides the focus for
Chapter 1, which also looks at the narrative strategies by which women's
desires for independence and sexual expression were made legitimate.
Such strategies, we argue, helped to accustom the reading public to

changes in the feminine ideal, and specifically, to the need to recover female sexuality.

Another way in which sexuality was manifestly out of control became increasingly apparent as the century wore on and the problems of prostitution and sexually transmitted diseases forced themselves on the public consciousness. By 1851 there were 42,000 illegitimate children born in England and Wales, and William Acton (author of a number of influential works on female sexuality and prostitution) estimated that as many as 'one in twelve of the unmarried women in the country above the age of puberty have strayed from the path of virtue'.[16] An article on 'Prostitution' published in the *Westminster Review* (1850) claimed that at least 50,000 prostitutes were known to the police in England and Scotland, 8,000 of them residing in London alone.[17] The vast number of prostitutes is often cited as evidence in support of the hypocritical attitude of Victorian society to sex, largely on the basis that the widespread use of prostitutes serviced and in some senses legitimised the sexual double standard. Among other things, it was argued that men's sexual urges were regrettable but normal, while a woman who admitted to similar desires (and William Acton reassured the public that these were very few) was regarded as unnatural, ill and deviant. The relationship between prostitutes in real life and their use in literature very readily reveals the tensions and contradictions in Victorian attitudes to women and sexuality, and points once again to the untenable nature of the dyadic model and the ways in which it was subverted, and even overtly challenged. Similar, and closely related, readings can be made of the clothing worn by Victorian heroines (in the semiotics of Victorian arts and letters, apparel is an infallible indicator of virtue) and the phenomenon of the New Woman. The New Woman and her young side-kick, the 'girl of the period', disturbed Victorian consciousness by challenging dress and behavioural codes and so blurring the neatly classified distinctions between acceptable and unacceptable representations of femininity. All of these issues are discussed in detail in Chapter 2.

Chapter 3 uses Victorian paintings to show that many of the most famous Victorian heroines are iconographically linked to sexually powerful and metaphorically complex images of femininity. This chapter offers a new model to replace the dyadic one which has dominated Victorian studies for several decades, and in the process identifies many different attempts to recover and restore middle-class women's sexuality. Because it was so thoroughly repressed, it is not surprising that female sexuality often returned (or its return was the subject of fantasy) in disturbing ways. One form this return took was sensation fiction. Chapter 4's exposition of the subject looks at the way in which sexualised images of femininity had the potential to threaten the middle classes' notions of their own respectability. Far from condemning feminine power, however, Chapter 4 shows that the adulteresses and murderesses who fill the pages of sensation novels provide a useful service. They are cathartic in that they enable middle-class readers to act out and so confront their fears about the repressed areas of society (including both repression of the lower classes and repression of sexuality), and they also give expression to a shared dissatisfaction with the 'feminine ideal' as heroine and role model.

The final chapter returns briefly to the issues of prostitution and the New Woman in a discussion of Sarah Grand's *The Beth Book*. Grand's villain runs a Lock Hospital for diseased prostitutes, and one of her heroine's tasks is to extricate herself from a marriage which is largely financed on the backs of women who have become victims of society's official refusal to accept that femininity and sex can be reconciled. Grand's novel is highly autobiographical. In our opening discussion of heroines we said that women were each other's heroines; nowhere is this more true than in the stories they tell about themselves. The closing chapter looks at the problems and possibilities women have identified in the process of writing about themselves. One solution has frequently been to fictionalise the self, thus allowing a version of the self to become a heroine for the writer as well as for other readers. As this chapter shows, fictionalised autobiography is not primarily narcissistic. Rather, it allows writers to explore and experience opportunities they have been denied. Moreover, the splitting of the self is often both symbolic, in that it externalises an internal sense of fragmentation, and metonymic – it is what women *were*. Perhaps most important of all, multiple selves are brought together in these texts to tell a collective story and to offer a specifically female approach to social relations and the construction of the self. This coda on collective identities is very much about the recovery of the sexual in the representation of femininity.

As we began by saying, the problems created by the artificial separation of good women and sex are manifold and complex; not least because many middle-class women had good reasons for upholding this model. It is important to remember that the feminine ideal was empowering as well as enfeebling, and the Victorian woman who wanted control over her body, her health, and the size and well-being of her family had much to gain from a cultural construction which made her sexually remote.[18] The following chapters look at representations of women in the literature of the period – both canonical and popular, and by men as well as women – in an attempt to trace the various strategies by which women and sexuality were reunited. Firmly enmeshed as part of middle-class ideology, the cult of the domestic ideal had to be dismantled gradually (although we suggest dissatisfaction with it was rapid and widespread). We look at the role played by literary representations of women in accustoming both sexes to the idea that change was necessary and acceptable. To this end we found it more effective to adopt a thematic rather than a chronological approach throughout. Each chapter raises questions about the categorisation of women, always remembering that both men and women were involved in creating the images of women we are examining, and that both had to live with the consequences of the separate spheres, virgin/whore dichotomies. We have also been conscious that often the best forum for examining the attitudes and ideologies of a period is provided by the literature it creates for the next generation. Writing for children tends to be more explicitly didactic and value-laden than that for adults, and thus by comparing the two throughout we have tried to be alert to the ways in which attitudes are often simultaneously deconstructed for adults yet largely reconstructed for young readers.

What we have attempted in *Victorian Heroines* is to examine the representation of femininity and female sexuality from a variety of perspectives and in relation to a range of official discourses. In the process, we have become increasingly convinced that our prevailing models of Victorian sexuality are in need of revision, and that it is less important to read these representations 'across the grain' than it is to seek areas of commonality in the problems they posed and solutions they offered for men as well as for women. Since we are inevitably products of the pasts which shape us, and since many of the patterns of sexual relationships which dominated Victorian life are recognisably with us today, extending our understanding of how these earlier models worked can only help us continue to dismantle divisions in experience and opportunity between the sexes.

The material in this book is the product of a collaboration between the two authors. However, both have taken primary responsibility for different sections. Each contributed first drafts for substantial sections of Chapter 1. Nicola Humble took overall responsibility for this chapter's final shape and for the first drafts of Chapters 2 and 4. Kim Reynolds was primarily responsible for the first drafts of Chapters 3, and 5 and the Introduction.

1 Purity or danger
Sexuality and the development of the Victorian girl

... this picture, I say, seemed to consider itself the queen of the collection.

It represented a woman, considerably larger, I thought, than the life. I calculated that this lady, put into a scale of magnitude suitable for the reception of a commodity of bulk, would infallibly turn from fourteen to sixteen stone. She was, indeed, extremely well fed: very much butcher's meat – to say nothing of bread, vegetables, and liquids – must she have consumed to attain that breadth and height, that wealth of muscle, that affluence of flesh. She lay half-reclined on a couch: why, it would be difficult to say; broad daylight blazed round her; she appeared in hearty health, strong enough to do the work of two plain cooks; she could not plead a weak spine; she ought to have been standing, or at least sitting bolt upright. She had no business to lounge away the noon on a sofa. She ought likewise to have worn decent garments; a gown covering her properly, which was not the case: out of abundance of material – seven-and-twenty yards, I should say, of drapery – she managed to make insufficient raiment ... On referring to the catalogue, I found that this notable production bore name, 'Cleopatra'.

(Charlotte Brontë, *Villette* (1853), chapter 19)[1]

Lucy Snowe's response to the picture of Cleopatra provides one of the clearest examples in Victorian fiction of an avoidance of the erotic. She resolutely resists the sexual import of the painting, an import we learn it certainly carried when we witness M. Paul's shock at finding her observing it. More, she displaces the erotic with the domestic, reducing the abundant sexual display to so much weight of flesh and yardage of drapery, expressing the righteous disapproval of the good housewife at the sight of the mythical Egyptian queen wasting the afternoon sprawled on her divan. This displacement is emblematic of the mental processes of the Victorian feminine ideal, the virtuous wife-mother, centre of hearth and home, repository of the conscience of the bourgeois industrialist state, devoted to the domestic crafts, entirely without sexual impulses. But Lucy Snowe's substitution of a banal discourse, that transforms Cleopatra's superb flesh into her last meal, for a symbolic erotic discourse fraught with danger, is a manoeuvre which, far from defusing the sexual import of the painting, serves only to attract attention to itself, and to the ideology that motivates such an elaborate substitution.[2] This passage exposes the willed nature of the sort of female sexual ignorance required by moralists such as William Cobbett, who, in his *Advice to Young Men and (Incidentally) Young Women* (1830) counselled that:

> Chastity, perfect modesty, in word, deed, and even thought, is so essential, that without it, no female is fit to be a wife. It is not enough that a young woman abstain from everything approaching in-decorum in her behaviour towards men . . . she ought to appear not to understand it, and to receive from it no more impression than if she were a post.[3]

Cobbett's own injunction, indeed, reveals in its use of the word 'appear' a covert awareness of a likely gap between actual and expressed sexual knowledge, even in the ideal woman of whom he speaks.

The denial of female sexuality was long seen as the dominant feature of Victorian culture and society. Until the mid-1970s, the received credo of Victorian studies was that the period witnessed a progressive desexualisation of the feminine. According to Françoise Basch's *Relative Creatures: Victorian Women in Society and the Novel 1837-1867* (1974):[4]

> Poets, moralists and philosophers embellished the domestic and family role of the woman with a universal and transcendental dimension. But the mutation of the Eve myth into the Mary myth, of temptress into redeemer, implied a fundamental process of desexualisation of the woman, who was bit by bit deprived of her carnal attributes; the housewife became at once the pillar of the home and the priestess of a temple. (p. 8)

Patricia Thomson, in *The Victorian Heroine: A Changing Ideal, 1837-73* (1956)[5] considered the issue of the 'Social Evil' of prostitution in terms of the culture that denied middle-class women the means to speak of the phenomenon, tracing the gradual incursions of radicals on the repressive cult of ignorance. The long-prevailing model of nineteenth-century sexuality as split between 'a prudish and hypocritical surface and the illicit, often perverse underground'[6] lies behind Steven Marcus's famous study of *The Other Victorians* (1977), with its focus on the underworld of pornography and vice and its incursions into bourgeois respectability.[7] Walter E. Houghton, in the chapter on love in *The Victorian Frame of Mind 1830-1870* (1957), concentrates almost exclusively on the sexual prudery of the middle-classes, while Duncan Crow devotes a large section of *The Victorian Woman* (1971) to an 'Anatomy of Prudery'.[8]

Shared by these readings of Victorian culture and society was the assumption that sexuality was systematically repressed in the nineteenth century. This 'repressive hypothesis' was famously attacked by Michel Foucault in *The History of Sexuality*, Vol. I, *An Introduction* (1976; trans. 1979).[9] He argues that sexuality was not so much repressed as regulated by the proliferating discourses – social, medical, legal, psychiatric – in which the nineteenth century spoke continuously about sex. Foucault's analysis has had such influence that few works on nineteenth-century sexuality published since 1976 have failed to make obeisance in its direction. Despite such apparent universal concurrence, Foucault's model is often only half-heartedly applied: as Nancy Armstrong notes in the introduction to her *Desire and Domestic Fiction* (1987), many writers who claim to concur with the notion of sexuality as a social construct eventually relapse into essentialism and end by positing 'a specific form of sexuality as natural, that is, as sex'.[10] There are, as several feminists have pointed out, significant problems with the application of Foucault's ideas to the discussion of a specifically feminine sexuality, particularly his tendency to marginalise women by treating the body and sexuality as curiously neuter.[11] Despite these reservations, most recent authorities rightly agree that Foucault's central revision of our notions of the mechanisms and purpose of nineteenth-century discourses about sexuality is crucially important. Which is why it seems curious that so few critics follow this argument to its logical conclusion.

The function of the nineteenth-century regulation of sexuality, according to Foucault, was 'to expel from reality the forms of sexuality that were not amenable to the strict economy of representation: to say no to unproductive activities, to banish casual pleasures, to reduce or exclude practices whose object was not procreation' (p. 36). If Foucault is right, the only place that sexuality could legitimately operate for the Victorians was within marriage, yet the very official Victorian discourses that are Foucault's subject insist that women naturally feel no sexual impulses at all. The much-respected doctor, William Acton, for example, published in 1857 an influential treatise on *The Functions and Disorders of the*

Reproductive Organs, in Childhood, Youth, Adult Age, and Advanced Life, considered in their Physiological, Social and Moral Relations[12] in which he provided considerable fuel for the increasingly accepted nineteenth-century myth that 'normal' women were passionless:

> The majority of women (happily for them) are not very much troubled with sexual feelings of any kind. . . . The best mothers, wives and managers of households, know little or nothing of sexual indulgences. Love of home, children, and domestic duties, are the only passions they feel.[13]

Acton offers this information only as a reassurance to young men frightened of marriage in case 'the marital duties they will have to undertake are beyond their exhausted strength';[14] he has little interest in female sexuality *per se*, seeing it only as the aberrant property of nymphomaniacs (a term invented in the nineteenth century), and prostitutes, whose sexual insatiability was legendary, and who were likely to have provided the young man's first sexual experience. In his entire lengthy and detailed work Acton has only two brief passages about the sexuality of women.[15] The paradox of the Victorian exaltation of marriage and family and the simultaneous insistence on the passionless nature of the good woman becomes more startling if we compare the cultural products of this period with major examples from other eras. Shakespeare's middle-period comedies, in particular *A Midsummer Night's Dream* and *As You Like It*, extol marital harmony based on erotic love by representing it as the highest form of comic resolution, while the novel of the early eighteenth-century, as epitomised by the fictions of Richardson and Defoe, allows its heroines to experience sexual pleasure and yet remain heroines.

Foucault, and many later writers on Victorian femininity and sexuality such as Nancy Armstrong, Martha Vicinus and Philippa Levine[16], account for the specific nature of Victorian sexual attitudes with a shared central hypothesis: that the regulation of sexuality in this period of rapid, unparalleled economic expansion served the purpose of outlawing non-marital, non-procreative sexual activity, with the function of ensuring the safe transfer of the newly increased wealth and property of the middle classes. What they don't explain is why this overwhelming social imperative is not matched by discourses extolling the pleasures and virtues of marital sexuality. In fact, there are such discourses operative in the period: one of them is the novel. The project of this book is to examine the ways in which the novel, and other cultural products such as Decadent art, and autobiography, seek to engage with and reformulate contemporary constructions of femininity. In the case of the novel, one such engagement is its attempt to resolve the paradox created by the contemporary insistence on the asexuality of the middle-class wife, and to advance the cause of procreation through allowed pleasures. Far from upholding the stereotype of the sexually ignorant female as an ideal, the Victorian novel treads a moral tightrope: attempting to provide heroines with knowledge and experience of sexuality without compromising them and so invalidating them as role models.

It has been suggested, most notably by Nancy F. Cott, that the notion of passionlessness had distinct advantages for women. In 'Passionlessness: An Interpretation of Victorian Sexual Ideology, 1790-1850',[17] she argues convincingly that the idea of women's superiority, which developed out of the late eighteenth- and early nineteenth-century Evangelical assertion of their passionlessness, was the base from which much feminist campaigning in the later nineteenth century drew its strength. She points also to the space the idea of their lack of carnal instincts gave women to develop other aspects of their personalitites and talents, and attributes the developments in women's education in the period to the fact that it was no longer seen as primarily for the purpose of increasing their ability to attract men. These points are a valuable reminder of the double-sidedness of this ideology, and indeed, we saw in the figure of Lucy Snowe with which this chapter opened, someone who has much to gain from what Havelock Ellis dubbed 'sexual anaesthesia'.[18] As the narrative of *Villette* amply demonstrates, Lucy devotes much of her physical and psychological energies to avoiding the profound dangers posed by passion and sexuality. The sense of passion as dangerous, however, is one that we receive most strongly, not from outside forces, but from Lucy's fear of her *own* passions. (The spectre of Genievre Fanshawe's 'fall' is a minor element in the text's processes, occurring 'offstage', when our attention is elsewhere.) Far from being passionless, Lucy Snowe battles constantly to subdue her passion, in line with the societal strictures she has internalised. It is this divided consciousness, one which, as we will demonstrate, is found repeatedly in the images and accounts of Victorian women, that Cott's analysis ignores. It also fails to acknowledge the fact that the concept of a 'natural' lack of passion was only ever extended to certain women. The prostitute or fallen woman was considered 'naturally' prone to physical passions, and the young girl, as this chapter will discuss, was considered in constant danger of following this debased creature in her fall. Even the pure wife, who undoubtedly, as Cott avers, benefited from the moral superiority the ideology of passionlessness accorded her, attempts in the Victorian novel – often very successfully – to have it both ways.

It is worth remarking that the term 'sexuality' tends to be used rather generally by many critics. Nancy Armstrong provides the classic definition when she insists that 'sexuality is the cultural dimension of sex'

(p. 11), but this still evades some important distinctions. It is certainly necessary to differentiate the act of sexual intercourse from the complex codes, ideologies and fantasies that surround it, but when examining the sexuality of the nineteenth-century fictional heroine it is equally important to consider whether the sexuality that attaches to her in a given representation is experienced *by* her, or has her as its object; to distinguish between her sexuality and a more pervasive sensuality; to determine a boundary between sexual knowledge and 'impurity'; to discover the relationship between the various types of passion attributed to her. It is precisely because the conventional nineteenth-century imagination knotted these elements indiscriminately together that it is imperative that we should untangle them, in order to see more precisely the pattern they form.

One of the most significant ways in which the novel achieves its revisions of the asexual feminine model is through its concentration on the figure of the young girl. It is conceivable that many writers on the novel and femininity have read the heroines of the Victorian novel as at least approximations to the passive, sexless cultural ideal only because an ideal is what they expect the heroine to be.[19] In fact, the ideal wife-mother, sexless and dutiful, is *not* the central concern of the typical novel of the period. Although an ostensible aim, she is significantly displaced in favour of the adolescent girl or young woman, and the story of her progress *towards* matrimony and virtue. This progress is necessary, because the girl, unlike the wife, was seen as highly sexualised – and at grave risk from this sexuality.

In the many non-literary writings about young women in the period – medical and evolutionary treatises on menstruation, sexuality and inheritance; handbooks for mothers; books and lectures (like Cobbett's) full of advice, warnings and instruction – there was general agreement that adolescent girls were sexual beings. When a girl reached the age of puberty, it was believed: 'the chief efforts of the organism are in some sort concentrated on the sexual parts'.[20] The mense, it was supposed, inflamed emotions and sensations, transforming the innocent child into the 'dangerous' pubescent girl who was to be confined and controlled to keep her from ruining her future. Even more important was the danger her inflammatory charms represented to young men, who might be provoked by them into making use of the equally unhealthy outlets of masturbation and prostitution.

Around this perilous condition there evolved both a rhetoric and a system of surveillance. It was the duty of parents to be watchful, to teach their daughters well, and by confining them and restricting their friends, discipline them into the habit of repressing sexual desires. Thus, the dangerous girl was kept from anti-social behaviour – that is, illegitimate sex – until she had attained the desired and presumed safety of marriage. Then she was to 'appear not to understand' anything which did not accord with the strict rules of modesty with which she had been inculcated. A more overt expression of Cobbett's injunction to conscious ignorance is provided by Dickens' Mrs General in *Little Dorrit* (1857), although her 'truly refined mind' is more a construction of class than of gender:

> Nothing disagreeable should ever be looked at. Apart from such a habit standing in the way of that graceful equanimity of surface which is so expressive of good breeding, it hardly seems compatible with refinement of mind. A truly refined mind will seem to be ignorant of the existence of anything that is not perfectly proper, placid, and pleasant.[21]

It is this paradox of the felt necessity of conscious ignorance from women declared naturally pure that the novel of the period simultaneously explores and attempts to resolve. Through the use of convention, omission, denial and suggestion we are provided in the novel with both a characteristically Victorian representation of the required development of the young girl into the ideal wife, and a challenge to the accuracy, validity and desirability of this model. Bakhtin's notion of dialogism is a helpful model for the relationship between these two impulses in the novel. He defines the dialogic as the characteristic mode of ideological communication in a society (in his formulation, all post-Enlightenment societies) that has lost the conditions to produce a single unifying ideology. Conflicting discourses in such a society establish no final hierarchy, but engage in an elaborate interplay, with the power or influence of one over another determined only at the moment of utterance. Thus, the single, or even repeated, articulation in the novel of opposition to the dyadic model does not easily achieve that model's overturning, rather the model and the oppositional discourses it produces are elaborately intertwined and contest for primacy.[22] If the novel attempts to heal the social dislocation caused by the separation of wives and sex, it does not do so unproblematically. It is precisely in its hints, elisions and contradictions that we find the – not always successful – challenge to the orthodoxy.

Girls into wives: paradoxical heroines

... get Dorothea to read you light things; Smollett – *Roderick Random*, *Humphrey Clinker*: they are a little broad, but she may read anything now she's married, you know. (George Eliot, *Middlemarch*, (1871–2), Chapter 30)[23]

When Mr Brooke makes this observation to the ailing Casaubon, he is assuming that his niece has made the transition from the dangerous stage of adolescence to the presumed safety of married womanhood. This recognition contains a series of complex and sometimes contradictory assumptions evolving from the conventional conception of the desirable development of a young woman. It begins with the fundamental belief underlying the masterplan, that marriage was the unquestioned goal of a girl's life.[24] According to the official model, Dorothea should now become the 'angel in the house'; her refined sensibilities should temper her husband's rougher nature and provide him with a haven of peace and virtue into which to retreat from the hurly-burly of the world. It is possible that Mr Brooke was suggesting that such a paragon could now read the 'broad' literature which in her youth might have incited unwholesome thoughts and sensations, for in her metamorphosed state she would be as insensible to it as Cobbett's post. However, it is equally possible to read Brooke's remark more cynically and suggest that he is expressing relief that Dorothea has managed to get respectably married without going astray under his guardianship. Brooke is free from the need to be watchful, and takes the view that Dorothea married is no different from Dorothea unmarried except that now she can know and do what she likes almost with impunity. The goal has been achieved.

But has it? In *Middlemarch*, with a few notable exceptions, married women rarely evolve into the 'Angel in the House' of convention. Dorothea attempts a variation of this role in her ministrations (both academic and medical) to her husband, and finds it ultimately barren. Her first marriage, like most others in the novel, is a failure. Moreover, the hint of sexual scandal which Casaubon's codicil invites never threatens her as a girl in that potentially dangerous incubation, but comes about as a direct consequence of her marriage. Thus Eliot, while seeming to provide a generally conventional structure to the life of Dorothea at the outset of *Middlemarch*, in fact raises questions about the assumptions upon which such conventions were based.

It would, of course, misrepresent the novel to suggest that Dorothea herself was ever presented as an ordinary young woman: the puritanism implicit in her fantasy of herself as Saint Theresa establishes doubts, from the very start of the novel, as to just what it is she is trying to damp down in herself. However, the pattern of her development set out in 'Miss Brooke' conforms in many ways to the conventional. Her life is restricted because she is a young lady; her education suffers on this account; action has to be effected through men, and she is as sexually unaware as a Cobbett could desire. Dorothea's choice of Casaubon, though surprising to her family and friends, is certainly in a familiar tradition of father–daughter styled marriages in Victorian literature (Dr Strong and Annie, Little

Dorrit and Arthur Clennam, Jane Eyre and Mr Rochester).[25] It is only after marriage that the orthodoxy begins to crumble. Eliot negates the marriage to Casaubon, in which Dorothea has been increasingly taking on the shape of the passionless Victorian wife, and provides her with a thoroughly unconventional replacement in her marriage to Will Ladislaw. Though there are undoubtedly ambiguities surrounding this match as well, Will offers qualities which the reader is expected to appreciate, and among them is the undeniable physical attraction between himself and Dorothea. When she marries Will, Dorothea is no longer the innocent girl whom the textbooks insisted was the only suitable material for a wife. (Cobbett was thoroughly disgusted by women who remarried and thus underwent a second time 'that surrender to which nothing but the most ardent affection could ever reconcile a chaste and delicate woman'.[26])

While the experience gained through a previous marriage is not a prerequisite for successful relationships in nineteenth-century literature, there is good evidence to suggest that as far as can be gathered from literary representations of marriages like Dorothea's to Casaubon, the Victorian ideal of the pure and desexualised wife was proving unsatisfactory. Time and again are depicted the attractions of unorthodox, rebellious girls. For the majority of the century, these creatures are contained by being taught to renounce their 'unwomanly' qualities and discover the true joys of love and motherhood, but by the end of the century, the rebel was appreciated for her own sake.[27] This combination of pattern and shift suggests that the Victorians may have felt that somehow the officially approved nineteenth-century woman had become a monster. The separation of wives and sex must surely have left both partners unsatisfied.

The remedy for this state of affairs by the healing of the culture's divided consciousness in its image of women is repeatedly suggested in literature. The second marriage, like Dorothea's, was one way of representing the bond, for it made it possible to combine sexual experience with the type of woman society would sanction as wife and mother. This solution is rarely unaccompanied by ambiguities or ambivalences (the marriage between Thackeray's angelic Amelia and Dobbin is a good example). However, a more interesting drive to unite the antithetical aspects of women emerges in the treatment of heroines' adolescence and its subsequent impact on their womanhoods.

Two ways of representing the period from puberty to womanhood predominate in Victorian literature. The first of these relies on the silent discourse, where the plot is structured so as to effect an absence or removal of the young woman at this time. Dickens frequently employs this device. In *David Copperfield* (1849–50), David's free and innocent intercourse with Little Em'ly is interrupted by his return home and subsequent removal to boarding school and finally to the care of his aunt. The next time David

sees Em'ly, she is represented as a young woman in the dangerous state of
adolescent sexuality (lest the pitfalls be forgotten, Dickens provides her
with a shadow in the form of the fallen Martha). David first learns about
the change in Little Em'ly from the 'funeral furnisher', Mr Omer. Omer
informs him that the local women have taken against Em'ly because of her
beauty and her wish to become a lady. According to John Reed's study of
Victorian literary conventions, this is a clear use of convention to infer
meaning. 'Destructive females in Victorian literature', he writes, 'are
generally motivated by pride or physical passion.'[28] Recognition of the
convention colours the whole of Chapter 21 and the subsequent events.
More importantly, it makes it impossible to regard Little Em'ly solely as a
victim. She is a destructive woman, whose actions disrupt the lives of all
who love her and bring about the death of Steerforth. Her destructive
potential is released through the sexuality she embodies in her person.

A similar pattern exists in *Great Expectations* (1860–1). Pip and Estella
are separated on the brink of adolescence, when he goes off to London for
his education. When Pip next sees her, he at first fails to recognise Estella –
she has turned into 'the lady whom I have never seen before'. When
recognition dawns, the overpowering sexuality of the new Estella
permeates the chapter:

> she was so much changed, was so much more beautiful, so much
> more womanly, in all things winning admiration had made such
> wonderful advance, that it seemed I had made none. . . . O the sense
> of . . . inaccessibility that came about her! . . . She gave me her
> hand. I stammered something. . . . Estella laughed. . . . she treated
> me as a boy still, but she lured me on.[29]

In *Great Expectations*, the sexually flirtatious, powerful Estella is set in
opposition to the domestic angel Biddy: the official Victorian divided
consciousness is clearly represented. In the earlier but more autobiographical *David Copperfield*, however, Dickens seems to have attempted a
fusion of the two aspects of women. He does this in two ways. The first,
and least effective (though more conventional), of these is the redemption
of Little Em'ly. Saved from a fate worse than death by the love of her
guardian and the efforts of Martha, she sets off for a new life in Australia,
where she becomes a beloved member of the community. The second
attempt at fusion comes about through the rather bizarre relationship
between Dora and Agnes, which emerges as the book progresses. David is
attracted to Dora at a time when she displays all the symptoms of the
sexually charged but juvenile state of adolescence. Their marriage is a
failure, presumably because it was grounded on physical attraction and
Dora was premature in assuming the demands of married life. Agnes is

situated at the opposite end of the scale of passion. Her life of celibacy and service prevents David from any conscious sense of attraction to her. But the separate characters of Dora and Agnes: temptress and angel, are forced to merge. Agnes is not only present at the wedding of David and Dora, but she holds Dora's hand throughout the ceremony. Dora's deathbed wish is that Agnes replace her as David's wife. This is impossible as long as Agnes is desexualised and inaccessible, but David's own experience gradually awakens him to the fact that Agnes is a woman and not an angel. While the language he uses about her remains elevated, Agnes becomes the object of David's passion, and thus in her character, however unconvincingly, Dickens attempts to bring together the disparate images of Victorian women.

The second way of dealing with female adolescence so that the mature heroine is permitted to retain something of her sexuality relies on the technique of inversion. Arnold van Gennep's study of rites of passage, of which the transition from child or unmarried person to adulthood/marriage is one, explains how such a stage threatens stability and therefore requires control and licence. These are often provided by acting out a ritual of inversion. The ritualised inversion is an expression of the change and the period of instability, but it is also a 'state of meaningful status reversal, one that expresses . . . the reasonableness and necessity of hierarchical principle'.[30]

In nineteenth-century literature, the most frequently used inversion associated with this rite of passage is that of sex-role swapping. In addition to its cathartic function and means of retaining the status quo, the inversion technique is also applied to the problem of the divided images of women. When order is restored, the heroine has usually made the passage into womanhood and marriage but is allowed to retain some aspects of her sexuality.

Two vivid examples of this behaviour are provided by George Eliot's heroine Maggie Tulliver, and Charlotte Brontë's Shirley Keeldar. As a child, Maggie is a trial to her mother and her aunts because of her tomboyish looks and behaviour and her unsuitable bookishness. In her adolescence, Maggie tries to renounce her desire for knowledge and experience through sheer effort of will. She imposes on herself the regimen which would make her socially acceptable, and in the sixth book is presented with a veneer of sophisticated respectability. But Maggie's renunciation is in fact a repression which leaves her unsatisfied. She is unable to forget that dynamic part of her nature which has caused her to desire – and know herself capable of understanding – the intellectual apparatus through which men control her world. She continues to act independently and to educate herself; Maggie is unable to reconcile approved behaviour with her intellectual and emotional insights. Because of this failure to forget or successfully control her appetite for unladylike knowledge, Maggie is capable of exciting active and illegitimate love. She is not desexualised and cannot therefore be reclaimed by marriage. Her inversion is never completed by reversion to the natural order.

Brontë's Shirley Keeldar, on the other hand, also manifests many unfeminine characteristics and chases men's education and power. She styles herself a man, and has to be discouraged from describing herself as a gentleman, whistling, and otherwise affecting 'masculine manners'. The difference between Shirley and Maggie is that Shirley's period of inversion is a product of her adolescence; she abandons all tokens of manly qualities when she marries for love and assumes her conventional role.

Perhaps the most interesting and complete experiment with the use of inversion to mark the passage into womanhood and at the same time effect a fusion between the sexual and desexualised images of women is provided by Tennyson's *The Princess* (1847-50).[31] The poem in fact contains a double inversion. The young prince begins the framed poem as an androgynous boy ('blue eyed, and fair in face . . . with lengths of yellow ringlets like a girl'[32]) who disguises himself as a girl in order to win his bride and achieve manhood. Ida, on the other hand, tries to divest herself of all feminine attributes. She aspires to equality with men and attempts to possess male education and authority. The body of the poem shows this pair in their inverted relationship. Ida is the leader and intellectual superior. Her conversation is full of classical allusions, and when showing the Prince and his friends around her college for women, she is seen in the role of teacher to the Prince's naive and romantic girlishness. Terry Eagleton suggests that in taking on the masculine role, Ida has desexualised herself; in fact, Tennyson uses the inversion to instil sexuality. Ida, like Maggie and Shirley, is presented as a woman men desire. She is acutely aware of the need to control her own sexuality if she is to acquire influence in the world of men. Moreover, that the Prince desires her is a necessary ingredient in any meaningful reading of the poem, for if there is no love between them and the Prince wants merely to subdue and enslave Ida, then he is no better than his father who insists 'Man is the hunter; woman is his game'.[33] The impetus of the poem is not to reassert this view as approved orthodoxy, but to implant its antithesis: the need for mingling the two sexes in equal and harmonious proportions. In the love debate which concludes Book VII, each speaks of their future union in these terms, finally agreeing, 'Not to be like to like, but like in difference. / Yet in the long years, liker must they grow; / The man be more of woman, she of man: / He gain in sweetness and in moral height, / . . . she mental breadth'.

Tennyson's use of the convention of inversion also seeks to show that the division of women into two mutually exclusive categories – pure Mary and dangerous Magdalene – is insufficient. Ida's assumption of the male role casts her in the part of experienced woman. It is certainly never suggested that she has had actual sexual experience, but her grasping for power, venturing into the male world, and the need to be instructed in suitably womanish attitudes and emotions is a great remove from the passive, 'Thy will be done' of the typical Mary. Ida is technically sexually pure, and achieves the goal of marriage without a real fall. Nevertheless, she is seen to require a kind of redemption or at least a renunciation of her wrong ways before marriage is possible. She is thus both the Holy Mother (a point highlighted by the Prince's idealised evocation of his own mother immediately prior to Ida's acceptance of him, the juxtaposition of the two women serving to encorporate Ida into the maternal role), and the sexual-but-redeemed Magdalene.

A separate but complementary way of reading *The Princess* is to see the use of inversion as indicating a tension between the official role of women and challenges to it from a new generation. Ida corresponds in many ways to 'the girl of the period' who was to metamorphose not into the angelic wife, but the New Woman. The inversion in adolescence, as well as denoting sexual tensions, could also signal dissatisfaction with the conventional options available to the well-brought-up Victorian daughter. The new image of women which was emerging was anathema to those who saw themselves as the guardians of conventional morality. In her famous article on the subject, Mrs Linton declared that university girls, the epitome of 'the girl of the period', 'All drink, smoke, swear, use vulgar language, and are represented as knowing and talking about unfitting subjects'.[34] These negative characteristics are all stolen from male preserves and were associated with loose morality. Charlotte M. Yonge told the readers of *Womankind* that those women who sought equality with men were on a fool's errand: 'His independence she has, and a very doleful thing she finds it . . . and while she strips herself of all grace and softness, she becomes ridiculous and absurd in his sight.'[35]

While non-literary publications asserted that discontent with the role of women would only lead to greater discontent, in fiction the girls who refuse to conform to expectations by attaining and relishing the roles of either wife and mother or of dutiful spinster are increasingly portrayed as victims of an intolerant society. Literary texts begin to present both the dilemma, and the suggestion that the models offered by society were inadequate. In *Shirley* (1849), Caroline Helstone encapsulates the con-tradictory attitudes which must have been held by a great many of what Gissing called the 'odd women': unmarried or potentially unmarriageable women in a society which offered marriage as the only truly satisfactory ambition in a girl's life:

I shall never marry. What was I created for, I wonder? Where is my place in the world? . . . that is the question which most old maids are puzzled to solve: other people solve it for them by saying, 'Your place is to do good to others, to be helpful whenever help is wanted.' That is very right in some measure, and a very convenient doctrine for the people that hold it; but . . . Is this enough? Is it to live? . . . Does virtue lie in abnegation of self? I do not believe it. Undue humility makes tyranny. . . . the Romish religion especially teaches renunciation of self, submission to others, and nowhere are found so many grasping tyrants as in the ranks of the Romish priesthood.[36]

Shirley herself tries to resist the pressure to conform in her adoption of male characteristics. As in *The Princess*, this employment of inversion is limited to adolescence, and Shirley, like Ida, surrenders all obvious signs of independence and masculinity when she marries. Thus a pattern emerges in the literary treatment of young women during the sexually potent period between puberty and the realisation of full womanhood as wives and mothers. It is a pattern whose function is to integrate the two disparate aspects of femininity, either through the use of convention and the fusion of characters, as we saw in the Dickens novels, or by granting to this time a period of misrule and inversion resulting in behaviour which corresponds to the Victorian notion of sexual experience, because a girl could not be both 'pure' and unladylike. The heroines of such works appropriate masculine behaviour and attributes, and challenge the conventional roles to which they eventually succumb. Thus one heroine, in the lifetime a text allowed her, could represent both terms in the conventional dyadic model that separated pure from tainted women. The combining of these binary opposites in a single woman represents a significant disruption, if not an outright challenge, to this model. The climax of these works (with the possible exception of *The Mill on the Floss* (1860) in which death serves the redeeming function in lieu of marriage) is on the reclaiming of the young woman from dangerous sexuality to safe purity. However, the concentration of attention is on the denial and rejection of the norm; the marriages and compromises which constitute redemption at the end of these texts are therefore subservient to the bulk of the work. The married woman may renounce her past, but for the reader it is the actions she is rejecting that have established and now comprise her character. The effect is to cause us to view the rejection with mistrust and to instil, if only subliminally, the sense that the new wife will continue to be informed by the knowledge and experience she has gained.

It is precisely the developmental narrative processes of the novel form that allow such negotiations to be effected. The demands of propriety are satisfied by the conventional closure of marriage, but the sexual elements of the young girl's persona, signalled by narrative conventions and inversions, are not entirely subsumed in the wife's requisite purity. It is through its concern with character, motivation and relationships, and its exploration of their development over time, that the Victorian novel has the means to explore, challenge and reformulate its society's conventions of femininity. Because its heroines can be shown *developing*, there is room to show them flawed, less than perfect; but because literary heroines offer a model of behaviour, attitudes and possibilities to their readers, minor flaws and divergences from the ideal could become gradually incorporated into a new, more complex and multifarious model of femininity.

One of the most subtle and far-reaching reformulations of femininity achieved by the Victorian novel is enacted on the level of character and plot convention, and yet again focuses on the girl as a site of rebellion: this is the orphan-convention, which provided the heroine with vast new spaces – both physical and psychological – in which to operate.

Girls alone: the dangers and rewards of orphanhood

The orphan-convention is so widely used in Victorian fiction that we could be forgiven for assuming that orphanhood was the typical condition of children in the period. All three of Charlotte Brontë's major heroines – Jane Eyre, Lucy Snowe and Shirley Keeldar – are orphans, as are Dickens' Oliver Twist, David Copperfield, Esther Summerson, and Pip. Emily Brontë's Cathy is orphaned early in *Wuthering Heights*, and Heathcliff's status as outsider is a function of his absolutely orphaned state – without parents, friends, family, home or class. George Eliot uses contrasting pairs of female orphans in *Adam Bede* and *Daniel Deronda*. Nina Auerbach and John Reed, both of whom survey the literary implications of the orphan-convention, mention between them in excess of fifty mainstream Victorian novels which revolve around the lives of orphans.[37]

We could, of course, account for this phenomenon in realist terms, arguing that parental, especially maternal, death was simply a fact of life for the Victorians. Disease, disaster, desertion, war and, particularly, childbirth meant that many children lost one or both parents at an early age. The real-life figure of the orphan was one which generated in the public a strong sense of guilt, unease, helplessness and resentment – rather like the many homeless young people today living in cardboard boxes on the streets of our cities. However, the orphan that we see in the Victorian novel is *not* simply a reflection of the sociological reality.

As far as legal and charitable institutions were concerned, orphanhood was a condition affecting only the lower classes: to all intents and purposes, middle- and upper-class orphans did not exist. Of course many children in these economic groups lost one or both parents, but legal and social structures provided for their *de facto* absorption into other known, relational categories. In most cases, relatives or an appointed guardian assumed care and responsibility for the child until he or she came of age. In the relatively few cases where this standard apparatus for absorbing parentless children broke down, legal provisions were available: the child became a ward of court and a guardian was appointed. Perhaps because of his experiences as a court reporter, Dickens was particularly interested in the legal machinery which was intended to protect orphans, and in novels such as *Nicholas Nickleby* (1838–9), *David Copperfield* (1849–50), *Bleak House* (1852–3), and *Great Expectations* (1860–1) explores the merits and demerits of every condition of middle-class orphanhood. Invariably those orphans who find surrogate parents or guardians (for instance Esther Summerson and David Copperfield) do better than those left to the vagaries of an anonymous and self-obsessed legal system.

That the child in this position was in no sense perceived by officaldom as lacking the necessary social structure normally provided by the family is evidenced by the fact that adoption – the formal integration of a child into a new family – did not exist even notionally. It was not until 1926, with the coming of the Adoption of Children Act, that adoption was technically possible, and then it was not established with a view to increasing the security or well-being of these relatively well-to-do orphans. Instead, in keeping with historical concerns, adoption was bound up in issues of legitimacy and the care of waifs and strays.[38]

No matter how unsatisfactory the system may have been for middle-class orphans, they were not generally perceived to be problematic and were, therefore, officially undiscussed. Social debate revolved around two categories of children likely to be at risk: bastards and orphans of the poor. Andrew Mearns' *The Bitter Cry of Outcast London* (1883) was typical of the call for legislation and effective action to protect children by eradicating the unwholesome environments in which they were forced to dwell. Life amongst 'thieves, prostitutes, and liberated convicts,' Mearns argued, bred: 'infancy that knows no innocence, youth without modesty or shame, maturity that is mature in nothing but suffering and guilt, blasted old age that is a scandal on the name we bear'.[39]

Certainly there was a school of nineteenth-century fiction deeply committed to reform and which, in its depiction of the conditions of urban life for the poor, anticipated Mearns' plea for legislation and action. *Oliver Twist* may have been the most famous example, but this strategy was central to and widely promulgated by Evangelical writers such as Hannah More (who began writing in this vein in 1829) and Hesba Stretton, whose best-selling stories, *Little Meg's Children* (1868) and *Alone in London* (1869), focused on the problems of preserving childhood innocence in the face of circumstances and bodily requirements which conspired to corrupt all but those in direct communication with the Almighty. Such works used the figure of the orphan to gain sympathy and rouse public indignation and were important in establishing the orphan-convention as one of social comment. They also explored the problems of alienation and injustice: Dickens provided an early and enduring example of this use of the orphan in *Bleak House*'s 'poor Jo'.

The major tendency in Victorian fiction is, however, to focus on those otherwise neglected orphans of the bourgeoisie. Further, the most cursory survey of nineteenth-century literature reveals the high percentage of works in which the central characters (and often a large number of their associates) are both orphans and female. This discrepancy between social and literary practices suggests that these orphans were primarily functioning in a symbolic rather than a realistic capacity, and that it is specific aspects of their symbolic function which made orphans particularly useful to women writers.

Before going on to look at these in detail, the term 'orphan' needs to be clarified: here it is being used loosely, so that it includes both the familiar meaning of the child actually deprived of one or (more usually) both parents, and the child who has temporarily or symbolically lost its parents. Thus Florence Dombey, whose mother has died and whose father neglects and rejects her, and Mary Barton, whose father ceases adequately to fulfil his parental duties after the death of his wife, are as much orphans as are Becky Sharp, David Copperfield and Jane Eyre. Perhaps more contentiously, all orphans are nominated 'she' because, whatever the designated gender of the fictional orphan, orphanhood as a condition operates to highlight dependency, and dependency in the Victorian separation of sex roles is in the domain of the female. Thus, as long as her orphaned status is the principal factor governing the character's situation in the novel, that character is in the position of a female.

The symbolic emancipatory function of the orphan motif was early noticed by Florence Nightingale, who declared in 'Cassandra' (1852-9) that 'the secret charm of every romance that ever was written . . . is that the heroine has generally no family ties (almost invariably no mother)', or, if she has, these do not interfere with her entire independence'.[40] The independence the orphan-convention lends to its heroines is allowable precisely because it is controlled by the narrative processes of the texts in which it occurs – almost invariably the narrative moves to remedy the orphan's lack: to find lost parents or to supply surrogates or spouses to provide the missing family structure. In the narrative strategies of orphan-novels, this assimilation of the orphan into family life tends to be part of a drive towards resolution and closure.

Closure of this kind was useful in enabling women to explore radical alternatives to conventional behaviour, but it also served other functions for Victorian readers of both sexes, and it is important to remember that women writers and readers of the period were frequently less conscious of perceiving the world as women than we are today. When imagining the woman reader, and perhaps to a lesser extent the woman writer, of a hundred years ago it is useful to think of her as wearing bifocal lenses: sometimes she read and understood through the large, outside lens as a general member of the Victorian reading public; sometimes through the lens which was more and more focused on 'women's issues'; and sometimes she was aware of the two lenses existing side by side, but offering very different views of the world. Thus the woman reading *Jane Eyre* or *Wuthering Heights* was likely to respond on a variety of levels, one of which would certainly evoke general social concerns. From this latter perspective, the orphan could be said to appeal to the Victorian reading public, living in the consciousness that industrialisation, mechanisation, urbanisation – progress generally – were cutting them off from the past and their origins. This was the first age to experience a profoundly schizophrenic attitude to itself and its origins, seeking on the one hand to demonstrate its organicism through researching and publicly celebrating its links with the past, while, on the other, constantly articulating both pride and anxiety about being new, different and self-created. Closure, which works in these texts through completion, resolution, the creation of a new stability, and, usually, marriages promising union and renewal, thus reassured readers of both sexes. This kind of ending implicitly promised a viable future, and so seemed to reaffirm the presence and intervention of some kind of spiritual parent (God or Nature) of whose existence it was increasingly difficult to be certain.

Looking through the 'woman's lens', though it might seem paradoxi-cal, it is precisely the orphan's dependence which attracted women writers and readers; not so much because it exaggerated their own dependency and the constraints it imposed, but because the orphan's dependence differed from that of most women in that it was frequently construed as both *necessary and legitimate* for the orphan to try to become independent. Fictional orphans could be shown making decisions, negotiating the world, and exploring paths traditionally barred to middle-class girls. Though their privations may be many, they are at least spared the outrage, frustration, and bitterness experienced by ambitious girls from good families[41] and so were, to some extent at least, to be envied.

Probably through a combination of pathos, vulnerability, the tension created by possible failure, and the legitimate need for independent thought and action, the parentless young woman had appealed to women writers from the earliest days of the novel (think of Jane Austen's many real and symbolic orphans). From mid-century onwards, Victorian female novelists appropriated the orphan-convention, with its established traditions of social critique and alienation, and added to it a sophisticated combination of psychological projection and political comment, making this one of the most versatile and effective of all literary conventions. In the hands of writers such as the Brontë sisters, George Eliot and Elizabeth Gaskell, the orphan became an emblem which, when decoded, is seen to be fraught with radical implications. The first of these is centred on the orphan-heroine's freedom to act, and to work.

The orphan who lacked financial independence was less likely to meet resistance or hostility if she proposed to be trained to earn her own living than the girl of modest means living with her parents or guardians; indeed Jane Eyre is sent to Lowood to prepare her to earn her own bread. Even the orphan who has been used to living relationally often has to learn to make her own way, as Lucy Snowe discovers in Charlotte Brontë's *Villette* (1853):

> Thus, there remained no possibility of dependence upon others; to myself alone could I look. I know not that I was of a self-reliant or active nature; but self-reliance and exertion were forced upon me by circumstances. . . . I must be stimulated into action. I must be goaded, driven, stung, forced to energy.
>
> (Chapter 4, 'Miss Marchmont', pp. 95–7)

For the orphan, then, action is not only possible, it is often positively necessary.

In addition to the exploration and legitimation of freedom and independence, women writers added a second, yet more radical, symbolic layer to the orphan-convention. This was a biological refutation of the patriarchal system of inheritance and its implications for marriage. Again, Florence Nightingale's observations about novelistic conventions and their relation to actual practices provide a useful focus. Nightingale writes about the usual ways in which couples of her day came to marry and how these are represented in novels. She begins by looking at the most common kind of unions: those comprised of people 'thrown together as children', observing that this state of affairs is sometimes reflected in fiction for, 'in novels, it is generally cousins who marry, and *now* it seems the only natural thing – the only possible way of making any intimacy'.[42] This, she argues, is a thoroughly unsound practice on purely biological grounds alone:

> we know that intermarriage between relations is in direct contraven-
> tion of the laws of nature for the well-being of the race; witness the
> Quakers, the Spanish grandees, the royal races, the secluded valleys
> of mountainous countries where madness, degeneration of race,
> defective organisation and cretinism flourish and multiply.[43]

The circumstances which would promote personally and biologically sound marriages are, according to Nightingale, rare in real life, but 'always provided in novels . . . whether the accident of parents' neglect, or of parents' unusual skill, or of having no parents at all, which is usually the case in novels'.[44]

Cassandra was written between 1852 and 1859, and clearly reflects contemporary interest in evolution, natural selection, and heredity. Recent work on these themes in nineteenth-century literature supports the idea that one function of the orphan in writing by women of the period was to provide a symbolic alternative to in-breeding and unnatural selection.[45] How this is so and why it should have been a topic of intense interest for women novelists emerges from the psycho-social context provided by Gilbert and Gubar in *The Madwoman in the Attic*. Their researches suggest that women writers were particularly alert to the ways in which their patriarchal society promoted female sickness as a goal. Women were surrounded by 'images of disease, traditions of disease, and invitations both to disease and to dis-ease'.[46] Contemporary debate about the position and definition of women's role helped to foreground the fundamental objectification of women which made them a kind of currency of exchange on a marriage market. This recognition, combined with the increasingly widespread dissemination of Darwin's theories in the second half of the century, provided both a concept and a vocabulary for rejecting the traditional role, and this rejection is often manifested, particularly in women's writing, in the figure of the orphan. It is as if in relation to her all the symptoms of all the diseases from which society was ailing are brought together and given a biological cause, as the foundation for a metaphor directed against class and gender prejudices and inequalities.

The orphan, for a variety of reasons, is uniquely suited to fulfil the necessary emblematic function required to make the strategy effective. First and most obvious is the orphan's lack of family connections which, in the universal principles of kinship but not in the social world of Victorian England, is a necessary precondition for an approved marriage. Proper kinship structures are founded on the elimination of closed biological groups as well as on alliances of material benefit. In the small world of the Victorian middle and upper classes, the latter consideration predominated, leading to frequent intermarrying of the kind described by Nightingale. Divested of immediate family, the orphan became the symbolic equivalent of the healthy exogamous marriage (one outside a given group).

A second reason for using orphans to make this point is that they provided the opportunity for showing what was wrong with social structures by contrast, rather than by naming ills directly, thus allowing readers to draw their own conclusions and to be less offended by a novelist's criticisms. Orphans could and did do the unconventional and thus threw convention into relief for examination, but as most orphan-heroines are ultimately commendable and their novels end with fulfilment and harmonious, traditional resolutions such as marriage, their behaviour is not regarded as compromising, ruinous or necessarily threatening. The orphan therefore provides the means of pricking consciences by the iteration of unofficial values while simultaneously making those values acceptable because ultimately the orphan conforms to traditional expectations and so never directly seems to incite those who are not orphans to radical behaviour.

That the literary orphan has an exagamous quality is further substantiated by the frequency of cross-class marriages in which they participate. Thus Dorothea Brooke marries her fellow orphan, the impoverished 'gipsy', Will Ladislaw; Mr Rochester marries his orphan-governess; Shirley Keeldar marries her tutor; Margaret Hale marries manufacturer Thornton, and so on and on. These orphans and their unconventional marriages embody the fundamental attraction of the orphan to women writers of the last century: the orphan's ability to act as an independent individual defied attempts to lump her under gross labels such as 'Angel in the House' or 'madwoman in the attic'. The orphan not only resisted categorisation, but through showing herself to be liberated from conventional, often stereotyped, behaviour she questioned its validity. With her ability to act, freedom to think, individuality and biological separateness, the orphan was capable of cutting across the conventions which quarantined people on the basis of class or gender and thus promoted psycho-social diseases arising from isolation, repression, division and frustration. In other words, the diseased condition of society, evidenced particularly in the large number of mental and physical ailments affecting women and members of the working class, was implicitly shown to be man-made: the result of masculine organisation, decisions, and values dominating society. These unnatural conditions could, it is suggested, be remedied by readjusting the balance through such things as universal suffrage, education and tolerance. This is one of the preoccupations of Mrs Gaskell's *North and South* (1854–5) – a text full of ill and dying characters – which ends not only with the symbolic marriage between northern manufacturing energy and interest and southern tradition and culture, but also with a new relationship between masters and men predicated on mutual respect and the need for all men to live decently and be properly educated and represented.

The fact that the new orphan–convention shaped by women writers almost invariably depended on the classic-realist convention of marriage-as-closure indicates the limits of its radicalism: it sought, not to abolish the family or devalue its significance, but to adjust the social balance by limiting patriarchal power and questioning the validity of a hierarchy organised according to artificially biased social constructs of class and gender. This is done in part by providing examples of bad fathers and bad patriarchal institutions, but more effective is the demonstration of capability and admirable conduct on the part of the orphan. Interestingly, some of the earliest examples of this means of criticism and instruction are provided by a male writer. Charles Dickens' constant care for women and other social victims inspired him to anticipate many of the strategies later employed and developed by women writers. Almost every one of his novels contains at least one orphan, and most of these have moved away from the bathetic appeal of Oliver Twist – who is the classic Romantic child, beautiful, pure and defenceless – to explore the personal costs and possibilities of being parentless. *Dombey and Son* (1848) is a particularly fine example of Dickens's use of the orphan–convention as in it he twins orphans of bad parents (Florence and Edith), explores the power of orphanhood to make or break character, and uses orphans to criticise male institutions, values and lack of self-knowledge.

The relatively simple orphan–convention of the first decades of the nineteenth century, which essentially exploited the sentimental, vulnerable and/or pathetic attributes of the orphan, was elaborated and redeployed during the middle years of Victoria's reign; especially by women writers, many of whom used it to make topical observations about the position and problems of women so that the orphan was established as a vehicle for radical comment, capable of providing alternative behaviour and roles to the domestic ideal without directly threatening the structure of the family. The orphan thus provided an emblem on which could be built a symbolic structure capable at once of articulating *and containing* the tensions and contradictions circulating around the changing image of women. This revitalised convention became thoroughly established and linked with the questioning of women's roles and, to a lesser extent, issues of class by the end of the century. The strength of the revitalised convention can be seen, paradoxically, in the way that its radical implications are strenuously undermined by the many writers for girls who adopt the device towards the end of the century.

Bringing the girls into line: the orphan in nineteenth-century girl's fiction

Writing for *Blackwoods Magazine* in the 1890s, Hugh E. M. Stutfield observed that as an ideal of feminine behaviour, 'self-sacrifice is out of fashion altogether in our modern school of novelists, and self-development has taken its place'.[47] To Stutfield, as to Mrs Linton, Grant Allen and the many other voices regularly and loudly raised against women's bid for liberation from the old domestic role, self-development was selfish, potentially harmful, and to be discouraged. The vigour with which they cry out against the symptoms of New Womanitis suggests its spread was endemic. Those who have written most about nineteenth-century girls' fiction start from this premise and see its confirmation in the profusion of girl-rebels who are also heroines featured in books published during the closing decades of the last century. For example, in *The Impact of Victorian Children's Fiction*, J. S. Bratton observes that new currents of thought in mid-century were increasingly reflected in writing intended for girls and were 'aimed at the moulding of aspirations and expectations to fit readers for a social role which was being newly defined'.[48] Examination of a wide range of nineteenth-century fiction for girls, from early Evangelical tracts through the imported Katy stories of Susan Coolidge, shows that this is simply not the case. In girls' fiction, the old ideal of self-sacrifice and service is perpetuated, not eradicated. The tenacity of this traditional representation of acceptable womanhood is immediately apparent in a comparison of the disparate uses made of the orphan in women writing fiction for adults and those addressing girl readers.

By the end of the last century, two principal kinds of orphans had developed in children's literature. First came the free-spirited, adventurous, conquering orphan featured in boys' stories. These young heroes ventured out into the world with all of their manly attributes in a nascent state. On their adventures they were tried, proved and rewarded. The orphan of these adventure tales had the innocence and honesty of the Lockian youth, and the latent power of a great empire to boot. Orphanhood was a gesture towards verisimilitude which made it reasonable for a young man to set off on his own without seeming callous or irresponsible in his duty towards his family. The boy-orphan inculcated respect for independence, self-reliance, and the entrepreneurial spirit. His ideological orientation was one of aggression, mastery and patriotism.

The second type of orphan was devised for books intended to be read by girls and written almost exclusively by women. It is too simple to say that these girl-orphans were concerned with providing models of passivity, renunciation, self-sacrifice and service. In fact, girl-orphans were often associated with wild, wilful and unconventional behaviour. They were outspoken, clever and frequently instigated outrageous schemes. Nevertheless, these 'naughty' orphans are not intended to facilitate the mental, emotional and social liberation of the girls for whom they were created. Where the orphan in women's writing for an adult market was advocating the need for social change, women writing for girls were promoting a conservative – even reactionary – message.

Because there is such an abundance of this kind of orphan-fiction for girls, I have chosen to limit examples to the work of a single, representative author. All of the stories described below were written by L. T. Meade, one of the most popular and prolific children's writers of the last century. Even today Meade's output is rivalled only by Enid Blyton. Between 1870 and 1915 she published approximately 250 books, edited a journal for girls, and wrote a range of journalistic features. Meade's work is now generally dismissed as formulaic and predictable, but these aspects make it highly useful for identifying and analysing conventions. A large proportion of Meade's books have as their central characters children who are permanently or temporarily orphaned. Of these, I have selected three for discussion: *Polly: A New-Fashioned Girl* (1889); *The Rebellion of Lil Carrington* (1898), and *A Sister of the Red Cross* (1901).

Despite its title, *Polly: A New-Fashioned Girl* is the book in which Meade is most obviously concerned with denying the attractions of the New Woman as role model. Her technique for doing this relies on one well-established theme of the motherless girl in Victorian literature, viz., 'the mere memory of a good mother is often pictured as having as beneficial an influence as a mother who is actually alive'.[49] Set against this sentimental evocation of motherhood is the behaviour of Polly Maybright, second oldest daughter in a large, country-doctor's family. Mrs Maybright dies in childbirth in the opening pages of the book. Significantly, Polly misses her mother's last blessing because, typically, she has left the house for the freedom of the heath.

As she is first described to the reader, Polly is, 'lanky and cross and disreputable, with bits of grass and twigs sticking in her hair, and messing and staining her faded, washed, cotton frock'.[50] Her tendency to wander freely, her familiarity with nature, constant state of dishabille, impetuous – often unthinkingly selfish – behaviour, and colloquial use of language all associate Polly Maybright with what Mrs Linton had termed 'The Girl of the Period'. Linton's article on this subject (1868) had disparaged this newfangled creature, 'whose sole idea of life is fun; whose sole aim is unbounded luxury . . . [she has] done away with such moral muffishness as consideration for others and purity of taste'.[51]

Perhaps surprisingly, having established Polly as one of these 'new-fashioned' girls, Meade seems to ask sympathy for her. She is externally naughty, yes, but not lacking in the internal values of tenderness, love, sympathy and intelligence. What Polly lacks is the practical guidance provided by good parents. While her dead mother's memory ultimately keeps Polly from corruption, she needs the regulation which is not provided by her overworked and nearly blind father. As the story unfolds, Polly learns to give up her love of fun and her determination to have her own way. In the process, she comes to respect domesticity, to care for others' well-being, and to delight in serving her family. With the model, of her departed mother as her mainstay, Polly teaches herself the error of her ways. All her mistakes serve as moral lessons. This is important as *Polly* explores many of the mistakes and pitfalls likely to bedevil a girl lacking correct parental guidance and seeks to make its warnings clear. One such message is encoded in issues of dress and deportment. Initially Polly refuses to dress and conduct herself as becomes a young lady. She is often hatless, untidy, and grass-stained. She appears in public places unchaperoned, and places herself in situations which may be morally compromising. In the semiotics of respectability in Victorian society each of these attributes indicates that Polly is in a precarious moral and social position and needs to be restrained before she goes further and plunges to 'a fate worse than death'. Polly's problems come about through the loss of her mother and the subsequent disruption of family life. When Polly learns to take on the role of mother herself and so unites the family again, domestic harmony is restored and Polly's future secured. Meade's insistence on the need for females of all ages to maintain or resume their places at the centre of domestic life and not to be seduced by the siren songs of the New Woman encapsulates the anxiety of those who feared that changes in the role of women would inevitably lead to the destruction of family life and ultimately of society.

Thus, far from repudiating the old values and putting in their place those of the 'new-fashioned' girl the book's title suggests Polly will be, Meade confirms them. For Polly, the independence and action of adolescence are simply a period of licence between childhood and the assumption of adult responsibility. (This attitude can usefully be compared to that discussed in relation to adult literature in Chapter 1). She promises to conform to the domestic ideal and show how, in the words of one typical turn-of-the-century handbook for parents, the tomboy could develop from, 'a rosebud set with little wilful thorns',[52] to become a sweet, ornamental and thoroughly conventional houseplant.

Lil Carrington, too, has to learn the virtues of obedience, passivity and service. *The Rebellion of Lil Carrington* uses the same device of twinning antithetical orphans frequently used in adult fiction. Indeed, familiarity with this convention in works for a mature audience adds an interesting dimension to Meade's characterisation. In adult fiction, women writers tended to use one member of the pair to represent domestic ideals and the other to embody worldliness and sexual experience. The former is generally successful and rewarded with marriage and motherhood while the latter fails with the loss of her virtue. Thus Dinah Morris, for all that she wanders unescorted (except by God) in her capacity as Methodist preacher, is the only young woman who could possibly clean and cook to old Mrs Bede's satisfaction. Eventually she makes the ideal wife for Adam, bears him a goodly family, and gives up her preaching. Hetty Sorrel, on the other hand, is weak, vain and pleasure-loving. Lacking proper parental guidance she is predictably led astray. The pair show how orphanhood can be the basis for making or marring character, and this convention underlies a book such as *Lil Carrington*.

Meade twins Lil with her sister Sibyl. Lil is gauche, awkward and dark. Her late father's favourite she has, according to Sibyl, 'grown up to have her own way in everything, and is . . . a little wild'.[53] By contrast, Sibyl's 'pretty daintiness, fair complexion, and winning gentle manners . . . ingratiated her with everyone' (p. 7). Together this pair of orphans comprise the warring roles for the modern young girl of their day; the active life, with its potentially sexual and subversive overtones, and maidenly passivity. Lil is bright, quick at her studies and witty. She is also reckless and attractive to men. As in the case of Polly Maybright, the possible moral and social problems which may await an unregulated girl are suggested in Lil's disregard for proper dress. In an early chapter she runs half-dressed through the woods to the railway station to reach her uncle ahead of the despised aunt into whose charge she has provisionally been given. The uncle and all the spectators are shocked and disgusted to see this middle-class adolescent girl hatless, shoeless, with hair uncombed and clothes rumpled and stained with mud and grass. At this point Meade redeems Lil by infusing her with the powerful innocence of childhood and having it overlay latent womanly charm so that her uncle realises that,

> Whatever he was, he must be truthful in her presence. He admired her, too, for awkward as she was now, he knew she had plenty of character, and he had very little doubt that by-and-by, she would be handsome – the sort of woman to take men by storm. (p. 36)

Lil rebels against her aunt and her regime of propriety. She puts herself under the guidance of a pair of disreputable New Women from America, and with them begins to lead her prim sister astray in London. The girls' reputations are in grave doubt after an evening's visit to the theatre. This bold display of independence and disregard for convention causes even Lil's staunchest allies to criticise her. She repents, confesses to God and her aunt, and from that moment is a reformed and dull character. The closing lines of the book signal her acceptance of the need to leave behind adolescence and the independence of orphanhood and to prepare for the domestic responsibilities of womanhood. 'When you give up trying to have your own way,' Lil tells her young friend Gooseberry, 'you get a strange sort of peace all over you' (p. 205).

The last of Meade's orphan-stories I've selected is the extremely popular *A Sister of the Red Cross*. The narrative revolves around another pair of orphaned sisters, Mollie and Kitty. Mollie is dark, intelligent, serious, and in her capacity as a Red Cross nurse, active in the war in South Africa. Kitty is fair, vain, and whereas Mollie has cut herself off from domestic life and romance in order to dedicate herself to her vocation, Kitty has precipitously fallen in love with the son of her guardian. The story is in many ways the girls' equivalent of a sensation novel. Its plot includes murder, drugs, crossed love, blackmail and heroism. Both girls end up on the battlefront. Mollie becomes an 'angel in the ward', and several men fall in love with her. One of these is her sister's fiancé, Captain Keith. Keith has been tricked into the engagement to save Kitty's reputation, but tries to remain loyal to his commitment and to ignore his love for Mollie. Kitty proves herself unequal to the role of helpmeet to a defender of the empire. She has nervous hysterics under fire, and funks her only attempt at nursing by scalding her lover's open wound.

Eventually the war proves the making of both girls. Mollie learns that devotion to a career is inferior to dedication to a husband and family while Kitty is forced to accept that she must not rely on pretty but potentially corrupting ways. She frees Keith so he may marry Mollie, who then assumes a life of domestic service while Kitty abandons her pampered life to take on the management of a series of homes for wounded soldiers. Once cured of her weaknesses bred of over-refinement, Kitty too promises to be rewarded with marriage and motherhood.

While clearly encouraging a period of unselfish social activity, *A Sister of the Red Cross* is as strenuous as its predecessors in its recommendation that the Victorian feminine ideal be retained. Girls are encouraged to see beyond the glamour of modern ideas of independence and to accept the quieter but more noble heroism found through dedication to service and lives of obedience. By following the trials and the progress of orphan heroines such as those created by L. T. Meade, girl readers were taught to appreciate the families which both protected them and provided opportunities for service, self-sacrifice, and preparation for wifely duties. These stories reminded girls to be grateful for parental guidance which could save them from the lapses of a Kitty or the inappropriate behaviour of a real-life Lil Carrington. The books cast a jaundiced eye over what they regard as the superficial and temporary attractions of the New Woman, and celebrate instead the traditional domestic ideal. The orphan-convention in girls' fiction is not a springboard for rejecting oppressive stereotypes, but provides the opportunity to praise the family by showing the consequences of its demise.

The contradictory nature of the orphan-conventions in adult and girls' fiction provides a useful insight into the complexities of late-Victorian attitudes to changes in the construction of femininity. While some women writers were addressing their peers and urging them to work for change, to prepare the way so that the next generation of women could enjoy freedoms and possibilities hitherto only dreamed of, apparently unbeknownst to them, others were reacting to these texts by writing their own. These reactionary books sought to ensure that the next generation would in fact reject the goals and ideals advocated by women writing for other women. Perhaps not surprisingly, it was a man who provided the parable which encapsulates the bitter irony of these two opposing efforts to shape the minds of women. As we'll see in the following chapter, Grant Allen's *The Woman Who Did* (1895) ends with the disillusioned suicide of Herminia Barton, the woman who had spent her whole life making stands against the orthodoxy which restricted women, in order that her daughter could live the life of a free woman. That same daughter is embarrassed by her mother's actions and rejects her in favour of her terrible patriarch of a grandfather and the life of a petty bourgeois wife.

2   The old woman in new clothes?
Sexual and body politics post-1848

The ambivalence of the response to the literary phenomenon of the New Woman, described in the previous chapter, scarcely surprises us. With her bohemian dress, free-spokeness, and principled challenge to the notion of asexual femininity, this creature surely represents too violent a disruption of the Victorian feminine model to have been taken seriously. But does she? This chapter will examine the sort of social and sexual challenge posed by the New Woman, and then consider similar literary challenges that, far from provoking outrage, went largely unremarked earlier in the century.

The fictional New Woman is a caricature of the late nineteenth-century feminist. Mobilising, from the middle of the century, around various single-issue campaigns (against slavery, for women's education, for the foundation of hostels for fallen women, for the reform of divorce law and the laws dealing with married women's property), the feminist impulse had become clearly recognised as such by the 1880s. The galvanic force that allowed overt feminism to become speakable – and successful – during this period was the intense shock and anger produced among women by the Contagious Diseases Acts.[1] These Acts, designed to eradicate venereal disease, gave police and officials in port and garrison towns the right to forcibly detain and physically examine women suspected of being prostitutes. Those suffering from venereal diseases were detained in the infamous Lock Hospitals for involuntary medical treatment. Stories of the barbarities perpetuated in the Lock Hospitals, and the arrest of non-prostitutes, added to the outrage of the middle-class women campaigners, but the central focus of the campaign for the repeal of the Acts (which ran, under the leadership of Josephine Butler, from 1864 to 1884) was the inequity of punishing women for what, they declared, was exclusively the product of male vice. The campaigners shifted the focus of attention from the prostitute to her client, shocking the

Victorian public – and each other – with accounts of male vice and brutality. One significant effect of the campaign was that the veil of conscious ignorance was finally torn aside – as Elaine Showalter puts it: 'How could a lady refuse to call a spade a spade when that utensil was digging the grave of her sisters?'[2] The campaign was not merely restricted to a few cranks: the manifesto published in the *Daily News* of 31 December 1869, which called for the abolition of the Acts, was signed by 124 prominent women, among them Harriet Martineau and Florence Nightingale.

Notably, therefore, the focus for overt feminist campaigning during the last forty years of the century was a specifically sexual issue. Several critics and historians have noted that the vocalised feminist disgust at male sexuality was not very far from the emotions traditionally expected of the domestic Angel.[3] We would not, in fact, expect it to be, because it was precisely the widely accepted ideology of woman's spiritual and sexual superiority that put feminist campaigners in a position to speak and be heard: 'Aggrandizement of the True Woman, sanctifying family, fueled the legislative triumphs of the New Woman, galvanizing society, for conservatives and radicals alike believed in woman's transforming power.'[4]

In the fictions of feminist women writers of the period, this ideology of male vice and the female power to cleanse it is strongly apparent. The unpleasant husband of Beth Caldwell in Sarah Grand's *The Beth Book* (1897) (discussed in detail in chapter 3) is a physician in a Lock Hospital, a fact which causes Beth to be ostracised by feminists, until they realise her total ignorance of such an institution and its purpose. In the short stories of 'George Egerton' (Mary Chavelita Dunne), published as *Keynotes* (1893) and *Discords* (1894), women are brutalised by sexually rapacious men, and oppressed by their own lack of sexual knowledge. In 'Virgin Soil', in *Discords*, a daughter castigates her mother for having failed to give her the sexual education that would have enabled her to see her husband for the philanderer he is. In 'Gone Under', in the same volume, a woman kills herself after having tried to live with the knowledge that her lover had arranged for the midwife to murder their bastard child. Olive Schreiner's powerful *Story of an African Farm* (1883) allows its heroine Lyndall only a brief rebellion, before she dies giving birth to an illegitimate child. In all of these texts, there *is* a sense of female sexual response: the suicidal woman of 'Gone Under' confesses painfully to having taken another lover after the murder of her child:

> You don't know what it is to have nothing to hold one back. I had no control over myself, something used to possess me; it is always like that, one stifles the memory of the first with the excitement of the

second. Afterwards I wanted to kill myself straight away, that is
God's truth, but I was afraid.[5]

Her sexual desire is imaged as shameful, beyond her control, productive of
more pain than pleasure. This is true, also, of Schreiner's novel, which
depicts its female characters in images recalling grotesque pregnancies,[6]
and enacts a textual 'punishment' for its heroine's sexual indiscretions
which is as damning as anything in the pages of Mrs Henry Wood. Sarah
Grand's Beth is finally allowed an ideal union with a man, but it is notably
depicted in romantic, rather than sexual terms, the novel ending as he rides
over the fields to claim her. Schreiner, in particular, was very interested in
the work of Freud, and depicts female sexuality as painful and distorted if
expressed, and productive of dangerous neuroses if repressed.

Given the strong parallels in the attitudes to sexuality expressed by
feminist campaigners and in the New Woman literature of women, it
seems perverse, to say the least, that *male* writers of New Woman
literature used their texts to extol the virtues of free love and sexual
liberation. The fact that it is their New Women – Hardy's Sue Bridehead,
Gissing's Rhoda Nunn, and Meredith's Diana – who survive into
posterity has distorted our sense of the whole New Woman debate.
Nevertheless, even in these texts that seek to reform sexual relations, do
away with marriage, and abolish the hypocrisy surrounding sexuality,
there remains a profound ambivalence about the nature of *female* sexuality.
The tenacity of the ideology of female sexual passivity can be observed by
focusing on two of the infamous male-authored New Woman novels:
Hardy's *Jude the Obscure* and Grant Allen's *The Woman Who Did* (both
published in 1895). Both novels posed a significant – and overt – challenge
to the notion that marriage should be the goal of a woman's life. Herminia
Barton, the heroine of *The Woman Who Did*, rejects marriage on principle,
offering herself to the man of her choice as his sexual and emotional
partner, but not as his wife:

'Unless one woman begins, there will be no beginning . . . Think
how easy it would be for me, dear friend', she cried with a catch in
her voice, 'to do as other women do; to accept the honourable
marriage you offer me, as other women would call it; to be false to
my sex, a traitor to my convictions; to sell my kind for a mess of
pottage – a name and a home; or even for thirty pieces of silver – to be
some rich man's wife – as other women have sold it. But, Alan, I
can't. My conscience won't let me. I know what marriage is – from
what vile slavery it has sprung; on what unseen horrors for my sister
women it is reared and buttressed; by what unholy sacrifices it is
sustained and made possible. I know it has a history. I know its past: I

know its present: and I can't embrace it. I can't be untrue to my most sacred beliefs. I can't pander to the malignant thing, just because a man would be pleased by my giving way, and would kiss and fondle me – and I love you to fondle me. But I must keep my proper place, the freedom which I have gained for myself by such arduous efforts.'[7]

Her passionate logic contrasts markedly with the covert, encoded objections to contemporary prescriptions of women's roles found in novels earlier in the century. There is even an acknowledgement of female sexual response in the aside – 'and I love you to fondle me'. The *passivity* of the desire imputed to Herminia, however, is as much a mark of the anxieties raised in this text by the issues of women's sexuality as it is an indication of a radical rejection of the previously prevailing model. Throughout the novel there is a desperately overdetermined insistence on the essential, 'natural' passivity of the 'good woman'; an insistence that sits ill with its self-conscious espousal of a feminist politics. It is the still-powerful thrashings of the ideology of the sexless woman, captured here in its death-throes. An awareness of this contradiction emerges in the following passage, in its curious mixture of absolute biological deter-minism and assertions that man's power over women is a 'usurpation':

Herminia was now beginning to be so far influenced by Alan's personality that she yielded the point with reluctance to his masculine judgement. It must always be so. The man must needs retain for many years to come the personal hegemony he has usurped over the woman; and the woman who once accepts him as lover or as husband must give way in the end, even in matters of principle, to his virile self-assertion. She would be less a woman, he less a man, were any other result possible. Deep down in the very roots of the idea of sex we come on that prime antithesis – the male, active and aggressive; the female, sedentary, passive, and receptive. (p. 83)

Ultimately, despite the overt authorial approval lavished on Herminia's high-minded and self-sacrificing project, every narrative card is stacked against her. 'The man of her choice' is not good enough for her, but in any case dies on their honeymoon. The daughter she intends as the saviour of womankind, 'the first free-born woman', is unfortunately 'genetically' materialist, an admirer of the accoutrements of respectable bourgeois life:

'Incredible as it seemed to Herminia, in the daughter of such a father and such a mother, Dolores' ideas – nay, worse, her ideals – were essentially commonplace. Not that she had much opportunity of imbibing commonplace opinions from any outside sources; she redeveloped them from within by a pure atavism. She had reverted to lower types. She had thrown back to the Philistine. (pp. 191-2)

Finally Herminia, whose drive to live out her political principles has been largely motivated, like Dorothea Brooke's, by her 'instinct for martyr-dom', kills herself to allow her daughter to marry, without shame, into a bourgeois family. She thus sacrifices the absolute principle for which she had lived to the more pressing exigencies of a mother's love, because:

> Every good woman is by nature a mother, and finds best in maternity her social and moral salvation. She shall be saved in child-bearing. Herminia was far removed indeed from that blatant and decadent sect of 'advanced women' who talk as though motherhood were a disgrace and a burden, instead of being, as it is, the full realization of women's faculties, the natural outlet for women's wealth of emotion. (p. 145)

The overt political purpose of *The Woman Who Did*: the rejection of marriage, and the legal, sexual and economic bounds it attached to women, is smothered in the weight of its anxiety to assert the security of gender distinctions. That the smothering was successful is attested to by many of the reviews that greeted this ostensibly shocking novel.[8] 'There is not a sensual thought or suggestion throughout the whole volume', assures *The Academy*, 'Though I dislike and disbelieve in his gospel, I thoroughly respect Mr Grant Allen for having stated it so honourably and bravely.' This sets the tone for the many other reviews, which praise the 'purity and innocence' of the tale while distancing themselves from its politics. The most aggressive reviewers consider that the book actually answers its own questions; as the *Sun* puts it, 'The book (for it is well-written and clever) ought to be the last note in the chorus of revolt. For it proves to demonstration the futility of the attempt.' Grant Allen himself anticipates precisely the tone of the response to his text when he describes the *Spectator*'s review of Herminia's own novel:

> 'Let us begin by admitting', said the Spectatorial scribe, 'that Miss Montague's book (she had published it under a pseudonym) 'is a work of genius. . . . Its very purity makes it dangerous. The book is mistaken; the book is poisonous; the book is morbid; the book is calculated to do irremediable mischief: but in spite of all that, the book is a book of undeniable and sadly misplaced genius.'
> If he had said no more, Herminia would have been amply

satisfied. To be called morbid by the Spectator is a sufficient proof that you have hit at least the right tack in morals. And to be accused of genius as well was indeed a triumph. (p. 151)

The irony here directed at the *Spectator*'s prurience might be suspected on occasion to be directed at the heroine herself. While notions such as Herminia's daughter as a 'throw-back' because of her conventional desires and politics may be unintentionally comic, other passages cast severe doubt on the authorial voice's declared partiality towards Herminia and her enterprise. Her intellectual pretensions – and hence the legitimacy of her arguments – are mocked and undermined, 'for a woman is a woman, let Girton do its worst' (p. 57). Feminist campaigners were eager to distance themselves from Allen's text. Suffragist Millicent Garrett Fawcett reviewed it unfavourably, denouncing Allen as 'not a friend but an enemy' of the women's movement.[9] The debate about whether male-authored New Woman texts were pro- or anti-feminist continues today. Patricia Stubbs, Gail Cunningham and John Goode all support at least one of the Hardy–Gissing–Meredith triumverate as pro-feminist, while expressing doubts about the others.[10] Terry Lovell perhaps provides the answer to the dilemma in the assertion (of Gissing) that 'his deep hostility to the marriage practices of his class, and towards "femininity", gives him some common ground with feminism, in spite of his misogyny'.[11] It is an analysis that certainly rings true for Grant Allen.

The ambivalence which characterises Grant Allen's approach to the issues of women's roles is also a marked feature of Hardy's depiction of Sue Bridehead. Another principled rebel against societal conceptions of female roles, Sue is also an hysteric and a capricious tease. She marries an elderly schoolteacher on a whim, rejecting her cousin Jude, then returns to Jude, but insists on living with him unmarried, ultimately returning to the ex-husband she finds physically repulsive because re-convinced of the sanctity of marriage by the violent deaths of her children. Although these reversals serve Hardy's apparent purpose of demonstrating the tenacious hold of his society's ideological bonds even on those who would escape them, Sue's actions remain fundamentally inexplicable because we have no sense of her as a desiring subject. She confesses her repulsion from Philotson in terms which make it unclear whether it is her husband or the sexual act itself that she finds repulsive:

'. . . though I like Mr Philotson as a friend, I don't like him – it is a torture to me to live with him as a husband' . . .

'I have only been – married a month or two', she went on, still remaining bent upon the table, and sobbing into her hands. 'And it is said that what a woman shrinks from in the early days of her marriage she shakes down to with comfortable indifference in half-a-dozen years. But that is much like saying that the amputation of a limb is no affliction, since a person gets comfortably accustomed to the use of a wooden leg or arm in the course of time.'[12]

Hardy's depiction of his New Woman as sexually frigid has been welcomed by critic Patricia Stubbs as psychologically radical. She argues that Sue's mental and sexual masochism are symptoms of her inability to break free emotionally from an ideology she rejects intellectually. It is these conflicts, Stubbs asserts, that make Sue 'such a perverse and contradictory, yet prophetic figure'.[13] But while Sue's confusion is presented as deeply structured, it is surely not an unproblematic psycho-political portrayal on Hardy's part. For a male author, there is a great deal invested, at this particular historical moment, in the depiction of a female sexual radical as entirely without active sexual desire. Sue's sexuality is completely bound up in her sense of herself as a desired *object*: 'I should shock you', she tells Jude, 'by letting you know how I give way to my impulses, and how much I feel that I shouldn't have been provided with attraction unless it were meant to be exercised. Some women's love of being loved is insatiable' (p. 214)

Like Grant Allen's, Hardy's text goes to some lengths to free its female protagonist from any imputation of an active sexual desire. Indeed, in the curious evasions and contortions of Grant Allen's moral philosophy, the absence of such a desire is the element that absolutely separates Herminia from a prostitute: it is the fact that she acts from the highest principles alone that constitutes her contravention of the social convention with regard to unmarried sexual intercourse as a rise, rather than a fall:

Here, of my own free will, I take my stand for the right, and refuse your sanctions! No woman that I know of has ever yet done that. Other women have fallen, as men choose to put it in their odious dialect: no other has voluntarily risen as I propose to do. (p. 46)

Of course, in both cases, the mere articulation of objections to the institution of marriage placed the texts firmly in the camp of the sexual rebels and the literary avant-garde, but the precise tenor of the sexual gospel preached is surely of supreme importance. As Foucault pertinently notes:

it would be a mistake to see in this proliferation of discourses merely a quantitative phenomenon, something like a pure increase, as if what was said in them was immaterial, as if the fact of speaking about sex were of itself more important than the forms of imperatives that were imposed on it by speaking about it.'[14]

The quantitative assumption of which Foucault speaks has informed much of the critical debate about nineteenth-century sexuality and has led to an acceptance of the male-authored New Woman literature as representing an essentially new and productive articulation of a politics of female sexuality.[15] In fact, this literature, like that of the earlier part of the century, articulates a tension between a sexless ideal and a desire for more active models of femininity. The covert and overt assumptions may represent a reversal of those in the earlier novels, with free love the ostensible ideal, and female sexual desire evaded, but the tension between the two elements continues to exist. These New Woman novels are an attempt to resolve the problem of the cultural disjunction between wives and sex, but in the service only of masculinity. The pure, impeccably marriageable heroines of this fiction are eroticised by being possessed outside the sanitising institution of marriage, and are saved from 'falling' by being themselves scrupulously uninterested in sex. This literature is not, as some critics have claimed, a reversal of a repression of sexuality operative throughout the rest of the century, but one of a variety of attempts to straddle the gulf that lay between sex and the middle-class woman.

The male-authored New Woman literature is not, of course, a univocal discourse. The figure of Arabella, the artificial, sexually aggressive barmaid in *Jude the Obscure*, provides a startling counterpoint to the high-minded heroines that people these fictions. Arabella, understandably, was D. H. Lawrence's favourite among Hardy's females. She is lewd and lascivious, attracting Jude's attention by hurling a pig's penis at him. Her first articulation of her aim to 'have' Jude is couched, not in terms of the economic advantages he might have to offer (as we might expect in the light of her later actions) but purely in terms of desire:

> In a few moments Arabella replied in a curiously low, hungry tone of latent sensuousness: 'I've got him to care for me; yes! But I want him to more than care for me; I want him to have me; to marry me! I must have him. I can't do without him. He's the sort of man I long for. I shall go mad if I can't give myself to him altogether! I felt I should when I first saw him.' (p. 47)

Arabella is not only desiring, she is highly desirable: she transfixes Jude with the force of her sexuality, 'the unvoiced call of woman to man'. Patricia Stubbs notes the ways in which Arabella's narrative role reverses some significant literary conventions:

She seduces Jude, where the male villain would normally seduce the innocent virgin (for example Alec d'Uberville and Tess); she dupes him into marriage with her by pretending she is pregnant when she is not – the woman, really pregnant, would normally be abandoned at this stage of a more conventional novel (for example, Hardy's own Fanny Robin and George Eliot's Hetty Sorrel), she commits bigamy without thinking twice about it (at least Lady Audley was hard put to it to cover up her crime) and she finally re-seduces Jude and persuades him to re-marry her when according to convention she should, by this point in the novel, have been an abandoned whore dying in the streets. She even has another prospective husband lined-up for when Jude dies. (pp. 65–6)

On one level, Arabella's role is to point up the hypocrisy of a code of sexual morality that will allow her, with her easy amoralities, to remain eminently respectable, but will simultaneously condemn the loving and committed Sue and Jude for their rejection of marriage. She is more than just a figure of society's hypocrisy, however. She represents a female sexual energy which, if not politicised, is at least not ultimately masochistic and self-defeating.

The preceding discussion has attempted to map both the extent and the limitations of the representations of female sexuality in the New Woman literature of the last decade of the century. The rest of this chapter will explore other such representations, with the aim of demonstrating that the same imperatives and ambivalences govern the treatment of the theme of women and sex in the middle years of that century as they do at its end.

Prostitution and retribution

As Patricia Stubbs' remarks on Arabella reveal, an articulation of an active female sexuality would almost invariably be accompanied, in nineteenth-century fiction, by a symbolic retribution. Nowhere is this process more clearly apparent than in the figure of the prostitute.[16] The preoccupation of the Victorian novel with effecting a union between wives and sexuality is paradoxically underlined by the fact that, though we had no difficulty in finding symbolic and narrative encodings of sexuality in association with 'pure' women, we find great difficulty in reading the novel's representations of *prostitutes* as anything other than punitive. The near-impossibility of reading the prostitute as a sexualised figure shows how localised is the attempt to eroticise women and provide them with sexual knowledge: the prostitute in most novels of the period is less an individual in her own right than a marker of the limits of the socially tolerable. Her fall is a warning of the bounds beyond which the author cannot allow the heroine to pass.

It has been frequently remarked that the fictional representation of prostitutes was highly inaccurate. The interviews of journalists like Henry Mayhew with women working as prostitutes, and the annual reports of The Society for the Suppression of Vice and of The London Society for the Protection of Young Females and the Prevention of Juvenile Prostitution, and the reports and statistics of the Metropolitan Police reveal a picture of rampant prostitution, with the West End of London liberally bespattered with brothels. Contemporary commentators recognised the link between vice and the terrible social conditions in which it proliferated. W. R. Greg, in *The Great Sin of the Great Cities* (1853), made the explicit association between poverty and prostitution, speaking of those 'for whom there is no fall . . . for they stood already on the lowest level of existence'.[17] Frederick Engels also, in his savage indictment of *The Condition of the Working Classes in England* (1887), drew continual links between prostitution and the degraded condition of life in the city slums. The difference between these depictions of the phenomenon of prostitution and that espoused by most novelists of the period is neatly summarised by Henry Mayhew, who vigorously refutes the 'foolish idea . . . which still lingers in the minds of both men and women that the harlot's progress is short and rapid, and that there is no possible advance, moral or physical'.[18] Mayhew's own interviews with prostitutes provide an effective riposte to this notion. In particular, his account of a conversation with an 'occasional prostitute' reveals the ways in which prostitution could function as a source of supplementary income, rather than as an irrevocable choice about identity. Remarkably, also, through the inevitably distorting lens of Mayhew's reporting, we get a sense of an individuality and strength of character that transcends the sordidity of her profession, and allows her to analyse her own condition, seizing the sociologists' tools for her purpose:

> I met a woman in Fleet Street, who told me that she came into the street now and then to get money not to subsist upon, but to supply her with funds to meet the debts her extravagance caused her to contract. But I will put her narrative into a consecutive form.
>
> 'Ever since I was twelve', she said, 'I have worked in a printing office where a celebrated London morning journal is put in type and goes to press. I get enough money to live upon comfortably; but then I am extravagant, and spend a great deal of money in eating and drinking, more than you would imagine. . . . I am attached to a man in our office, to whom I shall be married some day. He does not suspect me, but on the contrary believes me to be true to him, and you do not suppose that I ever take the trouble to undeceive him. . . .

I sometimes go to the Haymarket, either early in the evening, or early in the morning, when I can get away from the printing, and sometimes I do a little in the day-time. This is not a frequent practice of mine; I only do it when I want money to pay for anything. I am out now with the avowed intention of picking up a man. . . . Birth is the result of accident. It is the merest chance in the world whether you're born a countess or a washerwoman. I'm neither one nor t'other; I'm only a mot who does a little typographing by way of variety. Those who have had good nursing, and all that, and the advantages of a sound education, who have a position to lose, prospects to blight, and relations to dishonour, may be blamed for going on the loose, but I'll be hanged if I think that priest or moralist is to come down on me with the sledge-hammer of his denunciation. You look rather surprised at my talking so well. I know I talk well, but you must remember what a lot has passed through my hands for the last seven years, and what a lot of copy I've set up. There's very little I don't know, I can tell you. It's what old Robert Owen would call the spread of education.'

Although Mayhew has clearly re-shaped the words of this girl, his own distance from her self-justification is stated in his closing remarks:

The common-sense she displayed was extraordinary for one in her position, but, as she said, she had certainly had superior oppor-tunities, of which she had made the most. And her arguments, though based upon fallacy, were exceedingly clever and well put. So much for the spread of education amongst the masses. Who knows to what it will lead? (p.191)

Mayhew places this interview in the fourth volume of *London Labour and the London Poor*, entitled 'Those That Will Not Work': an interesting indication of the nineteenth-century refusal to view prostitution as *work*, and therefore an economic decision for those engaged in it; seeing it rather as a perversion of the sex instinct and of feminine modesty: a reading undercut by the voice of this unknown girl. The alterna-tive tendency – prevalent amongst novelists – of sentimentalising the figure of the prostitute is also denied by this account; as the girl freely admits to a taste for luxuries – a taste, however, that is recuperable back into the model of the prostitute as a prey to exotic and sensuous appetites.

Prostitution, in this account, is far from being the inescapable condition that it is in the novel of the period, where the girl's seduction begins an inexorable progress to her death in the gutter. It is extremely significant, however, that even the sociologists and journalists who place prostitution firmly in a material matrix continue to discuss it in the language of vice, sin and retribution. William Acton, who asserts unequivocally in the preface to *Prostitution Considered in its Moral, Social and Sanitary Aspects* (1857) that 'the great mass of prostitutes in this country are in the course of time absorbed into the so-called respectable classes', accompanies this socially devastating insight with a declaration of his desire to 'heal the sick prostitute, and to cleanse her moral nature'.[19]

Another common set of explanations for the prostitute's existence were the arguments, drawn from Darwinian notions, of the essentially animalistic sexual instinct of the fallen woman. W. R. Greg spoke of their 'unbridled indulgence in animal desire'[20], and Cobbett's reassurances to young men on the subject of the good woman's lack of sexual desire were motivated by his sense of the insatiable sexual appetites of the women of the street who would have provided the young man's sexual initiation. These impulses, it was increasingly believed, would physically and emotionally bankrupt both individual men, and the state itself. The belief that the men were at risk from women's sexuality continued well into the twentieth century in the surprisingly persistent myth that nymphomania was a medical condition requiring treatment.

There is, clearly, a fundamental paradox at the heart of Victorian notions of female sexuality, that sees the female ideal as 'naturally' sexless, and the fallen woman as 'naturally' libidinous. One resolution of the paradox is found in the dangerous figure of the young girl, navigating the choppy waters of adolescence, with the potential to rise to the ideal or fall into the abyss of sexual impulse and impurity. (Another is to be found in the decadent images discussed in the following chapter). Seduction figures largely in all accounts of the girl's fall: in those collected by journalists such as Mayhew, and in the representations of fiction.

The character of Esther in Elizabeth Gaskell's *Mary Barton* (1848) functions as an awful warning to her niece Mary of the results of allowing oneself to be seduced. Esther's suitor abandons her and her illegitimate child, leaving her no choice but to turn to prostitution to feed them. The very notion of 'seduction' implies a culpability on the part of the woman in this discourse. It is Esther's frivolity and love of clothes that initiates her fall, and Mary's delight in Harry Carson's admiration, and her naive day-dreaming about the luxuries marriage to him would bring, that place her in such imminent danger. In Elizabeth Barrett Browning's *Aurora Leigh* (1857), Marian's total innocence is maintained by the device of having her drugged to unconsciousness when she is raped in the brothel to which her parents have sold her. Had she been conscious during the ordeal, this device implies, some doubt would have been cast on her purity. Purity, for the nineteenth century, equates with ignorance: rape is no defence.

In both *Mary Barton* and *Aurora Leigh*, the fallen woman is paired with the pure heroine. In the case of Gaskell's text, the narrative relationship between the two is structured around the conventional warning. Esther's fate is that which could have been Mary's. In *Aurora Leigh* Barrett Browning significantly adjusts this model, having Aurora, rather than the putative hero Romney, lift Marian from the gutter, and – very radically – allowing Marian to claim the child of her rape as her's alone:

> . . . Ah God! I could not bear
> To see my darling on a good man's knees,
> And know, by such a look, or such a sigh,
> Or such a silence, that he thought sometimes,
> 'This child was fathered by some cursèd wretch' . . .
> For, Romney, angels are less tender-wise
> Than God and mothers: even *you* would think
> What *we* think never. He is ours, the child;
> And we would sooner vex a soul in heaven
> By coupling with it the dead body's thought,
> It left behind it in a last month's grave,
> Than in my child, see other than . . . my child.
> We only never call him fatherless
> Who has God and his mother . . .[21]

Marian refuses to compromise this claim by marrying, and so risking having other – legitimate – children whose status would mock that of her first born. It is Aurora's financial and emotional support that enables her to take this stand; the relationship between the fallen woman and the middle-class feminist lies at the heart of the poem.

Such pairings have more significance than that of simple contrast. It is possible to read the many good girl–bad girl pairings of Victorian fiction (Amelia Sedley and Becky Sharpe, Lucy Snowe and Ginerva Fanshawe, Dinah Morris and Hetty Sorrel) as not merely moralistic comparisons, but as a means of providing the heroine herself with a moral education that allows her at least a knowledge of and association with sex, if not the actual experience of the forbidden act. The fallen woman, in this reading, is not merely a more or less realistically represented figure, but is the opportunity for the sexuality displaced on to her culturally to return to contact with the main stream of femininity. In the case of *Aurora Leigh*, this overspilling of sexual 'experience' is arguably what allows the blue-stocking career writer Aurora to speak what is one of the most significant eroticisations of the male body by a desiring female in Victorian literature:

... Gradually
The purple and transparent shadows slow
Had filled up the whole valley to the brim,
And flooded all the city, which you saw
As some drowned city in some enchanted sea,
Cut off from nature, – drawing you who gaze,
With passionate desire, to leap and plunge
And find a sea-king with a voice of waves,
And treacherous soft eyes, and slippery locks
You cannot kiss but you shall bring away
Their salt upon your lips . . .
Methinks I have plunged, I see it all so clear . . .
And, O my heart, . . . the sea-king!
                                        In my ears
The sound of waters. There he stood, my king!
I felt him rather than beheld him . . .
– You Romney! . . . (Eighth Book, ll. 34–44, 59–62, 71)

The seductive, duplicitous figure of the mermaid is replaced in Aurora's vision by the sea-king, who transmutes into Romney Leigh – but a Romney Leigh subdued and blinded. This blindness, although evidently serving the same equalising purpose as that of Rochester, also ties Romney to the decadent images – to be explored in detail in Chapter 3 – of the *femmes fatales* who exist in a state of visionary trance. Although Aurora's usurpation of a masculine economic and social independence would account in part for her occupation of the position of spectator, rather than object, of such erotic imaginings, it is surely her philanthropic association with Marian that makes legitimate the sexual 'knowledge' that transforms her previously vaguely poetic references to 'passion' into an unashamedly sexualised fantasy.[22] Although this argument would allow for a reading of Victorian fiction as more concerned with eroticising its heroines than is usually seen to be the case, it is clear that this eroticising is still significantly encoded and displaced. Another place we might look for its encoding is in the representation of women's bodies and clothing.

Dressing the heroine

In the course of the nineteenth century, novelistic descriptions of heroines undergo some significant transformations. Departing from the vagueness of late eighteenth- and early nineteenth-century fictional descriptions (the heroines of Scott, Jane Austen and Maria Edgeworth, however complex their characterisation, are rather shadowy physical presences), later nineteenth-century novelists employ increasingly detailed and encoded taxonomies of the physical features of their heroines. Jeanne Fahnestock, in 'The Heroine of Irregular Features'[23] usefully notes the influence of the 'science' of physiognomy on heroine description between 1830 and 1870, establishing a taxonomy of elements of character associated with particular physical features, considering the different implications possession of a broad or a long chin, for instance, would have for the heroine's morality and likely fate. Fahnestock's account of the power of this pseudo-science in heroine description is convincing, but her sense of its existence as a tacit and complete code of characterisation means that she doesn't explore the narrative and ideological significance of the many elisions and evasions in the accounts of the physical appearance of heroines.

Laura Fairlie, heroine of Wilkie Collins' *The Woman in White* (1860), is the archetypal Victorian feminine ideal: fair, pretty rather than 'striking', demure, modest, and lacking in frivolity or vanity:

> The water-colour drawing that I made of Laura Fairlie, at an after period, in the place and attitude in which I first saw her, lies on my desk while I write. I look at it, and there dawns upon me brightly, from the dark greenish-brown background of the summer-house, a light, youthful figure, clothed in a simple muslin dress, the pattern of it formed by broad alternating stripes of delicate blue and white. . . . a little straw hat of the natural colour, plainly and sparingly trimmed with ribbon to match the gown, covers her head, and throws its soft pearly shadow over the upper part of her face. Her hair is of so faint and pale a brown – not flaxen, and yet almost as light; not golden, yet almost as glossy – that it nearly melts, here and there, into the shadow of the hat. . . . The eyebrows are rather darker than the hair; and the eyes are of that soft, limpid, turquoise blue, so often sung by the poets, so seldom seen in real life. Lovely eyes in colour, lovely eyes in form – large and tender and quietly thoughtful – but beautiful above all things in the quiet truthfulness of look that dwells in their inmost depths, and shines through all their changes of expression with the light of a purer and a better world.[24]

Despite the ideal nature of her beauty, this description of Laura is notably imprecise: her beauty of body and soul is represented synecdochally only by her eyes, which are remarkable mainly as conduits to a better world – the light shines *through*, not *from* them. Further, the figure itself is imprecise – her hair 'melts' into the shadow of her hat. The very process of picturing is vague: Laura is here described from a picture the narrator drew, from memory, of his first impressions of her. Such regressions act against the apparent simplicity of the depiction, leaving us with no sense of a character behind the physical form. Indeed, immediately after this description the narrator questions his ability to represent Laura in any terms other than those of cliché: precisely because she *is* an ideal, her body functions as a blank canvas on to which the observer's desires and fantasies can be sketched.

The vagueness of Laura's description is crucial in terms of the complex plot of the *Woman in White*: it is necessary that she should be so apparently unremarkable in appearance as to be easily confused with the mad Anne Catherick, with whom she is ultimately exchanged by the machinations of her villainous husband. It is equally necessary that Walter should have some absolute means of identifying the true Laura, and her eyes provide that means, since only someone who loved her would have gazed into them so closely.

The essential feature of the type of heroine Laura Fairlie epitomises is her bodily, and therefore sexual nullity. Such heroines, found particularly in the novels of Dickens, face an increasing challenge from the strong, dark passionate women who claim centre stage in the novels of women writers such as George Eliot and Elizabeth Gaskell. The physiognomy of the statuesque heroine – Maggie Tulliver, Margaret Hale, Dorothea Brooke – invariably speaks passion and strength of character: she has a strong jaw, full lips, and arms that are both sensually rounded and capable of effective action. Her bodily appearance parallels her career, with her large capacity for both action and passion. Because their physical features betoken sensuality, these heroines are often eroticised, if covertly, by male characters and narrators: something that is markedly absent from the textual depiction of Laura Fairlie. Interestingly, the most complete eroticisation of a female body in *The Woman in White* is Walter Hartright's description, not of his beloved Laura, but of his first sight of her half-sister Marian Halcombe:

> The instant my eyes rested on her, I was struck by the rare beauty of her form, and by the unaffected grace of her attitude. Her figure was tall, yet not too tall; comely and well-developed, yet not fat; her head set on her shoulders with an easy pliant firmness; her waist, perfection in the eyes of a man, for it occupied its natural place, it filled out its natural circle, it was visibly and delightfully undeformed by stays . . . The easy elegance of every movement of her limbs and body as soon as she began to advance from the far end of the room, set me in a flutter of expectation to see her face clearly. She left the window – and I said to myself, The lady is dark. She moved forward a few steps – and I said to myself, The lady is young.

She approached nearer – and I said to myself (with a sense of surprise which words fail me to express), The lady is ugly! . . .
The lady's complexion was almost swarthy, and the dark down on her upper lip was almost a moustache. She had a large, firm, masculine mouth and jaw; prominent, piercing, resolute brown eyes; and thick, coal-black hair, growing unusually low down on her forehead. Her expression – bright, frank, and intelligent – appeared, while she was silent, to be altogether wanting in those feminine attractions of gentleness and pliability, without which the beauty of the handsomest woman alive is beauty incomplete. (p. 58)

Marian's body is described with a lascivious textual attention, anatomised feature by feature, in marked contrast to the textual and visual evasions employed to describe Laura. Far from the revelation of Marian's ugliness forming a shocking reversal that would deny the previous eroticisation, it is precisely *because* she is ugly – and therefore not textually available as a wife for Walter – that she can be seen as an erotic spectacle. Also significant is the fact that her ugliness is constituted in her resemblance to a male. It is this partial masculinity that allows her to occupy her curious dual role as both Laura's girlish confidante and Walter's detective side-kick. Her remarkable physiognomy allows her to reject some, at least, of the constraints of her feminine role without being compromised in the novel's terms. Her elaborate stratagems to devise a suitable dress to allow her to climb out on to a window-ledge in the dark and wet to eavesdrop on the plans of the murderous villain are a clear indication of just how far she is allowed to go, and involve a curious textual strip-tease combined with almost ritual assertions of modesty:

A complete change in my dress was imperatively necessary for many reasons. I took off my silk gown to begin with, because the slightest noise from it on that still night might have betrayed me. I next removed the white and cumbersome parts of my under-clothing, and replaced them by a petticoat of dark flannel. Over this I put my black travelling cloak, and pulled the hood on to my head. In my ordinary evening costume I took up the room of three men at least. In my present dress, when it was held close about me, no man could have passed through the narrowest spaces more easily than I. (p. 342)

The physical restrictions of her feminine dress are only partially alleviated by this re-dressing: the petticoat, albeit single and black, remains an absolute essential, a representation of physical and, by implication, sexual modesty. It is this item of clothing that Marian had earlier identified as symptomatic of the restricted conditions of femininity: 'Being, however, nothing but a woman, condemned to patience, propriety, and petticoats for life, I must respect the housekeeper's opinions, and try and compose myself in some feeble and feminine way' (p. 221). As the petticoat clearly represents a modest concealment of the body, its use as a metaphor for women's oppression names that oppression as in part a physical, arguably a sexual, repression. The erotic overtones the garment carries for the male imagination, due to its intimate proximity to the female body, far from contradicting the idea that the petticoat images female repression, merely serves to bring to light the extent to which female physical restriction was eroticised for the nineteenth century.

Lucy Snowe, heroine of Charlotte Brontë's *Villette*, goes through somewhat similar manoeuvres when she refuses to assume a completely male garb when playing a man in a theatrical performance, instead devising a hybrid costume of a skirt combined with a man's jacket. While this hermaphrodite outfit could be read as a refusal to usurp absolutely a male role or appearance, whatever the circumstances, it also represents the curious way in which masculine elements in a woman's appearance were becoming eroticised. In the case of both Lucy Snowe's and Marian Halcombe's outfits, what is at stake in the adoption of a complete masculine guise is sexual modesty: there is a sense in which the male garments would too potently suggest their opposite. It is a sexual threat that is more fully realised in the contemporary furore over dress reformers and their attempts to introduce the scandalous 'bloomers'. The reverse process of sexual signification is in operation in the device of the nun's habit that floats through *Villette*, apparently uninhabited. The classic symbolism of female chastity associated with the nun is violently inverted by the revelation that the nun is in fact a man, present in the school for illicit – and hence, by implication, sexual – encounters with Genievre Fanshawe. Here, again, sexuality is encoded in the notion of cross-dressing. It is in an attempt to avoid such sexual associations that Lucy and Marian adopt their hybrid costumes; rather than playing with the rich complexities of gender roles in the manner of the heroine of a Shakespearian comedy, they seek to become neuter – to have no gender, rather than both.

The Woman in White evidences one of the most striking preoccupations with women's clothing to be found in the novels of the period. As well as Walter Hartright's meticulous documentation of the clothing and appearance of every woman he meets, there is the fact that both the story's plot, and the melodramatic 'plots' of the villains within it, turn on the physical similarities between the heroine and Anne Catherick, the woman in white. The latter drifts spectre-like through the narrative, her all-white dress inappropriate for the cold and dark in which she is usually encountered. The dress, we learn, is the result of a feeble-minded obsession with Laura's mother, who had had some of Laura's clothes altered for the child Anne, 'explaining to her that little girls of her complexion looked neater and better all in white than in anything else' (p. 84). Mrs Fairlie's motivation is concern at the 'sad want of taste in colour and pattern' with which Anne's own mother had dressed her. This initial act of class-motivated benevolence has transmuted into a physical representation of insanity by the time Anne reaches adulthood: a knowledge of appropriate dress-codes is revealed as an index of the class and – extremely – the sanity of the Victorian female. The subtlety of these codes is great: the echoes between Laura and Anne Catherick are most strongly evoked immediately before the revelation that allows us to name the woman in white as the child dressed by Mrs Fairlie. As Walter and Marian read Mrs Fairlie's letters, Laura paces the terrace, dressed in a simple white muslin gown, which Walter had previously interpreted as the physical manifestation of her 'natural delicacy of feeling and natural intensity of aversion to the slightest personal display of her own wealth' (p. 80). Anne Catherick's identical dress marks her out, however, as *un*natural. In dress, context is all: the semiotics are constructed around the representation of difference, rather than presence. Laura's white dress is not Anne's, and Laura and Anne are not identical, but Anne represents what Laura might become, and Laura, indeed, stands in the place of Anne when she is incarcerated in an asylum under her name.

The mother who dressed Anne with vulgar ostentation figures a crucial association for the Victorian imagination between immorality and a liking for clothing above one's station. Mrs Catherick is 'a heartless woman, with a terrible will of her own – fond of foolish admiration and fine clothes' (p. 487). The mystery of her involvement with the villainous Sir Percival Glyde is intensified when we hear of her husband's past discovery of 'a lot of lace handkerchiefs, and two fine rings, and a new gold watch and chain, hid away in his wife's drawer – things that nobody but a born lady ought ever to have' (p. 488). These revelations are made by an old acquaintance of Mrs Catherick's, but the woman herself pithily confirms the importance of fine clothing as a motivating force in her actions: 'The dress of Virtue, in our parts, was cotton print. I had silk' (p. 554).

It is in order to avoid the damaging association of fashion with frivolity at best, immorality at worst, that such stress is placed on the simplicity of the heroine's dress in so many nineteenth-century novels. Laura's blue and white striped muslin dress and straw hat vie for plainness with Dorothea Brooke's 'poor dress', which, as we are told in the first lines of *Middlemarch*, threw her beauty into relief. The most extreme association of clothing and immorality is in the depiction of the prostitute. Even relatively progressive analysts of the material basis of prostitution, such as

Henry Mayhew, named a love of clothing and a liking of male admiration as primary causes of a girl's fall. A classic articulation of this association is given in Elizabeth Gaskell's *Mary Barton*.[25] John Barton foresees the fate of his sister-in-law, Esther, in her dress: 'Says I, "Esther, I see what you'll end at with your artificials and your fly-away veils, and stopping out when honest women are in their beds; you'll be a street-walker"' (p. 43).

And, indeed, a street-walker she becomes. When John Barton next encounters her, he recognises her profession by her clothes:

> It was told by her faded finery, all unfit to meet the pelting of the pitiless storm; the gauze bonnet, once pink, now dirty white, the muslin gown, all draggled, and soaking wet up to the very knees; the gay-coloured barège shawl, closely wrapped round the form, which yet shivered and shook. (p. 168)

When he sees in the bedraggled, frozen form his wife's sister, he experiences hate: directed, most extremely, at her dress: 'But most of all he loathed the dress; and yet the poor thing, out of her little choice of attire, had put on the plainest thing she had, to come on that night's errand' (p. 169). It is not only the sordid and inadequate nature of her covering that marks Esther as a prostitute in this encounter: it is the gay colour of her shawl, and the delicate fabrics – gauze and muslin – which, utterly inadequate for any manual labour, were the preserve of the leisured classes. John Barton had made precisely this association in his earlier condemnation of Esther's clothes: 'she came downstairs, dressed in her Sunday gown, with a new ribbon in her bonnet, and gloves on her hands, like the lady she was so fond of thinking herself' (p. 43).

It is her usurpation of the clothes of the upper classes, made possible, as Barton again notes, by the intermittent economic independence afforded women by factory work, that is Esther's initial transgression. From these primary presumptions – of economic independence from men, and the foray into the frivolous excesses of upper class dress – Esther's fall is completed, not begun, by her descent into prostitution.

Helena Michie, in the discussion of pornography in her excellent study of *The Flesh Made Word*, also draws a connection between prostitution and dress. Arguing that the prostitute, for the Victorians, is 'a cipher of displaced lust', that her body is made invisible in its 'strangely fleshless fleshiness', she focuses on the use of the metaphor of dress to cover and reveal the prostitute, noting, for instance, that:

> The descriptions of Nancy and the other prostitutes in *Oliver Twist* focus far more obsessively on what they put on than on what they take off; Oliver's first observations, that they have 'a good deal of

hair' and 'a great deal of colour in their faces', emphasize dress and artificiality over nudity and sensuality. (p. 76)

Michie sees the impulse to clothe the Victorian prostitute as an attempt to 'cover up' her flesh; to displace her sexuality. I have argued that there is also a more material strand running through these depictions, which asserts that it is her love of finery that pre-disposes the prostitute to fall; however, the process of the displacement of sexuality Michie notices is one that is markedly operative in many texts. It is perhaps most elaborately invoked, as we saw at the beginning of the previous chapter, in *Villette*. Like *The Woman in White*, Brontë's is a novel obsessed by clothing. Characters are defined by what they wear: Madame Beck wears an Indian shawl which invests her with power and majesty – in her own as well as others' estimations. Lucy Snowe has none of the confidence required to carry off such an exotic garment; indeed she is overcome with horror at the prospect of wearing a pink dress to a party:

> Two days after came home – a pink dress!
> 'That is not for me,' I said hurriedly, feeling that I would almost as soon clothe myself in the costume of a Chinese lady of rank.
> 'We shall see whether it is for you or not,' rejoined my godmother, adding with her resistless decision, 'Mark my words. You will wear it this very evening.'
> I thought I should not; I thought no human force should avail to put me into it. A pink dress! I knew it not. It knew not me. . . .
> Without any force at all, I found myself led and influenced by another's will, unconsulted, unpersuaded, quietly over-ruled. In short, the pink dress went on, softened by some drapery of black lace. I was pronounced to be en grand ténue, and requested to look in the glass. I did so with some fear and trembling; with more fear and trembling, I turned away. . . .
> For the rest, the dress was made with extreme simplicity, guiltless of flounce or furbelow; it was but the light fabric and bright tint which scared me.[26]

The pink dress is invested with agency in the Gothic excesses of the language: it 'came home', apparently unaided; 'it knew not me'. It is an instrument of torture that Lucy will valiantly resist. She fears the colour for its ability to draw attention to her presence: to make her bodily by making her visible. *Villette* is a novel that challenges the modern feminist orthodoxy that representations of female sexuality are invariably emancipatory textual moments: Lucy Snowe's power to judge others and to control the text of her own life comes precisely from her bodily invisibility, and her consequent social marginalisation.

A murderous dress as Gothic as Lucy's figures prominently in the many nineteenth-century depictions of the fate of the seamstress. The famous *Punch* cartoon of 'The Haunted Lady or "The Ghost" in the Looking-glass' of 1863, which depicted a fashionable lady in an elaborate gown, with the figure of the dying seamstress who had rushed to finish the garment reflected in the mirror, is only one example of a large number of visual and textual depictions of this subject.[27] This figure of the sacrificed seamstress is one which lies very significantly behind the mirror of nineteenth-century depictions of the feminine. Her absence from the discourses of fashion is insisted on so ritually by so many nineteenth-century writers that she seems to be another of Foucault's speaking silences – where a society loudly speaks of that which it claims it cannot say. The many accounts of her very real physical sufferings (often sentimentalised and even oddly eroticised in these accounts) are, it seems possible, a displaced means of representing other – less fatal – sufferings bound up in the restrictions of the nineteenth-century structuring of the female body. She is a symbolic scapegoat, a ritual representation of her society's sense that there is something painful and punitive bound up in its images of female beauty and fashion.

Where the fictional representations of the young girl's progress to maturity often allow her to retain some of the physical exuberance and even forbidden knowledge of her youth, and the images of fallen women are used to bring such knowledge into association with the heroine, clothing in the nineteenth-century novel almost invariably makes visible the body in a way detrimental to the heroine. It produces her for the gaze of the spectator, and its qualities are generative of pleasure only for that spectator, and not for the woman herself. Whether the woman's body is tastefully erased, or made vulgarly visible by her dress, she is constructed as a spectacle for a putatively male observer. Walter Hartright, with his anatomising gaze and disproportionate interest in women's dress, merely articulates the response of the imagined male viewer for whom these images are constructed. Hartright's is the eye that reads the statements encoded in women's dress; that distinguishes Laura's innocent and modest white dress from Anne Catherick's mad one. So too, Esther is recognised as a prostitute through John Barton's reading of her dress. The only dress of those here surveyed that is explicitly interpreted by a woman is Lucy Snowe's pink dress – which is perhaps endowed with agency precisely to allow her to remain outside its determining folds. Even Lucy's judgement must later be confirmed by a male observer, M. Paul, who interprets Lucy herself as immoral, rather than the dress, thus amply justifying her earlier fears.

There is notably very little sense in Victorian literature of dress as explicitly pleasurable for women. It is rarely, for instance, represented in terms of its tactile qualities, or as an aesthetic phenomenon. Those women who do take pleasure in their dress are at best infantile, at worst morally debased – often, in fact, they are both, like the murderous Lady Audley, whose greatest pleasure in her bigamous marriage is the opportunity it gives her to sit in her lacy boudoir, playing with her piles of jewels, and trying on her silk dresses. One exception to this rule is that curious scene at the beginning of *North and South* (1855), where Margaret Hale stands as a lay-figure in her black silk dress, draped with the gorgeous, spicy Indian shawls that form part of her cousin's trousseau. Her pleasure in their scent, their glowing colours, and their sumptuous texture is clearly evoked; she is even allowed an innocent vanity in her appearance, 'the familiar features in the unusual garb of a princess'.[28] The vanity is innocent partly because the shawls are not her own – she is not puffing herself up with worldly pride – and partly because of their alien, exotic nature. The Indian shawl is too important a garment to be merely frivolous, it echoes the strength and passion of the woman who wears it. As was the case with Mme Beck, the wearing of the garment speaks power – it is significant that it is Margaret whom we see dressed in this way, and not the actual owner of the shawls, the kittenish Edith, who would be swamped by the expectations the garment creates. It is also noteworthy that the exception to the rule of women's dress not being represented as justly pleasurable to women should be a garment that betokens female power and agency. This fact seems to indicate an awareness on the part of these writers – if unconscious – of the extent to which women's appearance was a powerful cultural agent in their oppression. Women's dress, in these texts, does speak sexuality – but it is a sexuality that is both produced and owned by a male observer; one that can only trap a woman into limiting roles.

As we have seen, from at least the middle, to the final years of the century, it was possible to depict sexuality as closely associated with the heroines of fiction. Almost invariably, however – perhaps *because* it is represented directly – it is a sexuality that, at worst, damages the woman physically and psychologically and, at best, represents her as a sexual object, rather than a subject. The places where we might have expected the most productive challenge to the prevailing orthodoxy are barren. The female-authored New Woman literature figures female sexuality as painful and dark, while those texts produced by male authors, although overtly concerned to challenge the hypocrisy of the social insistence on marriage, leave unchallenged, indeed are desperate to bolster up, fundamental assumptions about the asexuality, or at least the sexual passivity, of the 'good woman'. Similarly, the representation of women's clothes and bodies, productive as it is for a reading of covert inscriptions of sexuality, inscribes finally only the objectification of women's bodies as an erotic commodity for a male market – either that of prostitution or of marriage – allowing little space for the naming of women's own desires and pleasures. The forms such desires might take, and the new ways found to name them – in encoded patterns of imagery, autobiographical constructions of the feminine subject, and the transgressive imaginings of popular culture – are explored in the following chapters.

3 Sightless seers

Decadence and representations of femininity

The paradigm of female sexuality has been the Gordian knot of nineteenth-century feminist studies, a knot which feminists themselves have often tightened over recent decades. The problem for feminists is that often they find themselves attracted to Victorian representations of women which intellectually they feel they ought to reject as products of a male-dominated and tyrannical society. They are particularly troubled by images which are in any way erotic because critics such as Griselda Pollock (1988) and Laura Mulvey (1975; 1989) have suggested that the pleasure they may produce is suspect as it offers no female perspective. Pollock is able to transform this defect, as she sees it, into a positive position for women by exposing the layers of patriarchal repression – the dominant ideological structures – thus reaching towards a more 'authentic' relationship with the subject of the representation by reading against the patriarchy which produced it.[1] Mulvey, on the other hand, maintains that this kind of representation of women (by men for men) requires the female spectator to adopt the male gaze or, as she puts it, to become a 'nominal transvestite'.[2] Neither denies that women are attracted to Victorian images of women (as no doubt they were at the time they were produced). Helena Michie sums up the oscillation between fascinated attraction and horrified repulsion well:

> Feminism has so frequently found its texts, mirror images, and enemies in Victorianism because of the nineteenth century's ambiguous and erotic stance vis-à-vis the female body. While some feminist work denies this eroticism and others acknowledge it or at

least bow to its possibility, clearly the fascination for the Victorian is in part erotically motivated.[3]

The antagonism between feminism and Victorianism is a direct consequence of the knot we have tied around our models of Victorian female sexuality. By unpicking its threads, a new and positive relationship between women and Victorian representations of femininity can be established.

At the heart of this knot is the paradox that female desire was officially classified as abnormal and therefore infrequently experienced, yet in both literature and the visual arts of the period, highly erotic images of women abound, as do those concerned with the consequences of 'unnatural' sexual appetites in women. What is important about this paradox is that we have come to accept it as containing the truth about Victorian attitudes to sexuality. Foucault, for instance, has pointed out that the Victorians both refused to acknowledge sex in everyday life yet (perhaps because of this) discoursed about it endlessly in acceptable (legal, medical, etc.) forums. The widely held belief that women were either passionless or sexually insatiable is largely part of this phenomenon – the medicalisation of female sexuality – as is the acceptance that female sexuality was inclined to deviance and therefore in need of examination and regulation.

While there is much that is useful in the identification of Victorian attitudes to sexuality as contradictory, the tendency to 'explain' female sexuality in terms of binary oppositions (madonna/whore; Angel in the House/madwoman in the attic; passive/aggressive; passionless/sexually voracious) has resulted in neat theories which often seem to impose meanings rather than to ask questions. We are predisposed to accept Victorian attitudes to sexuality as extreme. This way of thinking is laid down at a primary level in western culture. Probably the first thing that a child remembers learning about the Victorians is their prudishness concerning the body and sex, as evidenced by the covering of piano legs, the removal of genitalia from such things as primitive chalk carvings, and the residual tradition of referring to the turkey breast as 'white meat'. This delicacy is a far cry from the open discussion of and pleasure in sex recorded in the cultural products of the eighteenth century, yet rather than questioning the plausibility of a prolonged cultural repression/collective amnesia regarding a drive as powerful as sex, most critical studies confirm this sexophobic image of our Victorian forebears. The dyadic model, which insists that in this period the only good woman was the passive, fragile, passionless 'Angel of the House', while any female who dared to challenge this role was labelled abnormal – insane or immoral – persists. Yet even a cursory survey of depictions of women in the last century can hardly fail to call this highly polarised way of constructing femininity into question, and in the process reveal much that is strong, powerful, and affirmative in Victorian representations of women by writers and artists of both sexes.

The inadequacy of this dyadic model first struck me when, as an undergraduate, I was told to read Tennyson's *The Princess* (1847), and I encountered for the first time the famous love lyric:

Now sleeps the crimson petal, now the white;
Now waves the cypress in the palace walk;
Now winks the gold fin in the porphyry font:
The firefly wakens; waken thou with me.

Now drops the milk-white peacock like a ghost;
And like a ghost she glimmers on to me.

Now lies the earth all Danae to the stars,
And all thy heart lies open unto me.

Now slides the silent meteor on, and leaves
A shining furrow, as thy thoughts in me.

Now folds the lily all her sweetness up,
And slip into the bosom of the lake.
So fold thyself, my dearest, thou, and slip
Into my bosom and be lost in me.[4]

The palpable sensuality of this poem, with its images and lexis of penetration and enfolding, seemed unmistakable, yet I was assured that this quality would not have been consciously included or recognised at the time it was written. Indeed, this, my tutor told me, was exactly the kind of piece a young lady might recite to a gathering of friends. The sensuality of the poem, he declared, was the product of the repression of sex – it returned under the thinnest of disguises, and because of deliberately cultivated naivety and a shared reluctance to acknowledge the existence of 'unacceptable' desires in 'normal' adults, was not recognised.

This is not an unhelpful explanation, but it is incomplete. Certainly there is evidence of this kind of wishful innocence, even much later in the century. For instance, an 1895 review in *The Magazine of Art* described Frederick Leighton's often reproduced painting, *Flaming June* (in which a beautiful young woman, clad in diaphanous scarlet robes, lies curled up in a sleep which looks both feline and serpentine), as 'unsuggestive . . . and unemotional'.[5] Taking its cue from examples such as this, and particularly from the public pronouncements about sex which abounded in the last century, twentieth-century criticism has readily embraced the idea that the Victorians in particular did construct the world according to dyadic principles (good/bad; male/female; active/idle) and that this is how they experienced it. It seems that people, places, objects and feelings were all classified according to absolute principles and filed away in separate drawers. That one mind could be a virtual apothecary shop, with pure substances, curatives, and poisons alike, or that the contents of a single drawer could have different effects depending on the quantity, the circumstances and the individual seems not to have been explored. Moreover, particularly in the case of women, changes to the headings under which they were classified only went one way. 'Good' could become 'bad', 'pure' 'impure', etc., but once corrupted, the process could only be reversed by death.

This dyadic model is neat, but just as it was necessary to question whether or not the Elizabethans really believed in the 'world picture' so often referred to in their visual and literary products, so it is useful to query the widely adopted 'separate spheres' mentality of Victorian Britain. It may indicate what people wanted and were encouraged to believe (the value of such a code, with its emphasis on passive women and the nuclear family, to maintaining both patriarchy and industrial capitalism is undeniable), but it is highly unlikely that most people were able to live – and feel – according to it. Indeed, some of the most interesting interpretations of nineteenth-century literature have focused precisely on the tensions created by attempting to live under such a repressive regime.[6] One of the most provocative attempts to reassess the 'Victorian frame of mind' is Bram Dijkstra's *Idols of Perversity*, which argues that we have been misreading late-Victorian culture and that far from being naive and unconscious, the sexual element in *fin-de-siècle* culture was deliberately inscribed. According to Dijkstra, this was part of a game of visual *double entendre* which, 'the intellectuals of the turn of the century used incessantly as a rather transparent veil with which to shadow the icons of their libido against the intrusive censorship of the moral majority' (p. 293).

This reading succeeds in defamiliarising overfamiliar images, and certainly makes it necessary to scrutinise habits of mind which automatically categorize nineteenth-century constructions of femininity solely according to two antithetical versions of sexuality. Surprisingly, however, having opened up the possibility of consciously inscribed sexual content, Dijkstra then comes up with his own dyadic interpretation of the images of women he discusses. He presents the sexualised images of women produced at the end of the century as studies in evil which can only

1 Albert Moore, *Midsummer* (1887)

be fully understood by comparing them to the depictions of female
perfection which dominated early Victorian culture. Because he adheres
firmly to the dyadic model, Dijkstra can only understand eroticised
images of women as representing perversity. That they may instead be
attempts to restore aspects of femininity which had been banished or
mangled as the cult of the domestic ideal came to prominence is never
considered. Similarly, women's responses to these eroticised representations of femininity are rarely considered. For instance, on the basis that
most aspirant middle-class men were well read and kept themselves
informed of 'popular' scientific theories, he concludes that many of the
most famous Victorian paintings were constructing a single version of
womanhood. This was that woman was so sexually depraved that she

2 Frederick, Lord Leighton, *Flaming June* (1895)

would 'criminally abuse herself' at every opportunity – particularly in the
company of other women and/or with animals. She did this to such an
extent that, exhausted, she was unable to resist the urge to sleep.
Accordingly, paintings which show women asleep and women with
animals (Figures 1–2) are really male fantasies about the autoerotic aspects
of femininity, and, Dijkstra argues, the men at least knew it (Dijkstra is
not interested in the eclectic reading habits of middle-class Victorian
women, although these are well documented): 'No well-informed late-
nineteenth century man of the world could have mistaken the "scientific"
implications of the peculiarly languid sensuality of the women' (p. 76).
Such paintings warned parents to guard their daughters (particularly from

3 Benjamin West, *Cyrus Liberating the Family of Astyses* (1770)
(© Her Majesty the Queen. A clear example of the Neoclassical style,
undisturbed by Decadent elements.)

the pestilential atmosphere of boarding schools where it was believed girls
regularly masturbated *en masse* and to such an extent that they ruined their
health), and taught husbands the tell-tale signs to look for in a wife. The
primary symptom was excessive lassitude, apparently produced not by a
society which denied its women the possibility of mental or physical
activity and dressed them in garments which restricted breathing and
circulation, but through regular and vigorous masturbation.

> Physicians explained to horrified husbands that as blood drained
> from their wives' brains to rush to their excited reproductive organs,
> their minds as well as their bodies weakened, and soul and body alike
> would travel off into a sleep induced by erotic self-stimulation.
> (p. 75)

Taken literally, this way of reading images of sleeping women would
radically alter our understanding of many Victorian texts as well as
paintings. Look, for instance, at the beginning of Elizabeth Gaskell's *North*

and South, in which Margaret Hale observes her sleeping cousin and girlhood companion, Edith:

'Edith!' said Margaret gently, 'Edith!'
But as Margaret half suspected, Edith had fallen asleep. She lay curled up on the sofa in the back drawing-room in Harley Street, looking very lovely in her white muslin and blue ribbons. If Titania had ever been dressed in white muslin and blue ribbons, and had fallen asleep on a crimson damask sofa in a back drawingroom, Edith might have been taken for her. . . . the prospect of soon losing her companion seemed to give force to every sweet quality and charm which Edith possessed . . . in spite of the buzz in the next room, Edith had rolled herself up into a soft ball of muslin and ribbon, and silken curls, and gone off into a peaceful little after-dinner nap.[7]

Dijkstra's reading would add quite a new dimension to the chapter's title, 'Haste to the Wedding', and the reason for separating the two 'bosom' companions!

It is ludicrous and inadequate essentially to invert established wisdom and say that at least half of the Victorian public, far from being sexually unaware, were actively decoding erotic and frequently misogynistic messages encoded in any images of women which deviated from the narrow confines of the feminine ideal. Moreover, this explanation makes even more bizarre the phenomenon described at the beginning of this chapter: the young girl reading aloud to a mixed audience a sensuous love poem. While the frisson given to the (male) *cognoscenti* in the audience might provide a rationale for such performances, it seems highly unlikely that most Victorian patriarchs, brothers, husbands and suitors would enjoy the spectacle of their daughters, wives, sisters and beloveds reciting such a piece. Neither does it seem likely that most respectable Victorian men would have wanted to be known to read texts, or purchase, hang or see exhibited paintings which they understood to be about women revelling in the pleasures and satisfactions of self-stimulation. Given what seem to have been the Victorian male's problems in having satisfactory sexual relations with the kind of woman he was supposed to regard as the angel of his house, it may be the case that depictions of sleeping women – women so soundly asleep that it seems nothing (including illicit sexual intercourse) will rouse them – and women who manifestly have sexual appetites, were at an unconscious level highly appealing. But as long as a dyadic model is in operation, it is necessary to understand such images as wholly innocent or wholly perverted. This also tends to mean that the sexualised works of art and literature and the society which tolerated them are, as in Dijkstra's study, understood to be part of that brief moment in the Victorian period when sexual mores and taboos were openly flouted: the worldly and decadent *fin-de-siècle*. To believe this is to deny a tradition of representing women and ideas in art and literature which was well established by mid-century and which had profound implications for both the evolution of artistic theories and the construction of femininity.

In order to refute this argument and to show the dangers of relying entirely on the 'separate-spheres' model of Victorian attitudes for our understanding of how femininity was being constructed, it is helpful to digress briefly and to look at what is known as the Decadent Movement.

The Decadent mythology

There is a tendency to regard Decadence as a movement in British arts and letters which suddenly arose at the end of the nineteenth century, and just as suddenly evaporated.[8] This seems to be largely because those figures most closely associated with the movement (notably Wilde, Symons, Beardsley, Dowson and Johnson) spent much of their time devising and publicising a myth about themselves. The Decadents presented their movement as one which newly liberated artists from conventions which they claimed had been stifling the arts in their century, but (and this is where the connection with constructions of femininity can be made) the visual and literary evidence suggests that the self-styled Decadents were only making explicit developments which had been well established many decades before and which refused to disappear when the movement fell into disrepute. Because the Decadents' propaganda was generally accepted at the time it was produced it has continued to be taken as fact, and this has coloured much of our understanding of Victorian culture and particularly its attitude to female sexuality.

Before it is possible to embark on a history of Decadence, it is necessary to understand what the term means, though the problems of defining a movement which was by nature eclectic in a period noted for artistic diversity are manifold. Nevertheless, it is possible to find considerable consensus among those who were practising and writing about its creeds. According to Max Beerbohm, Decadence was characterized by, 'paradox and marivaudage, lassitude, a love of horror and all unusual things, a love of argot and archaism, and the mysteries of style'.[9] For Richard Le Gallienne, it was the 'euphuistic expression of isolated observation . . . limited thinking, often insane thinking'.[10] Arthur Symons, in many ways the doyen of the Decadent Movement, believed its pre-eminent features were, 'intense self-consciousness, a restless curiosity in research, an over-subtilizing refinement upon refinement, a spiritual and moral perversity'.[11] These writers saw themselves as expounding a philosophy of art that was new, original and radical. In fact, what was new was the social climate which, briefly, allowed *open* discussion of changes in artistic sensibilities and the resulting portrayal of Victorian society (frequently represented by its women) in terms other than ideal, respectable and self-righteous.

The concentration on Decadence as an end-of-century phenomenon generated by a small group of men has a tendency to submerge its origins and carefully controlled development earlier in the century and, more importantly for this discussion, the nature of the women who are at the centre of so much of its art. The *fin-de-siècle* label also suggests that Decadence in the 1890s was a complete and coherent phase, the principal characteristics of which can be identified, listed, and so contained and understood. In fact, the interesting feature of Decadence is its very reliance on contradiction and ambiguity and its concomitant refusal to offer resolution. Studies into the Victorian imagination and psychology[12] have made it possible to see that the disturbances and ambivalence characteristic of much Victorian art and literature can be understood as deliberate attempts to revise the existing language of representation to incorporate epistemological anxieties arising from life in the modern world without simultaneously jettisoning the established models for understanding the world. As the certainty that '*humanis generis progressus*'[13] was eroded by increasingly accepted evolutionary theories, social, political and economic changes, and the problems arising out of industrialisation and urbanisation, there was a collective psychological need for reassurance. Continuity of representation is known to be an important means of maintaining at least a myth of stability, unity, and confidence in the future during times of transition. For the generation of Victorian artists and writers working in the early and middle years of the century, it was therefore necessary to work within accepted conventions. As students of ideology are quick to point out, there is generally a correlation between actual social change and increased insistence on representations which seem to support the established, dominant ideology. Largely because of this conservative pressure, combined with our habitual dyadic approach to Victorian studies, although what came to be called 'Decadence' was well established by mid-century, its existence before 1880 has generally been unnoticed, denied or ignored. As a consequence, the closing decade of the century is often seen as an aberration in Victorian arts and letters: a period when sexual deviance had social cachet, and when a small group of innovators made a failed attempt to break the ground of Modernism.[14] This perception is erroneous, for in fact the positive aspects of Decadence had hardy roots, and though a few figures naively exaggerated the more sensational side of Decadent philosophy and called the movement into disrepute, the significant aesthetic and intellectual perceptions of earlier

Decadent experiments were merely obscured by their actions, not obliterated. Among these ideas were a movement towards decoration and abstraction (especially in the visual arts), an interest in the reflexive natures of time and memory, and a preoccupation with the symbolic potential of language and images.

The reasons for regarding Decadence as a kind of turn-of-the-century hiccup seem to be bound up in the myth-making of the 1890s. Those who devised the myth were also responsible for orchestrating its demise following Oscar Wilde's conviction and imprisonment for homosexual offences in 1895, and did it so effectively that Decadence appeared to have disappeared altogether. For instance, Arthur Symons, hitherto the staunchest ally of Decadence and who remained ever-faithful to its theoretical positions, instantly saw the necessity of publicly distancing himself from Decadent activities. In the 1895 prospectus for *The Savoy* he disclaimed any relationship with the discredited movement:

> We have no formulae and we desire no false unity of form or matter. We have not invented a new point of view. We are not Realists, or Romanticists, or Decadents. For us, all art is good which is good art.[15]

At the same time, Symons changed the title of the book on which he was then working from *The Decadent Movement in Literature* to *The Symbolist Movement in Literature*.

The retreat from Decadence was so complete that the movement *qua* movement *was* dead by the end of the century. Even those who owed an artistic debt to Decadence tended to accept that the movement was short-lived and its impact fugitive. According to W. B. Yeats,

> Then in 1900 everybody got down off his stilts; henceforth nobody drank absinthe with his black coffee; nobody went mad; nobody committed suicide; nobody joined the Catholic Church; or if they did I have forgotten it.[16]

Whether Decadence was a failed experiment, or, as can be argued equally strongly, the seedbed of Modernism, the fact is that for a long time very real changes had been taking place in attitude, subject matter and treatment in Victorian arts and letters. These changes came about gradually; not in the sudden burst of celebrity and notoriety attached to Wilde, *et al.* Many of these changes are bound up with the representation of female sexuality; specifically, they systematically subvert established conventions and orthodoxy surrounding the acceptable public image of the feminine ideal. They reinstate female sexuality as a positive feminine attribute: the eroticisation of these depictions of women is not merely an aspect of male sexual fantasy, but a recognition that, deprived of her sexuality, woman was insubstantial and incomplete. Separating respectable women and sex had been a disastrous policy, and if the repressed sometimes returned in a frightening way, that is hardly surprising. What is more surprising is the uneasiness we feel, more than a hundred years on, when looking at these sexualised representations of women. This uneasiness reminds us that in some ways we are not so very different from the Victorians – that it is taking a long time to dismantle their sexual ideology. Feminists' determination not to adopt the male gaze may have caused us to miss the strategies and qualities within these works which are emancipatory rather than repressive.

The way in which change was gradually effected and absorbed into the discourses of criticism can most easily be seen through examining the way in which Decadent elements were incorporated in the apparently unimpeachable genre of Neoclassicism. To this end, it is useful to adapt some of the terms and theories devised by Mikhail Bakhtin (1895–1975) to facilitate his discussion of the novel.[17] Although this part of Bakhtin's work is concerned specifically with linguistic structures, he regarded language and its changes as entirely the products of culture, and it is therefore equally legitimate to apply his theories to discussions of the languages of the visual arts as well as those associated with verbal culture.

Of particular interest to this discussion is Bakhtin's notion that the novel is comprised of different kinds of languages, juxtaposed in order to emphasise that they are in a condition of conflict. He makes a distinction between this kind of variform, interacting, or 'heteroglossic' language, and that belonging to 'monoglossic' communities. Monoglossia Bakhtin associates with stable, pre-capitalist societies which demonstrate a tendency to work for a unified, dominant language – one which refuses to acknowledge any gap between language and reality. The dominant language may absorb elements from dialects, slang and jargon: it is not rigid or impervious to change. However, once isolated, rogue elements are integrated into the dominant language; they become part of standard usage and lose their irregular status. They no longer have the power to disrupt the authority of the dominant voice. This process is consistent with – indeed, integral to – creating a unified vision of society. But if the dominant language is forced to be omnivorous because of widespread challenges and claims, then it breaks down, fragments and becomes heteroglossic. In this case oppositional, subversive voices are liberated to speak, resulting in 'a plurality of independent, unmerged voices and consciousness . . . which are not subject to the authoritative control',[18] including the control of the author/creator.

The reasons for the breakdown of a unified language are many; among them are the intense activity and cultural change brought about by such things as war, internal political and/or economic upheavals, interchange as a result of trade and exploration, and scientific discoveries. Monoglossia Bakhtin associates with stability, confidence, and the 'classical body' (for example, representations characterised by harmony, proportion, maturity, idealisation and an emphasis on things cerebral, pure, and serious). Heteroglossia's characteristic articulation of transition and the questioning of established values Bakhtin connects with the 'grotesque body' of misrule, inversion, anti-intellectualism, carnality, and the lower bodily functions.[19]

In Bakhtin's formulation, monoglossia is impossible after the Renaissance. The rise of the novel he cites as evidence that unified language can no longer exist. For the purposes of this discussion, however, it is useful to think of the early years of the nineteenth century as embodying many of the features of a monoglossic community and that this is reflected in its art. As the century progresses (particularly after Victoria ascends the throne) and there is increasing awareness of and anxiety about change, the languages of representation begin to break down and to include elements from the grotesque body. These, rightly recognised by Bakhtin as subversive, latterly came to be called 'Decadent'. What is most interesting of all is the alliance between heteroglossia, subversion and the construction of femininity in nineteenth-century art and literature, for it is by looking at these constructions as heteroglossic (and not according to the essentially monoglossic angel/whore dyad) that the complexity and range of attitudes to women and femininity emerge.

Decadence, Neoclassicism and monoglossia

As the nineteenth century proceeded, writers increasingly associated the early years of the century with past epochs, which seemed to have been characterised by a sense of order, stability, continuity and predictability. Nostalgia for a time when the world seemed to be knowable underlies much writing which dealt with the problems and possibilities of change. It is present in such non-literary works as Carlyle's *Signs of the Times* (1829) and *Past and Present* (1843), Ruskin's *The Stones of Venice* (1851), and Matthew Arnold's *Culture and Anarchy* (1869). Similarly, much of the poetry of Arnold, Meredith, Morris and Rossetti is concerned with the theme of loss through change. George Eliot's introduction to *Felix Holt the Radical* (1866) encapsulates the theme of change inherent in the novel by mid-century in its coach journey back through time with its recapitulation of all that had changed in the scant thirty-five years since

The great roadside inns were still brilliant with well-polished tankards, the smiling glances of pretty bar-maids, and the repartees of jocose ostlers; the mail still announced itself by merry notes of the horn; the hedgecutter or the rick-thatcher might still know the exact hour by the unfailing yet otherwise meteoric apparition of the pea-green, Tally-ho or the yellow Independent. . . . In those days there were pocket boroughs, a Birmingham unrepresented in Parliament . . . unrepealed corn-laws, three-and-six penny letters, a brawny and many-breeding pauperism, and other departed evils; but there were some pleasant things too, which have also departed.[20]

Each of these writers deals with rapid change as a new and ambivalent phenomenon. To be positive and progressive, they surmise, change must be gradual and organic. While much might have been wrong in the old world, much was also sound, and the old values had managed to see Britain into the new century without the violence and disruption of revolution. Adhering to the right principles while working for gradual reform is advocated as the recipe for successful social development. In this way, Birminghams get Parliamentary representation, Corn-Laws are repealed, and pauperism lessened without obliterating the pleasant things or erasing the lessons of history. In other words, the traditionally dominant values and discourses characteristic of the early nineteenth century are being constructed as monoglossic; able to absorb, accommodate and adjust change and dissent.

This literary sense of the early years of the century as being constructed as essentially monoglossic is substantiated by a survey of the art of the period, and particularly the vogue for Neoclassicism. Historians suggest 1770–1850 as the period when Neoclassicism was the dominant style in British art. With its emphasis on heroism, grandeur, reason, and man, Neoclassicism was welcomed as the style appropriate for representing the values and aspirations of a society experiencing the benefits and prestige of industrialism, empire, and the successful preservation of its constitutional monarchy. The work of Flaxman and West, and the popular 'etruscan' ware of the Wedgwood potteries give a representative picture of this stage of the British classical revival (Figures 3–4). They are wholly concerned with imitating classical subjects and styles for the purposes of celebrating contemporary people and events (and, of course, they appeal to the dominant cultural voice of the classically educated élite). This visual language, while not devoid of Victorian inflections, is unaffected by any conflicting modes or vocabularies. It is monoglossic, and accordingly takes the form of the idealized classical body.

After 1830, a new strand was being incorporated in the Neoclassical idiom. If Decadence is characterised by the rejection of the mundane, the

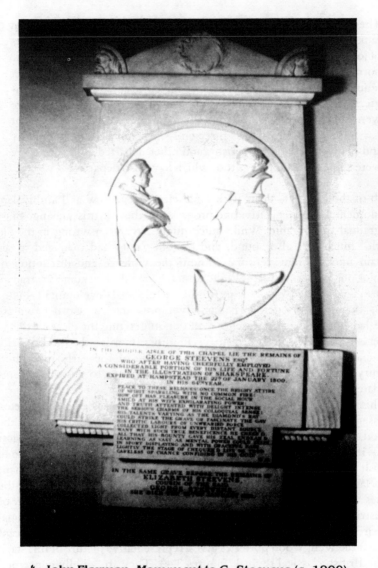

4 John Flaxman, *Monument to G. Steevens* (c. 1800)
(Flaxman (1755–1826) retained the monoglossic style of Neoclassicism typified by this heroic monument well into the second decade of the nineteenth century.)

embracing of the unusual and unnatural, an aesthetic celebrating beauty as entirely separate from morality, and an atmosphere of languor conveyed through a semiotic constructed around antiquity/archaism, then this new voice was that of Decadence (Figures 5–12). The point to be made is that

5 G. F. Watts, *Paolo and Francesca* (1872–4)
(First begun in 1848, Watts' painting includes the sightless eyes, exaggerated
gestures, dynamic robes, and suggestion of the horrific characteristic of
Decadence.)

Decadence, which would seem to embody values antithetical to those of
Neoclassicism, rapidly became established as an acceptable component in
mid-century Neoclassicism. Why is this so? How is it articulated? Why
has this phenomenon so often been ignored and misunderstood? How
does identifying the relationship between Neoclassicism and Decadence

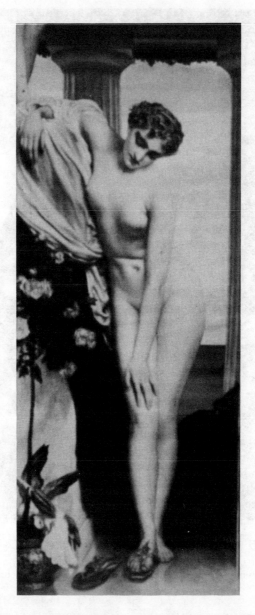

6 Frederick, Lord Leighton, *Venus Disrobing* (1866–7)
(In this early nude, the first to be exhibited at the Royal Academy for twenty
years, Leighton introduces the veiled eyes characteristic of his later sleeping
women. The sea in the background reflects the eternal though ever-
changing nature of time.)

promote understanding of the ways in which femininity was constructed in the last century? All of these questions could be explained as the by-products of the Decadent mythology which insisted that nothing interesting had happened in art before the end of the century. There is, however, a more interesting, and a more credible answer. This accepts that there was a well-understood 'dominant' discourse about what comprised acceptable and appropriate subject matter, and that this discourse not only dictated what could be shown and said, it also provided the means for challenging itself. This accepts Dijkstra's point that to some extent there was a difference in the way the Victorian public understood what they read and saw and the intention of the artists and writers who produced these cultural artefacts, but is more akin to Steven Marcus' understanding of the relationship between pornography and mainstream literature. In *The Other Victorians*,[21] Marcus describes Victorian literary languages as being divided between the elaborate, genteel and periphrastic discourses of public life and letters, and the plain, direct and deviant language of pornography. He shows how pornographic writers made use of orthodox literature through borrowings, inversions, and parodies, and builds up a convincing case to prove that Victorian novelists were aware of but deliberately excluded the worlds represented in pornography. Elaborating Marcus' model, it seems that Victorian writers frequently used what could be called 'dual address'. That is, they described one vision of the world – that which the middle-class reader was prepared to recognise – but did so in terms which mirrored the world of sexual exchange, need and fantasy characteristic of pornography. What was technically absent worked as a paralipsis and could readily be made present by readers who recognised the setting. An interesting example of this is provided by *The Diaries of Hannah Cullwick* (discussed in detail in Chapter 5). Hannah, a domestic servant and so someone with experience of both the genteel and the low sides of Victorian society, develops a technique for writing about herself which closely resembles the strategies Marcus identifies with Victorian novelists. It is known that Hannah read little fiction, so her reliance on the use of metaphor and substitution must be based on her understanding of what can and cannot be said in different social situations. Hannah's diaries were written for her gentleman-lover, and she wanted to please him without transgressing the bounds of respectability. Consciously or not, she manages to do this very effectively by describing those parts of herself which it was acceptable to mention (especially her hands and arms) in such a way that they call to mind the more private and exciting parts of her body to which she cannot overtly refer. For instance, her emphasis on the size, colour, temperature and texture of her hands is erotically suggestive though expressed in the perfectly legitimate discourse of domestic duty.[22]

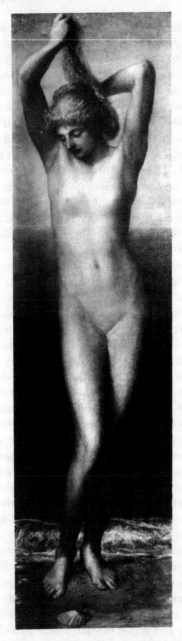

7 G. F. Watts, *Thetis* (1867–9)
(The classical subject rendered Watts' coy and self-conscious nude 'safe' for
Victorian viewers. Compare the use of the hidden eyes and the sea to
Leighton's paintings of Venus and Acatea.)

Recognising the erotic in representations such as this can come about in a variety of ways: consciously, through actually identifying correspondences in settings/situations or, as an 'ambiguous figure' in which one viewer sees one picture (classically a pair of vases) while another sees one which is entirely different (lovers kissing), though each can be taught to see the other's picture. Finally, there is the subliminal reading in which some readers are not consciously aware of comparisons, ironies, or humour based on the existence of the alternative view but may respond to it subconsciously and may, indeed, come to recognise it in time.

The ambiguous figure provides the most useful model for explaining the peculiar relationship between femininity and sexuality characteristic of much of the last century. On the one hand, a description or picture could be entirely innocent (a vase); on the other, suggestive (a kiss). The 'hidden' or alternative meaning does not have to be acknowledged if a picture is given a title or narrative function explicitly relating to the 'official' meaning. However, while it is impossible to 'see' the two figures simultaneously, it is possible to know that both exist; by adjusting the mind's eye the reader/viewer can rapidly alternate between the two. Thus, the omnipotence of the dominant languages of Neoclassicism and femininity could be broken down by inscribing within them new, different, and sometimes conflicting meanings. This tactic allows for treatment of subjects hitherto deemed inappropriate in their own right, as well as exploration and experimentation in form, technique and intention. Such an approach is not obviously rebellious or radical. It neither requires nor wants a label in the manner of the Pre-Raphaelite Brotherhood or the Decadent Movement, but instead finds the superficial adherence to traditional concerns to be actively beneficial. One benefit comes through allowing the established authorities (the monoglossists) to welcome new ideas without having publicly to alter their own positions. This may be a dangerous strategy in that new ideas can be absorbed and 'sanitised' by the dominant language, but it also has the potential to bring about a shift in perception. The retention of recognised structures makes it possible for views to be expanded through subtle adjustments at an acceptable rate. This tactic also avoids the suspicion and hostility likely to be aroused by incomprehension or shock on the part of the public and its approved arbiters of taste. Finally, conventions themselves are useful. They allow for a kind of 'short-hand': simply evoking a convention makes implicit much that need not then be presented in detail. Convention may also facilitate irony by providing a background against which the artist or writer can work, and aids the introduction of complication. Conventions can also be used to foreground disparities such as those which may exist between the choice of subject matter and the way it is treated. Thus the fact that a conventional form (Neoclassicism) or the conventional characteristics

8 Frederick, Lord Leighton, *Acatea, Nymph of the Shore* **(1868)**
(The provocative pose, the phallic fish, the echoes of Acatea's breasts and
body in the mountains all highlight the sexuality of this nymph.
Significantly, she looks not at the spectator, but into the distance. She sees
what we cannot. The associations with Pater's Mona Lisa and the Decadent
femme fatale are clear.)

of an ideological construction (such as femininity) was widely used
does not mean that thinking was necessarily conventional or regressive.
Rather, such 'conventions' can be used to encode a commentary which
questions official values, reflects the conflicts and interactions of a society
in transition, and ultimately helps to shape the emerging culture without
being overtly threatening. This is the process whereby a society learns to
cease thinking of itself as monoglossic and coherent, and accommodates a
heteroglossic world view. The process cannot be instantaneous, and
clearly residual discourses which have been central to the dominant
ideology (in this case the unity and grandeur of Neoclassicism and the
idealisation of femininity) will be retained longer than those which have
been less crucial.

The slippage between pure Neoclassical and Decadent constructions of
femininity is most striking in the visual arts, though once familiar with its
modes the corresponding tropes in the literature of the period are
unmistakable (as Michie observes, Victorian novels themselves frequently
point to the connection between written and painted metaphors for
capturing female likenesses[23]). For this reason it is helpful to look at a

9 Ernest Normand, *Playthings* (1886)

(The Royal Academy's 'Picture of the Year' and the most obvious example of an 'ambiguous figure'. To modern eyes it is difficult not to see this as an overtly erotic image; however, the treatment is not threatening. This siren-figure combines the sexuality of the *femme fatale* with the playful approval of the young mother.)

10 J. W. Waterhouse, *Hylas and the Nymphs* (1896)

(Here the connection between women and water is explicit, and the potentially destructive nature of female sexuality implied. The picture illustrates the moment in *The Odyssey* when Odysseus's beautiful companion, Hylas, is carried away by nymphs who fall in love with his appearance. While ambivalent towards female sexuality in its theme, the nymphs nonetheless unite the graceful and spiritual appearance of the feminine ideal with the sexuality of the *femme fatale*.)

11 Sir Edward Poynter, *The Cave of the Storm Nymphs* (1903)
(Completed shortly after Victoria's death, this painting shows the continued
combination of Neoclassical subjects and Decadent treatment which helped
to restore sexuality to representations of femininity.)

12   Sir Lawrence Alma-Tadema, *In the Tepidarium* (1881)

range of visual representations of femininity which includes female
sexuality before moving on to literary examples of this phenomenon.

The naked and the dead

When looking at the new brand of Neoclassicism which emerged in the
1860s it is important to remember that there was as yet a limited lexicon of
sexual signs and symbols and no specific vocabulary for the unconscious.[24] This facilitated the 'ambiguous figure' – like quality of many
paintings by allowing them apparently to conform to the separate-spheres
mentality which society was understood to approve while in fact
acknowledging the inadequacy of the model through images which it is
now possible to see were highly erotic and attributed considerable power
to women. The power of an acceptable label – in this case 'Neoclassical' –
to purify what should have been highly contentious images is manifest.
Under this label nudes and paintings which today it seems impossible to
construe as lacking erotic content were reintroduced to the Royal
Academy after an absence of twenty years.[25] Paintings which in the 1890s
would have been classified as highly Decadent were well received at this
time. Look, for instance, at the reproductions of paintings by Leighton,

Watts, Moore, Poynter, Waterhouse and Ernest Normand. Each fulfils the definition of Decadence as set out by its *fin-de-siècle* proponents, yet all were deemed unexceptionable and were in fact highly acclaimed. Normand's outrageously Decadent *Playthings* (Figure 9) was even voted 'picture of the year' in the Royal Academy's 1886 exhibition![26] Even today, the fact that these pictures make use of Neoclassical subjects and motifs tends to override their characteristically Decadent concern with *femmes fatales*, trance-like states, disruption of clock time, refinement, decoration, and their total rejection of moral content. Even pictures with only vestigial connections to classical subjects or treatment, under the hand of a painter associated with the genre, are disassociated from Decadent connotations. Thus, as late as 1903, Sir Edward Poynter's *The Cave of the Storm Nymphs* (Figure 11) was remarked upon for being, 'the finest of Poynter's academic nudes'![27] Alma-Tadema's erotic and langorous nude shown *In the Tepidarium* (1881, Figure 12) and Leighton's coy *Venus Disrobing* (1867, Figure 6) show well how Decadent elements were being deployed behind a veil of exotic classical disguises: Bakhtin's classical body had been invaded by the grotesque, but the masquerade was undetected until the decade of carnival orchestrated by Wilde and his associates.

This new version of Neoclassicism positively celebrates plurality, and in the process invites questions about the condition of art and society. Because women are at the centre of virtually all the work produced in this form, it probes particularly deeply into the gaps between being a woman, the way femininity was constructed in society, and how people actually felt about women. A painting such as Albert Moore's *Midsummer* (1887, Figure 1), with its references to empire, materialism and religion in conjunction with the central figure of the enthroned, dreaming woman provides an interesting example. The painting places a woman at its centre and buttresses her with two female acolytes. Although highly decorative, the women's surroundings are concretely realised and highly detailed. They exist and she possesses them. She is powerful, but her power is like Cleopatra's (who is evoked through the eastern influence of the design on her throne and the two 'serving women'), mysteriously Other. She is the object of the gaze, but seems to evade it for she is not really present. Her own gaze is directed away from the spectator and, perhaps because of the oriental setting, her dream has the quality of a trance. What she sees is beyond the mundane world of the spectator, who is excluded from her secret knowledge. Is this the dream of a woman suffering from self-induced sexual exhaustion? To me it looks like a fantasy about female power – power is clearly attributed – but what kind of power is it? The woman is no Amazon, she conforms to the feminine ideal in being both decorous and passive, yet she seems to possess both secret knowledge and the power signified by the very real throne. She is no Virgin enthroned, but because enthronement was so frequently associated with saints and martyrs she is both compared to them (as would have been consistent with the Angel of the House) and distinguished from them. Instead of the either/or reading required by the dualistic model, this painting invites the viewer to construct a very complex version of femininity in which experience, knowledge and power may be attributed to women without making them mad, evil or fallen. The passivity required by the feminine ideal becomes a symbol of power, and sleep indicates not masturbatory exhaustion, invalidism or ennui but the ability to transcend this world. While it is more usual to think of Victorian women as having to become invalids and finally to die to demonstrate their connection with the next world, images of healthy women able to enter into trance-like, visionary states abound in both literature and the visual arts of the period.

The dreaming or trance-like states of women depicted here anticipates visually the suggestion of hidden meanings and other worlds typical of much of the writing of the 1890s. It also gives expression to some of the serious, philosophical and aesthetic concerns of Decadence which have come to be overshadowed by its more sensational manifestations. These second-generation nineteenth-century Neoclassical beauties, with their visionary, timeless attitudes in antique settings which interact with modern treatments are the mothers and sisters of the *Mona Lisa* as described by Walter Pater. Like 'Lady Lisa' they 'stand as the embodiment of the old fancy, the symbol of the modern idea'.[28]

She is older than the rocks among which she sits; like the Vampire, she has been dead many times, and learned the secrets of the grave; and has been a diver in the deep seas, and keeps their fallen day about her; and trafficked for strange webs with Eastern merchants; and, as Leda, was the mother of Helen of Troy, and as Saint Anne, the mother of Mary; and all this has been to her but as the sound of lyres and flutes, and lives only in the delicacy with which it has moulded the changing lineaments, and tinged the eyelids and the hands. The fancy of perpetual life, sweeping together ten thousand experiences is an old one; and modern philosophy has conceived the idea of humanity as wrought upon by, and summoning up itself, all modes of thought and life.[29]

What is interesting about this passage is the way it both makes women the repositories of knowledge and history, and therefore significant for the reproduction of cultural values, and also celebrates the diversity of their experiences and contributions. It empowers women, yet sees in them both the traditional Victorian vampire/temptress waiting to suck men dry in every aspect of their lives, and the potential to give birth to the mother of God. For Pater, women are closely linked to history, the inner life, and the ability to register myriad impressions simultaneously. They are archaic and entirely contemporary.

While Pater's work is known to have influenced the Decadent Movement, it was in turn influenced by the works of his predecessors and contemporaries, not least those ostensibly written for children. As early as 1863 Kingsley had adopted a style which relied on innate contradictions for its meaning and set up a model of an alternative world in which linear time no longer exists and death is not problematic. Women feature prominently in The Water-Babies, and their sexual significance is central to the text. Kingsley's use of elaborate sexual symbolism in The Water-Babies has been widely remarked: a boy comes down a chimney into a young girl's virginally white bedroom and then rushes off in a frantic desire to cleanse himself. Later Tom meets the good and bad 'mothers' Mrs Doasyouwouldbedoneby and Mrs Bedonebyasyoudid and is eventually able to give himself up to the stroking and petting of the first's pure love. Humphrey Carpenter is the latest critic to suggest that Tom's fear and repugnance of sex represents Kingsley's own repressed homosexuality, and that his love for Mrs Doasyouwouldbedoneby is an expression of his displaced desire for his mother.[30] Whether or not this is the case, the book certainly constructs femininity as on the one hand provoking and responding to desire, and on the other as the route to altered states. Perhaps as a consequence of this, while The Water-Babies is unreal and impossible in terms of the physical world, emotionally, psychologically and spiritually it makes a great deal of sense. The Victorians often grouped women and children together (both, for instance, are linked with the past, intuition and other kinds of non-verbal knowledge, and with sexual deviance), and it is perhaps not surprising that so many male writers found an outlet for their erotic feelings in writing for children (think of Kingsley, MacDonald, Dodgson and Barrie). Children were a suitable audience because unlikely to be aware of the sexual dimension to their texts. (Indeed, whether the writers themselves were always aware of it is debatable.) In a similar way, visual artists located sexual desire in women, who if confined by the ideal as described by Cobbett (quoted in Chapter 1), ought also to have been incapable of recognising it.

In mid–century Kingsley began to explore what must be seen as Decadent ideas about art and female sexuality. Like many members of the later Decadent Movement, he linked women and sexuality to religion, resulting in some bizarre and highly erotic 'Christian' images including sketches he made of himself and his wife making love while ascending to heaven or tied, in mock crucifixion, to a cross.[31] Even earlier Tennyson wrote about the artist's dilemma in having to choose between social and ethical duty and the (Decadent) muse of imaginative beauty. In 'The Lotos-Eaters' (1832) he considers the attractions of existing for sensation and through it moving beyond this world and its limiting chronological existence to a state of 'long rest or death, dark death, or dreamful ease' (11.43–53). The siren call to abandon the hardships of reality for a life of contemplation, sensation and pleasure has traditionally been associated with women, and in the introduction to *The Palace of Art*, written in the same year, he presents the Decadent life (as it came to be called nearly sixty years later) as a 'glorious Devil' in love with Beauty. Beauty in this poem is feminine, one of three sisters, Beauty, Good and Knowledge, who as a triumvirate befriend men but can 'never be sunder'd without tears'. Beauty worshipped for her own sake results in Decadence, and thus the reader is warned to beware beautiful, vacant-eyed women (such as those who feature in the works of Moore, *et al.*) who may be *femmes fatales* and vampires, preparing to lead men from the paths of virtue and knowledge to certain ruin.

They may be *femmes fatales*, but they may also be real women made fatal to themselves alone through male fears of female power – the aspect of femininity written out of the Victorian domestic angel and so turned to evil by our dyadic orthodoxy.[32] Because we have accepted the truth of the stereotypes presented to us in the images of femininity provided by the last century, we have tended to overlook the fact that the function of a stereotype is precisely to reconcile conflicting identifications.[33] The need is to keep Beauty, Good and Knowledge together, not to deny the potential for each in women. The depiction of women with empty eyes suggests not only links to another world and the possibility of evil knowledge, but also the empty heads of the many Victorian women who were denied education and in whom intellectual powers were deplored. It is this idea which is explored in much Victorian fiction, and which I think provides the key to reconstructing attitudes to femininity in circulation at this time more accurately than we do by adhering to the angel/whore model. It also helps to understand how the Victorian public could accommodate, not ignore, exclude or miss, the sexual content manifest in many of its best-known images of women.

Fiction and femininity

Marian Evans (George Eliot) could be considered one of the century's most famous real-life *femmes fatales*: intellectually rapacious, she renounced religion, assumed a man's name (professionally), lived with another woman's husband, and on his death married a man twenty years her junior. She was admired and feared, celebrated and socially shunned, iconoclastic and wedded to intellectual integrity. Eliot felt herself to be a social pariah because of the irregularity of her relationship with G. H. Lewes, yet she knew herself to be valued by him, their circle of friends, and her reading public. The affirmation of her worth she experienced professionally seems not to have compensated for the rejection she felt from friends and family (particularly her beloved brother Isaac) when she set up house with Lewes, and though the virtues and fruits of that relationship were clear, and celebrated by her in letters and journal entries, psychologically she had to battle with an image of herself as destructive. This is the struggle which lies at the heart of her fictional autobiography, *The Mill on the Floss*, published in 1860, five years after she set up house with Lewes and Isaac severed all contact with her. In this text, Eliot constructs a persona for herself as narrator, and another as the central character, Maggie Tulliver. Each has characteristics of the Decadent *femme fatale*, yet in the end it is not a book which is concerned with the destructive properties of femininity. Rather, it explores female perceptions of time and memory, forms of female creativity other than childbearing, the connection between these and the female capacity for spirituality, and finally, the way society encourages girls to reject these qualities for the life of domestic routine and service.

Chapter 1 brings the narrating persona and the fictional alter ego overtly together, and it sets up the story to follow as a dream, a memory, a conversation, and a story created by an omniscient narrator:

> Ah, my arms are really benumbed. I have been pressing my elbows on the arms of my chair, and dreaming that I was standing on the bridge in front of Dorlcote Mill, as it looked one February afternoon many years ago. Before I dozed off, I was going to tell you what Mr. and Mrs. Tulliver were talking about, as they sat by the bright fire in the left-hand parlour, on that very afternoon I have been dreaming of.[34]

There are several significant things about this narrator. First, if we are to assume that she is Marian/Maggie, then she represents the living dead – a ghost or vampire – since at the end of the text we learn that Maggie drowns. It is not difficult to see this as a psychological statement about Marian, who at this time was a social ghost, shunned by society and made to feel that her very existence was objectionable to her brother. The text describes a figure who is obsessed with the past and for whom past and present exist simultaneously; indeed, the past is more real than the present, for it is recollected vividly whereas the present is experienced as a 'dreamy deafness'. The past is a dream, but a dream of a real world in which events play themselves out time and time again until the dreamer's wish to be reunited with her brother is fulfilled: 'In their death they were not divided' is the inscription on Tom and Maggie's shared tombstone.

Though this is a story told by a ghost about the sibyl-like Maggie Tulliver, it is not one which accepts society's rejection of its central character, Maggie's 'unfeminine' intellectual abilities and passionate feelings are surpassed only by her supremely feminine capacity for renunciation and self-sacrifice and her need for love which makes her always dependent and repentant. 'It is a wonderful subduer, this need of love – this hunger of the heart – as peremptory as that other hunger by which Nature forces us to submit to the yoke, and change the face of the world' (p. 31), observes the narrating persona. Accordingly, Maggie lives through others and defines herself only in relation to those she loves.

Maggie's death by drowning is prefigured several times early in the story, but first and most meaningfully in her own discussion of the illustration of the witch-drowning in Defoe's *The History of the Devil*. Maggie points out the paradox of this means of testing a woman to her father's friend Mr Riley:

> That old woman in the water's a witch – they've put her in to find out whether she's a witch or no, and if she swims she's a witch, and if she's drowned – and killed, you know – she's innocent, and not a witch, but only a poor silly woman. But what good would it do her then, you know, when she was drowned? Only, I suppose, she'd go to heaven, and God would make it up to her. (p. 11)

Maggie, of course, drowns and so her goodness is proven, even if, like the people in the picture, her associates have mistaken her as evil because she is thought to have broken a social taboo and so fails to conform to their public construction of femininity. Her 'transgression' is entirely their fantasy: all she has in fact done is to ride alone in a boat with a man she loves and who loves her. Through the omniscience of the narrator, the reader knows that Maggie is technically innocent, and is therefore made to reject the attitude of mind of a community which chooses to condemn a woman (Stephen is not punished in the same way) on the basis of rumour and rejects the truth when it is provided and corroborated. (Again, the parallels with Marian Evans' experiences are unmistakable.) The book not only undermines the dualistic model which allows for Maggie's being a paragon one day and a *femme fatale* the next; it deliberately complicates her emotional and sexual state throughout. As a child, Maggie is constantly placed in and compared to nature and to fallen women (like Eve, she has eaten of the tree of knowledge). As a woman, Maggie *is* one of the sightless seers so common in the Decadent paintings of the period. On the fateful river ride with Stephen she is in an 'enchanted haze', and 'only dimly conscious of the banks, as they passed them, and dwelt with no recognition on the villages' (p. 430). While she is in the boat all experience is reduced to a 'dreamy gliding' (p. 433) and the submerging of her own personality. Later, on the eve of her next and final journey on water, she sits by the window, with her back, as it were, towards the reader, and stares at the rising water as it passes:

> She sat without candle in the twilight, with the window wide open towards the river; the sense of oppressive heat adding itself indistinguishably to the burthen of her lot. Seated on a chair against the window, with her arm on the window-sill, she was looking blankly at the flowing river, swift with the backward-rushing tide – struggling to see still the sweet face in its unreproaching sadness, that seemed from moment to moment to sink away and be hidden behind a form that thrust itself between, and made darkness. (p. 473)

These are images exactly analogous to those found in the paintings of Leighton, Moore, Waterhouse, et al., and they make the same associations between women and the timelessness of water to disrupt the linearity of the narrative. These interludes take the reader back to the 'dreamy deafness' the narrator experiences on the river bank by the mill and so suggest a link to another time and world beyond that of the 'present' in the narrative. Maggie's links to this other world have been hinted at repeatedly throughout the text, and because the narrator can also be understood to be Maggie, her death is converted to a moment of transcendence. She physically leaves this world for the next, but her links with this world have not entirely been severed and she continues to inhabit both (Philip senses her presence, 'like a revisiting spirit' among the trees of the Red Deep). The text thus continues the themes with which it opened: the possibility of many realities existing simultaneously and the subjective nature of experience and truth. Maggie is like Pater's Mona Lisa, dead many times, knowing the secrets of the grave, a diver in deep seas and a trafficker in the strange webs of dreams. She may be a siren, luring men to destruction – Tom drowns in her embrace, and to 'the world's wife there had always been something in Miss Tulliver's very physique that a refined instinct felt to be prophetic of harm' (p. 452) – but Philip and Stephen survive, and, one suspects, have been made better by their attachment to her. Maggie is neither the Angel in the House nor the madwoman in the attic: she has fallen without sinning, is forgiven by those who love her and whom she loves, and is permitted to tell her own story. She is not made unfeminine through her intelligence, and her sensuality, though socially misunderstood, is neither denied nor construed as evil. Thus, largely through drawing on the iconography of Decadence, Eliot is able to show the falsity of the dyadic model, with its opposed, ideological, constructions of femininity, and to articulate in an empathetic way the tensions, conflicts and confusions it engendered.

Maggie Tulliver is not the only example of a Victorian heroine who combines the virtues of the good woman with the qualities of the *femme fatale*. Jane Eyre is another siren, whose links to another world are clear. She is compared to a mermaid and an elf; her paintings and drawings reveal the rich and complex nature of her fantasies, and she is apparently psychic, dreaming truths and on one occasion able to communicate telepathically with Rochester. She is first La Belle Dame sans Merci, and then the all-providing wife and mother. Emily Brontë provides Catherine Earnshaw with many of the attributes of a *femme fatale*, as do Oscar Wilde for his Salome and Thomas Hardy in the character of Sue Bridehead. Each of these characterisations defies attempts to categorize women as either entirely good or purely bad. A less well-known and more consciously feminist text which makes good use of the Decadent construction of femininity to reshape the dominant version is Sarah Grand's *The Beth Book* (1897).

Like *The Mill on the Floss*, *The Beth Book* is a fictionalised autobiography (though Grand herself denied this, the correlations between her life and that of the book's central character, Beth Caldwell, are unmistakable[34]). The difference between Eliot's text and Grand's is largely one of political conviction and emotional attachment. Where Eliot believed in gradual, organic change and attached the utmost importance to male educational values with their emphasis on rationality, Grand was supremely interested in women, dedicated to the Suffrage movement, and convinced of the superiority of female ways of knowing. She begins the book with two epigraphs (ironically both by men). Together they celebrate the powers of intuition, knowledge which is not academic in origin, links to Nature, and specifically the receptivity and prophetic potential of the female mind to grand, inspirational, visionary thought: 'And if you have not that within you . . . which my words may awaken, though they be indistinct and swift, leave me, for I will give you no patient mockery, no labouring insults of that glorious Nature whose I am and whom I serve' (Ruskin); 'The truth is in the air, and the most impressionable brain will announce it first. . . . So women, as the most susceptible, are the best index of the coming hour' (Emerson).

The Beth Book studies the coming to consciousness of an intelligent and sensitive young girl under domestic and social conditions which, through poverty and lack of understanding, exaggerated the repressions of the middle-class female child's lifestyle. Beth's sibyl-like qualities are highly reminiscent of Maggie Tulliver's though Beth is even more sensitive to criticism than Maggie and she is generally a more charismatic personality. The Decadent aspects of Beth's character are rapidly established. Like one born again, she has knowledge beyond her years and the power to enthral those around her with words and stories. In the superstitious atmosphere of rural Ireland, where her father is posted (and dies), Beth is accused of witchcraft, and fear of her is so great that the locals attempt to shoot her with a silver bullet. Beth is also linked with nature and especially the sea, thus again associating her with time beyond time and the female cycles of moon and tide. Though the witchcraft episode fades into the past, Beth continues to be invested with the power of prophecy and is used to explore the possibility of other realities. Once, in a trance-like state, she tries to explain the nature of her special knowledge to her Aunt Victoria, one of the few people in her early life who care for and respect her abilities. The description comes after Beth has heard a ticking sound which she and her Aunt recognise as the Death Watch:

> 'It does mean something,' Beth interrupted vehemently; 'I know – I always know. The smell of death has been about me all afternoon, but I did not understand, although the words were in my mouth. When things mean nothing, they don't make you feel queer – they don't impress you. . . . I sometimes feel as if I were listening, but not with my ears, and waiting for things to happen that I know about, but not with my head; and I try always to understand when I find myself listening, but not with my ears, and something surely comes; and so also when I am waiting for things to happen that I know about, but not with my head; they do happen. Only most of the time I know that something is coming, but I cannot tell what it is. In order to be able to tell exactly, I have to hold myself in a certain attitude – not my body, you know, *myself* – hold myself in suspense, as it were, or suspend something in myself, stop something, push something aside – I can't get it into words; I can't always do it; but when I can, then I know.' (p. 213)

She likens the experience to a pair of doors, one of which opens on to the reality we know, and another which opens when her physical self is suppressed. Aunt Victoria recognises that such knowledge need not be evil, though that is the way it is usually constructed by those who are unable to comprehend the possibility of something beyond the present. She accepts it as ancient, spiritual power – the power Pater attributes to his Mona Lisa of the rocks.

   Like Maggie, Beth's education is sacrificed for her brothers', and she too finds consolation in religious discipline and devotion. Also like Maggie,

Beth first admires and yearns after, then is disenchanted with, the masculine world of educational achievement. When her brother introduces Beth to his friends she is impressed by their assumption of superiority and surmises that it comes with knowledge of Latin. Once she learns that Latin is neither difficult to learn nor occult she swiftly realises that it is because she is female that she is diminished, and not because of what she knows. This is the beginning of Beth's respect for women's minds, which she realises could be at least as good as men's if they were properly trained and developed.

The sexual double standard is explored in *The Beth Book* in ways quite different from those adopted by Eliot. In part this must be attributed to the fact that the book was written nearly forty years later and from the perspective of one knowledgeable about birth control and the injuries done to women suffering from sexually transmitted diseases by men, who as a group were largely responsible for transmitting them. Unknown to her, Beth's brutish husband runs a Lock Hospital, a degrading institution designed to control the movements of women with venereal disease. Equally important, however, is the rejection of the dyadic model and to some extent the sexual double standard as well. Though not an admirable character, Beth's husband is presumably meant to represent many men when he declares that he doesn't believe in (or want) a passionless, unworldly angel for a wife. Such behaviour he deems 'conventional affectation' which results in sending husbands elsewhere for their amusements (p. 349). Nevertheless, Dan is highly conscious of public propriety, and though he carries on a bald flirtation with one of his patients, countenances none of Beth's friendly relationships with men.

It becomes increasingly clear that Beth's marriage is doomed to failure. Beth's yearning for an inner life which is both mentally satisfying and spiritual leads her to search for a private space in their house where she can work without fear of Dan's intruding upon her. Her exploration is reminiscent of Princess Irene's in Macdonald's *The Princess and the Goblin* (1870–1), as well as fairy tales such as 'The Sleeping Beauty' and 'Rapunzel', where tower rooms operate as metaphors for the female body.[35] In Macdonald's tale, Irene climbs a staircase she has never seen before and finds herself in a tower where she meets a *very* beautiful and *very* old lady, also called Irene. She calls herself the princess's great-great-grandmother, but as the story progresses it becomes clear that she is much more than this. The lady, whose presence can only be detected by those with faith, is older than anyone knows. She represents spirituality, cleansing, love, loss of self, and is also a replacement for Irene's dead mother. The tower room has several functions. It provides Princess Irene with a spiritual haven; symbolically the tower room also represents a retreat from her changing body. Irene is approaching puberty and finds herself under threat from the goblins who live beneath the ground. They want to capture her and force her to marry the goblin prince. Not only are the goblins repulsive to her (though for most of the book she does not know who they are or why she is frightened of them), but she is not yet emotionally or physically ready for marriage. They thus represent sexual threat on psychic grounds as well as a threat to her feminine purity. The ascent to the tower room can be seen as representing not simply the development of her spiritual self, but the repression of her emerging sexuality and the denial of her self as a sexual object. This meaning seems to be deliberately suggested in the text, for Curdie, the young miner who eventually saves the princess from the goblins and who in the sequel marries her, is prepared to wait for Irene until she is ready for a sexual relationship. Accordingly much is made of a kiss Irene has promised him and which he avoids receiving.

Just as Irene finds spirituality and the ability to act when in the tower room (at one point the old lady shows her how to save Curdie from the goblins), so Beth cultivates her inner self and finds an outlet for creative expression in her secret chamber. Irene feels instantly at home with her 'mother of grandmothers', but subsequently learns that most people, and especially most grown-ups can not see or do not believe in the old lady. Significantly, Grand describes the Beth who discovers the secret room as childish:

> At the far end [of the attic] . . . there was a pile of packing-cases and travelling-trunks. . . . The pile was too high for her to see over it, but by going down on her hands and knees where the sloping roof was too low for her to stoop, she found she could creep around it. It was the kind of thing a child would have done, but what was Beth but a child? (p. 346)

Irene's sense of being at home when with the old lady is mirrored in Beth's feelings of *déjà vu* in her new room:

> Beth dropped on to one of the dusty chairs and looked round. Everything about her was curiously familiar, and her first impression was that she had been there before. On the other hand, she could hardly believe in the reality of what she saw, she thought she must be dreaming, for here was exactly what she had been pining for most in the whole wide world of late, a secret spot, sacred to herself, where she could be safe from intrusion. (p. 347)

The mixture of dreaming and vision, discovery and repeated experience, links Beth again with the far-seeing, timeless Decadent *femmes fatales*. She seems both to have discovered past selves, and to have stumbled on her own destiny. As the final section of the book develops, this feeling becomes more profound. Beth begins to develop her creativity and independence, first through selling tapestries and then through her writing. She completes the separation from Dan (her goblin equivalent) and moves to London. This is perhaps the most difficult phase of Beth's life for feminist readers, for while in London Beth lives isolated, unrecognised, and, more importantly, starts to sacrifice herself caring for the young man in the flat opposite who has become seriously ill. The levels of repression and self-denial she forces on herself are enormously damaging, but they are also presented as formative. It is in this last phase of suffering that Beth's personality is completed. Her willingness to live for others also links this woman, who turns out to be a radical suffragette and public speaker, with the feminine ideal. She finds her 'natural gift' (in this text, Nature and God are inseparable) in public speaking, something which should be antithetical to femininity; however, the book ends with images of Beth as the apotheosis of Victorian womanhood. After a triumphant public appearance Beth returns to her cottage, and several pages are spent describing what she sees as, like Maggie Tulliver, she stands at her window and watches the transition from dusk to dawn. Maggie's distant gaze foretells that she is soon to leave this world, but Beth's shows her to be both in touch with a different reality and very much of this world. Seeing a watchman guarding some tools, she decides to bring him some refreshments. The man, who has been dozing, mistakes Beth for the Virgin Mary, and Beth, 'slipped away, leaving him in the happy certainty that a heavenly vision had been vouchsafed him' (p. 526). In this moment Beth *is* the Victorian feminine ideal, but she is also still knowledgeable and worldly. The final passages in the book reaffirm her links with the powerful women of Decadent art and letters, for as Beth watches, another vision rises before her. Arthur Brock, the young man in the attic, comes riding over the fields to claim her. Lines from Tennyson's 'The Lady of Shalott' come into Beth's head, yet where Tennyson's Elaine dies of unrequited love, Beth's knight has come for her. The mirror has indeed 'cracked from side to side', but the result is not deranged female power, disorder and death. Instead, it is life-affirming partnership and equality. Beth, with her ancient knowledge, her distant gaze, her intellect and public recognition, is nonetheless a positive representation of femininity.

4   Strange sensations

The aberrant heroines of sensation fiction

The foregoing chapters have highlighted a range of subtle adjustments to the role of the heroine in the nineteenth-century novel; challenges to the stereotype of the domestic Angel that yet remain within the bounds of respectability, and are recuperable back into the establishment model of acceptable feminine behaviour. This chapter examines the phenomenon of sensation fiction, which in the 1860s posed an outright and gleeful threat to both social proprieties and the conventions of heroine construction, and considers what its immense popularity has to tell us about contemporary frustrations with the circumscribed nature of the feminine role.

So what is a sensation novel? M. E. Braddon's evocation of horrible crime and dark secrets beneath the hospitable roofs of bourgeois England provides a remarkably clear demonstration of both the identifying features of sensation fiction and the ways in which it threatened conventional values:

> What do we know about the mysteries that hang about the houses we enter? If I were to go tomorrow to that common-place, plebeian, eight-roomed house in which Maria Manning and her husband murdered their guest, I should have no awful prescience of that bygone horror. Foul deeds have been done under the most hospitable roofs, terrible crimes have been committed amid the fairest scenes, and have left no trace upon the spot where they were done. I do not believe in mandrake, or in blood stains that no time can efface. I believe rather that we may walk unconsciously in an atmosphere of crime, and breathe none the less freely. I believe that we may look into the smiling face of a murderer and admire its tranquil beauty.[1]

Violent crime is placed in a lower middle-class setting; the action primarily of a named woman and only secondarily of her male accomplice. It is an affront against basic social decencies: they murder their guest. More, it is invisible – evil is not immanent in the scene of a crime, or even in the face of a murderer: it is something hidden, to be searched for beneath the dissimulations of ordinary social interactions. Crime, and the evil that engenders it, are no longer imagined, as in the Gothic novel, to be necessarily associated with squalid or foreign surroundings: they can be, and frequently are, found in the rural idyll of the English Home Counties. Crime and perversion – the darker elements of human behaviour – are associated with secrecy, with the English middle classes, and with women: these are the essential features of the sensation novel, which sprang into life at the start of the 1860s and dominated the book trade, via the circulating libraries, for that decade.

The sensation novel differed from its generic predecessors – the Gothic novel of the late eighteenth and early nineteenth centuries, and the Newgate novel of the 1830s – in its depiction of sensational events occurring in domestic settings, and in times and places familiar to its readers. Eschewing the supernatural, which had provided both terror and explanation in the Gothic genre, the sensation novel employs the dark side of contemporary life to scare and titillate: murder, bigamy, illicit sexuality, prostitution, illegitimacy and mistaken identity replace the diabolical villains and ruined monasteries of Henry Lewis and Mrs Radcliffe. As Winifred Hughes, author of one of the most comprehensive accounts of sensation fiction, notes of M. E. Braddon: '[she] knew what would scare people most effectively and she knew that it had nothing to do with monks in medieval castles'.[2] What it did have to do with was lifting the stone of studied bourgeois respectability to see what scuttled out from underneath.

As the above list of sensations indicates, many of the crimes and perversions on which these novels focus are committed by women. Female protagonists figure prominently in this fiction – as murderesses, bigamists, swindlers, prostitutes and detectives. In this, sensation fiction represents one of the major contestations of female roles operative in the nineteenth century – and is responsible for initiating significant changes in the representation of women in later fiction.

Contrary, perhaps, to the expectations raised by this statement, sensation fiction was not written only by women. The earliest exponent of the genre in its definable form was Wilkie Collins, whose *The Woman in White* (1860) is usually credited with creating the market for tales of domestic sensation. Two years later Mary Elizabeth Braddon published the equally influential *Lady Audley's Secret* (1862). Among the other major sensation novelists were Charles Reade – *Hard Cash* (1863) and *Griffith Gaunt* (1866) – and Mrs Henry Wood – *East Lynne* (1861). Braddon, Collins and Mrs Henry Wood will be taken as exemplars of the following arguments about the nature and influence of sensation fiction, first because they were the most popular, and most imitated of the sensationalists, second, because between them their major texts represent the most significant trends within the genre, and finally, because their novels are available in recent paperback editions.

Elaine Showalter, reading the novels of female sensationalists as overturning the conventions of what she calls 'feminine fiction', has dismissed Wilkie Collins' four novels of the 1860s as 'conventional' in their 'social and sexual attitudes'.[3] Her evidence is a fairly perfunctory reading of *The Woman in White*, which rejects Marian Halcombe as a positive female role model because of her moustache. She does not consider *No Name* (1862), in which Collins provides in Magdalen Vanstone a female protagonist at least as active, powerful, sexually attractive and sympathetic as Braddon's Aurora Floyd, or *Armadale* (1866), whose Lydia Gwilt, forger and poisoner, is a far more animated villainess than Braddon's bigamous Lady Audley. Showalter's dismissal of Collins is a key element in her chapter on sensation fiction in *A Literature of Their Own*, which occupies a pivotal point in her consideration of developments in women's writing in the nineteenth century. The sensation novel she sees as the end point of 'feminine fiction', with its dismissal of that fiction's stereotypes clearing the way for the 'feminist fiction' which was to follow in the 1880s. It is clearly imperative for her argument that this essentially female literary tradition should not have been galvanised by male writers. But if Showalter's contention that only women sensationalists wrote subversive female characters is wrong, what explanation can be found for the radical challenge the heroines of sensation fiction pose to the conventional orthodoxy?

One explanation for the subversiveness of the genre might be found in an examination of the biographies of its authors. Many of the most successful sensation novelists had personal reasons to scorn conventional social pieties. M. E. Braddon's life reads like one of her stories: she worked on the stage under an assumed name, wrote for money, and lived unmarried with her publisher John Maxwell – with whom she had five illegitimate children – because his wife was in a mental institution. Knowledge of the writer's unconventional life fuelled much of the objection to her work – as is demonstrated by Henry James' distaste at the prospect that Braddon had had experience of the bohemian society of which she wrote:

> She knows much that ladies are not accustomed to know, but that they are apparently very glad to learn. The names of drinks, the technicalities of the faro-table, the lingo of the turf, the talk natural to a crowd of fast men at supper, when there are no ladies present but Miss Braddon, the way one gentleman knocks another down – all these things – the exact local colour of Bohemia – our sisters and daughters may learn from these works.[4]

James' reference to things that 'ladies are not accustomed to know' returns us to Cobbett's injunction to conscious ignorance, discussed in Chapter 1: as James implies, the popularity of Braddon's novels with women suggests a profound dissatisfaction with such codes of reticence. Wilkie Collins suffered a life-long opium addiction, and established as his mistress a Mrs Caroline Graves, the original of the Woman in White, whom he met on a dark night when she was escaping from a private lunatic asylum. He had two children by another mistress, Martha Rudd, and lived alternately with the two women until his death. Charles Reade remained unmarried as a condition of his Oxford fellowship, but lived for many years with his mistress, the actress Mrs Laura Seymour. The detrimental effects of enforced celibacy are a preoccupying theme in many of his novels, which also deal with sexual obsessions and perversions. Reade's life was as dramatic as his works, filled with lawsuits, violent quarrels, and accusations of plagiarism against fellow authors. Like Collins he was vocal in his opposition to private lunatic asylums, taking escapees from these institutions into his home. Perhaps understandably, given the correspondence of his life and fiction, Reade insisted on the documentary basis of even his most outlandish sensations, pointing for evidence to his extensive collection of newspaper cuttings dealing with contemporary crimes.

Unusually among sensation novelists, Mrs Henry Wood lived a life of unimpeachable respectability. As Steevie Davies notes in her introduction to the Everyman edition of East Lynne, the choice of the double patronymic for her pen-name was a clear assertion of this respectability: 'Such a pseudonym declares the author's active and militant conservatism, her willed acknowledgment of the binding power of patriarchal norms: it may even suggest a potentially interesting tendency to extremism in this direction.'[5] As we might expect, her East Lynne poses none of the overt challenges to social and moral conventions of the works of Braddon, Reade and Collins; however, its employment of an adulteress as heroine – even though much of the novel consists of her elaborate expiation of her sins – suggests that a challenge to propriety is an in-built feature of the sensation form, and not restricted to the works of maverick and bohemian authors.

Another quality shared by this group of authors is that they were, for the most part, career writers: professionals able to make an adequate living from their novels. The sensation craze created a voracious popular demand, and to supply it the most successful novelists wrote rapidly and often, and gave the public what they wanted – suspense, fear and titillation in carefully measured doses. They were rewarded with striking commercial and popular success: East Lynne and Lady Audley's Secret were the best-selling novels of the entire century.[6] As Showalter notes, such widespread commercial success was a new thing for women writers: 'All the commercial, competitive, self-promoting aspects of the literary life that had been played down or ignored by the first two generations of nineteenth-century women writers were conspicuous in the careers of the third generation' (p. 154). Louisa M. Alcott, herself an author of several sensation stories, has Jo March progress from writing 'very mild romances' to sensation novels. Her first story

> was as full of desperation and despair as her limited acquaintance with those uncomfortable emotions enabled her to make it, and, having located it in Lisbon, she wound up with an earthquake, as a striking and appropriate dénoument.[7]

Alcott's amused acknowledgement of the disparity between the passion of the typical sensation story and the polite upbringing of the average middle-class woman writer – or reader – is more strongly echoed in the shocked denunciations of women sensationalists that packed the periodical press. Francis Paget's outburst – in fact in his parody sensation novel *Lucretia; or the Heroine of the Nineteenth Century* – is a fair example:

> And the writers of these books, ay, of the very foulest of them, – authors who have put forth confessions of the darkest profligacy that an utter reprobate could make, and who have degraded women's love into an animal propensity so rabid and so exacting, as to profess an opinion that its gratification will be cheaply purchased at the cost *of an eternity in hell*, – these writers are, some by their own admission . . . women; and the worst of them, UNMARRIED WOMEN![8]

Although Jo's father expresses gentle and 'unworldly' disparagement of her chosen form, the money she earns from her 'rubbish' 'turned into comforts for them all': ' "The Duke's Daughter" paid the butcher's bill, "A Phantom Hand" put down a new carpet, and "The Curse of the Coventrys" proved the blessing of the Marches in the way of groceries and gowns' (p. 42).

Like M. E. Braddon, Jo responds to the latest popular literary demand to support her family. Rather, however, than such popularism devaluing the sensation genre for a twentieth-century consideration, it is precisely their formulaic qualities, and their appeal to the popular imagination that renders these novels so useful as a source of evidence of the fantasies and fears of the mid-Victorian reading public.[9] The fears tapped by the sensation genre are those of the outsider within – the governess, the upper servant, even the trusted wife, who is not what she seems – and the danger of the insider becoming an outsider: the intense insecurity of class and economic status that afflicted the Victorian bourgeoisie in their rapidly changing society is reflected in the many plots that revolve around a sudden loss of fortune or a revelation of illegitimacy. For the female reader in particular, reading with that dual lens identified in Chapter 1, the same situations that are productive of fear may simultaneously be a source of pleasure: sensation novels invite identification with their heroines in their attacks on the propriety, and even the wealth, of the bourgeois patriarch.

Critics have offered various accounts of the sudden genesis of the sensation form, and attempted explanations of the opprobrium attached to the novels by contemporary reviewers. Winifred Hughes, in *The Maniac in the Cellar*, sees Dickens as the immediate influence for the sensation novelists' insinuation 'of elements of crime and mystery into the lives of ordinary, respectable middle-class characters' (p. ix).[10] The moral certainty that Dickens brings to, for instance, his account of the life and fate of Lady Dedlock, is replaced in sensation novels by a moral ambiguity that can allow a bigamist such as Aurora Floyd to end her days forgiven and remarried by her second husband. As Hughes remarks:

> If Braddon or Collins had written *Bleak House*, Lady Dedlock would not only have become the central character, she would probably have married her original lover, committed bigamy, then patched things up with Sir Leicester. Or else she would have been an out-and-out villainess, doing away with both lover and blackmailer before she got caught. (p. ix)

Thomas Boyle, in his idiosyncratic *Black Swine in the Sewers of Hampstead*,[11] finds the genesis of the sensation impulse not in literature but in the increasingly graphic accounts of brutal crimes such as child murder and abuse, rape and bestiality that pack the newspapers of the period. The sensation novel, according to Boyle, results from an intense anxiety produced by the real-life sensations of an ever-more chaotic urban society; his argument implies that the fictional genre, where the crimes are for the most part considerably less vile than those reported in the press, was a means for Victorian society to act out, in a controlled form, the fear produced by its environment.

Boyle's curiously personal book devotes its first two thirds to a discussion of real-life crimes and their reporting in the press.[12] Three sensation novels are given a rather perfunctory reading, while his most productive insight into the reasons for the rise of the sensation novel at that particular historical moment is contained in a brief and undeveloped association of ideas:

> The mass media treatment of crime which was inspired by the Palmer case in turn inspired a reaction in many ways comparable to the 'convulsions of the national mind' brought on three years later by the publication of Darwin's *Origin of Species*. . . . Each was a landmark . . . bringing into focus . . . certain realizations. Chief among these

was the rediscovery of an old truth that mankind, to paraphrase
Tennyson in *In Memorium*, had not yet worked out the beast. (p. 76)

What Boyle reads as merely parallel cases of texts (newspaper crime
reports and a scientific document) producing profound shocks to the
popular imagination can be more productively read as the necessary
conditions for the birth of the sensation novel: a proliferation of reports of
violent bestial crime, and Darwin's assertion of the animal heritage of the
human race. The fact that both occur immediately prior to the publication
of Wilkie Collins' catalytic *The Woman in White* is a persuasive explanation
for the phenomenon of the appearance of such a genre, devoted to the
gradual uncovering of crime from beneath the patina of civilised culture.

The modern critical consensus that sensation fiction represents a radical,
socially disruptive literary form arises not just from the fact of its dealing
with illicit subject matter, but from the furore its appearance occasioned in
the press.[13] Influential authors including Geraldine Jewsbury, Mrs Linton
and Mrs Oliphant objected publicly to the new literary craze. A feature
particularly singled out for moral outrage was the lack of purity evinced in
the representation of passionate women, and the failure of many authors
to punish their female characters for such passion. Mrs Oliphant, writing
in *Blackwood's* magazine, expresses this disgust most clearly:

> What is held up to us as the story of the feminine soul as it really
> exists underneath its conventional coverings, is a very fleshly and
> unlovely record. . . . Now it is no knight of romance riding down
> the forest glades, ready for the defence and succour of all the
> oppressed, for whom the dreaming maiden waits. She waits now for
> flesh and muscles, for strong arms that seize her, and warm breath
> that thrills her through, and a host of other physical attractions,
> which she indicates to the world with a charming frankness. . . .
> were the sketch made from the man's point of view, its openness
> would at least be less repulsive. The peculiarity of it in England is . . .
> that this intense appreciation of flesh and blood, this eagerness of
> physical sensation, is represented as the natural sentiment of English
> girls, and is offered to them not only as the portrait of their own state
> of mind, but as amusement and mental food.[14]

The final remark is the crux of the matter: the sexually aroused heroines of
sensation fiction are so repugnant to many contemporary literary
authorities because these authorities believe the heroine of the novel to
provide a behavioural model for the instruction of the young female
reader. It is notable that many of the most heated objections to the
sensation novel emanate from other novelists: writers of realist novels. For

them, the notion of the novel as a moral and social barometer, and thus a worthy exemplar for young women was hard – and comparatively recently – won. The sensation novel, with its often frivolous, ironising tone (particularly in the case of M. E. Braddon) and overturning of cherished moral precepts, threatened to topple the novel from its pillar of respectable instruction. In an anonymous article in *All the Year Round* of December 1894, the writer examines 'A Century of Feminine Fiction', extolling Fanny Burney as the first of the novelists to transform the genre into something respectable:

> She first showed that a tale might be written in which both the fashionable and the vulgar life of London might be exhibited with great force, and with broad comic humour, and which yet should not contain a single line inconsistent with rigid morality, or even with virgin delicacy.

The author, using precisely the arguments mounted thirty years earlier against the sensation novel, criticises the New Woman literature for threatening this high moral status. The threat, in both cases emanates directly from the heroine, because, as another anonymous writer pointed out in a *Saturday Review* article in 1883,

> the heroine of fiction is, let us remember, the ideal woman of the period, the mould of form with which our young women naturally compare themselves. Her example will outweigh, with them, all the exhortations of their guardians, and for them, therefore, there is the pleasant prospect of seeing the attractive qualities described, reproduced in their daughters and wards.[15]

Perhaps the most radical feature of the sensation novel was its deconstruction of the ideal Victorian heroine. In a variety of ways these novels mock, decentre and undermine the passive, angelic female, rendering her so ridiculous that they effectively laugh her off the pages of the Victorian novel. Where the orphan was able to enact a symbolic and legitimate female independence, and decadent constructions of femininity allowed it to incorporate power and sensuality, such revisions of the cultural norm were of essence covert and encoded. With a conspicuous absence of any such subtlety, the sensation novel declares open season on the Angel in the House.

Who is the heroine?

As we remarked in Chapter 2, the ostensible ideal of Victorian fiction – the passive, blue-eyed, ringleted blonde – is often notable by her absence from centre stage. Novelists such as Eliot and Gaskell assure us of the unusual nature of their dark, passionate, statuesque heroines, yet the tacit ideal is really only to be found in the pages of Dickens, whose women often acquire accretions of mythic signification by virtue of their utter blankness. (Lucie Manette, who inspires the fervid devotion of Sidney Carton is a case in point; it is curious how very many doll-like women in both realist and sensation novels bear the name Lucy.) In much Victorian fiction the demure, passive ideal is often shunted to the side to become the foil to the more tempestuous heroine: Edith Shaw to Margaret Hale, her cousin Lucy to Maggie Tulliver. More, the faults of the ultra-feminine character are often exposed, particularly by women writers. Elizabeth Gaskell's Edith is idle and frivolous, and rather too interested in material luxuries; George Eliot's Lucy is timid and equivocating; and Louisa May Alcott's Beth is virtually incapacitated by her unworldly goodness. Such criticisms are light rebukes rather than damning swipes – largely because the characters involved have minimal roles in the narratives – but they are indicative of a pervasive dissatisfaction with the culturally sanctioned ideal. It is a dissatisfaction that is played out much more overtly on the stage of the sensation novel.

Sensation fiction employs an unusually large number of female characters – even in those novels written by men. Their various representations and roles allow us to question who precisely the heroine *is* in Victorian fiction. There are three possible answers to this question: she is the ideal; she is the object of the hero's affections; she is the protagonist (these, of course, are merely the structural roles available; as we have demonstrated in the course of this book, there are a wealth of complex and subtle *narrative* roles occupied by heroines in the nineteenth-century novel). In many sensation novels each of these formal roles is assigned to a different woman, effectively splitting the 'heroine' into separate parts. This could result in a diminution of female significance in the narrative, and a lack of a focus for the (female) reader's identification, but in fact it invariably represents a radical expansion of the possibilities for female identity and behaviour. The technique often disturbs the reader's narrative expectations: providing another source of suspense, as doubt is cast on which woman represents the authorial ideal, or which preoccupies the hero in his secret thoughts. Winifred Hughes suggests that most plot devices in sensation fiction rely on the principle of doubling – of which the notion suggested here of a split heroine role (and hence two or more heroines) is an element – seeing both the recurrent themes of bigamy and the dead returned to life as revealing a 'preoccupation with the loss or duplication of identity' (pp. 20–1). Such concerns return us to the subject matter of the previous chapter: the loss or transcendence of individual identity that is achieved by the visionary women of the decadent imagination, and anticipates the discussion of the collective identity of the speaking subject of feminine autobiography in Chapter 5. Such connections suggest further reasons for us to take seriously the proposition that sensation fiction offers revisions of the feminine role as radical as those found in less populist genres.

The splitting of the heroine in fact acts *against* that tendency to stereotyping that is one of the major objections of contemporary reviewers to the sensation genre. The following extract from a review article of 1863 is typical of such objections:

> A sensational novel, as a matter of course, abounds in incident. Indeed, as a general rule, it consists of nothing else. . . . The human actors in the piece are, for the most part, but so many lay figures on which to exhibit a drapery of incident. Allowing for the necessary division of all characters of a tale into male and female, old and young, virtuous and vicious, there is hardly anything said or done by any one specimen of a class which might not be said or done by any other specimen of the same class. Each game is played with the same pieces, differing only in the moves.[16]

In fact, as Henry James notes in his criticism of M. E. Braddon, sensation fiction does provide copious detail to distinguish characters, but it is invariably material, rather than psychological in nature. Lady Audley, he complains, is 'a non-entity, without a heart, a soul, a reason. But what we may call the small change for these facts – her eyes, her hair, her mouth, her dresses, her bedroom furniture, her little words and deeds – are so lavishly bestowed that she successfully maintains a kind of half illusion.'[17] As a genre, sensation fiction is precluded from supplying the sort of psychological and social motivations that deepen our sense of character in the work of James or Eliot, since precisely the suspense in these novels – as in their descendants the detective novels – lies in hidden and unexplained motivation and elements of character. This does not necessarily result in wooden stereotypes. Indeed, in its representation of character as equivocal and shifting – a function as much of social niceties and conventions as of deep structures of identity – the sensation novel anticipates many modernist developments.

The split heroine and her sisters the libidinous heroine, the detective heroine, and the doll-like villainess represent significant variations on the heroine-roles available in the conventional Victorian novel, but they also allow us to take another look at the mechanics of heroine-construction in those main-stream novels.

The ideal

> Wherever she went she seemed to take joy and brightness with her. In the cottages of the poor her fair face shone like a sunbeam. She would sit for a quarter of an hour talking to some old woman, and apparently as pleased with the admiration of a toothless crone as if

she had been listening to the compliments of a marquis; and when she tripped away, leaving nothing behind her (for her poor salary gave no scope to her benevolence), the old woman would burst out into senile raptures with her grace, her beauty, and her kindliness, such as she never bestowed upon the vicar's wife, who half fed and clothed her. For you see Miss Lucy Graham was blest with that magic power of fascination by which a woman can charm with a word or intoxicate with a smile. Everyone loved, admired, and praised her. . . . her employer; his visitors; her pupils; the servants; everybody, high and low, united in declaring that Lucy Graham was the sweetest girl that ever lived. (*Lady Audley's Secret*, pp. 6–7)

Lucy Graham is one of the masterpieces of nineteenth-century fiction: she performs the charitable duties of the heroine with more charm than a Dorothea Brooke; her personality beguiles with its childish exuberance and gaiety; her looks are the acme of the ideal. Those looks exert an immediate power over her future husband:

He could no more resist the tender fascination of those soft and melting blue eyes; the graceful beauty of that slender throat and drooping head, with its flaxen curls; the low music of that gentle voice; the perfect harmony that pervaded every charm, and made all doubly charming in this woman; than he could resist his destiny. Destiny! Why, she was his destiny! (p. 7)

Indeed she was, for Lucy Graham thus becomes the notorious Lady Audley – a doll-like villainess, finally revealed as a bigamist and attempted murderess. M. E. Braddon's *Lady Audley's Secret* was an instantaneous best-seller, seducing its readership with its taut suspense, and with its daring placement of a bigamous villainess at centre stage. Lady Audley is always the focus of attention in the novel, effortlessly dwarfing her hoydenish and tempestuous step-daughter Alicia, and the intense and commanding Clara Talboys through the sheer audacity of her portrayal. The heroine's central position is thus usurped by the villainess.

The reader's suspicions of Lady Audley mount gradually throughout the novel, fuelled by the investigations of her newly acquired nephew Robert Audley. Robert's old friend George Talboys returns to England from Australia, having made his fortune, only to discover his young wife recently dead. Visiting Audley Court with Robert, he fails to meet Lady Audley, but the two young men are shown into her chambers, through a secret passage, by Alicia Audley, and there encounter a 'pre-Raphaelite' portrait of Lady Audley. On seeing the portrait George falls strangely silent, and disappears soon afterwards. Investigating his disappearance, Robert soon uncovers a conspiracy to make it appear that George has returned to Australia, and begins to fear that his friend has been murdered. Aided in his investigations by George's beautiful and inspiring sister Clara, Robert secures the evidence that links Lady Audley with the apparently-dead Helen Talboys. He finally confronts his aunt with the evidence, accusing her of having murdered her first husband, George Talboys. She responds by setting fire to the inn in which Robert is staying, having first locked him in his room. Escaping, Robert forces her to confess her bigamy to Sir Michael Audley, and is commissioned by his distraught uncle to deal with her. This he accomplishes by escorting her to a private lunatic asylum in Belgium – Lady Audley having finally revealed her great secret: not her bigamy, or the murder, but an inherited tendency to madness. Robert weds Clara; George Talboys returns alive from America, and tells of how he crawled from the well into which his wife had pushed him; and Lady Audley dies a year later in the asylum, leaving, as Braddon assures us, 'the good people all happy and at peace'.

While this plot summary evokes some of the techniques of suspense and investigation that so hooked Braddon's audience, what it fails to communicate is the pervasive and delicate irony with which she approaches her subject. Lady Audley does not hide her villainy behind her childlike exterior: her surpassing selfishness and her evil actions stem precisely *from* her occupation of the position of cultural ideal. She merely carries the stereotype to its logical limit – sacrificing everything to attain the requisite ideal of marriage and position:

> 'I had learnt that which in some indefinite manner or other every school-girl learns sooner or later – I learned that my ultimate fate in life depended upon my marriage, and I concluded that if I was indeed prettier that my schoolfellows, I ought to marry better than any of them.' (p. 374)

The reader's sympathy for Lady Audley begins to be eroded long before any specific evidence against her has been introduced: she is simply too close to the ideal, revealing it in its most facile and infantile guise:

> That very childishness had a charm which few could resist. The innocence and candour of an infant beamed in Lady Audley's fair face, and shone out of her large and liquid blue eyes. The rosy lips, the delicate nose, the profusion of fair ringlets, all contributed to preserve to her beauty the character of extreme youth and freshness. She owned to twenty years of age, but it was hard to believe her more than seventeen. Her fragile figure, which she loved to dress in rustling silks, till she looked like a child tricked out for a masquerade, was as girlish as if she had just left the nursery. All her amusements were childish. She hated reading or study of any kind, and loved

society; rather than be alone she would admit Phoebe Marks [her maid] into her confidence, and loll on one of the sofas in her luxurious dressing-room, discussing a new costume for some coming dinner party, or sit chattering to the girl, with her jewel-box beside her, upon the satin cushions, and Sir Michael's presents spread out in her lap, while she counted and admired her treasures. (p. 57)

On the surface, Lady Audley poses no threat to the culture of respectability: she extols all its values, and is devoted to her role as the ornament of Sir Michael's house. She is entirely untainted by any imputation of sexual passion, marrying both her husbands for social status, rather than out of any physical desire – as she assures Sir Michael: 'The common temptations that assail and shipwreck some women had no terror for me. I would have been your true and pure wife to the end of time, though I had been surrounded by a legion of tempters' (p. 375). Rather than undermining its codes of propriety, she threatens bourgeois culture by too closely parodying its ideal, and revealing it as a hollow idol. Somewhat perversely, Elaine Showalter reads Lady Audley as a feminist icon, assuming that it is the female reader's identification with her that necessitates Braddon's use of the 'secret' of madness to account for her character's crimes:

> Lady Audley's unfeminine assertiveness . . . must ultimately be described as madness, not only to spare Braddon the unpleasant necessity of having to execute an attractive heroine with whom she in many ways identifies, but also to spare the woman reader the guilt of identifying with a cold-blooded killer. (p. 167)

Showalter offers scant justification for what is a contentious reading of a novel which very early presents its central female character as silly and frivolous, and steadily pulls aside successive veils to reveal her as mysterious, duplicitous, violent, bigamous and insane. While the woman reader may indeed find that Lady Audley's actions gratify her own desire to attack the patriarchal home, the villainess is neither a conscious rebel, nor an attractive character, in the way that other aberrant females – such as Braddon's own Aurora Floyd – certainly are.

The cultural ideal is represented in virtually every sensation novel, with a varying intensity of focus. In *The Woman in White* its exemplar is Laura Fairlie, whose curious blankness of both character and visual appearance were explored in Chapter 2. Laura is the ideal unquestioned – generous, sweet-natured, kind and demure – but it is Laura, not her ugly sister Marian, who so easily loses her grip on her sanity that the villain, Count Fosco, is able to incarcerate her in an asylum. Like the classic heroine of popular melodrama, Laura passively accepts her arranged marriage to Sir Percival Glyde, who is soon revealed as a cruel and heartless fortune-seeker. The truly innocent heroine, to be vulnerable to the machinations of the villains, needs to be rather stupid: appropriate physical fragility is paralleled by mental weakness.

In another of Braddon's very popular works, *Aurora Floyd* (1867), the foil to the heroine is her cousin Lucy:

> She was a fair-faced, blue-eyed, rosy-lipped, golden-haired little girl, who thought Felden Woods a paradise upon earth, and Aurora more fortunate than the Princess Royal of England. . . . She was direfully afraid of her cousin's ponies and Newfoundland dogs, and had a firm conviction that sudden death held his throne within a certain radius of a horse's heels; but she loved Aurora, after the manner common to these weaker natures, and accepted Miss Floyd's superb patronage and protection as a matter of course.[18]

Braddon is unequivocal in her assertion of Lucy's belonging to the class of 'weaker natures', and almost gleefully assigns her the fate of the meek and pure woman; to suffer her love in silence, unlike her tempestuous cousin Aurora, who speaks her passion clearly, and therefore gains (too many of) its rewards:

> But it is hard upon such women as these that they feel so much and yet display so little feeling! The dark-eyed impetuous creatures, who speak out fearlessly, and tell you that they love or hate you – flinging their arms round your neck or throwing the carving knife at you, as the case may be – get full value for all their emotion; but these gentle creatures love, and make no sign . . . concealment, like the worm i' the bud, feeds on their damask cheeks; and compassionate relatives tell them they are bilious . . . They are always at a disadvantage. Their inner life may be a tragedy, all blood and tears, while their outer existence is some dull domestic drama of every-day life. (p. 135)

Braddon's contempt for the self-sacrificing, modest ideal is manifest: poor Lucy gets the man of her secret desire, the fantastically pompous Talbot Bulstrode, who is a parody of the Victorian patriarch. Talbot congratu-lates himself at the end of the novel that his Lucy has escaped the heroine's role, giving the clearest of indications of the author's sense of the profound restrictions of the conventional feminine sphere: 'Thank Heaven, my poor little Lucy has never been forced into playing the heroine of a tragedy like this; thank Heaven, my poor little darling's life flows evenly and placidly in a smooth channel!' (p. 373).

The possessor of another such smoothly channelled life is Norah Vanstone, the eldest of the two illegitimate sisters in Wilkie Collins' *No Name* (1862). Our first introduction to Norah, the ostensible heroine at this point, is frankly equivocal in its judgement, seeing her as a weaker, paler echo of her more unconventional mother. 'If we dare to look closely enough', Collins suggests, 'may we not observe, that the moral force of character and the higher intellectual capacities in parents often seem to wear out mysteriously in the course of trans-mission to children?'[19] Although she is not the fair and slight physical embodiment of the ideal, Norah is morally unimpeachable – the Angel in the House in person. She is also very quickly revealed to be dull and irritating, imposing her superior moral judgements through silence and resigned disapproval: 'Whether the motive was pride, or sullenness, or distrust of herself, or despair of doing good, the result was not to be mistaken – Norah had resolved on remaining passive for the future' (p. 51). Although Norah reveals strength in her fortitude when faced with her parents' death and the revelation of her and her sister Magdalen's illegitimacy, it is a strength to endure, not to act. At the end of the novel, after the elaborate and ingenious stratagems in which Magdalen has engaged to win back their fortune have run their course, it is Norah who quietly marries the new heir to the fortune, and so secures passively that which Magdalen had hoped to win through active – if morally equivocal – endeavour. There is little doubt with which enterprise textual sympathy rests. While in *The Woman in White* the heroine's role is split between the beautiful Laura and the characterful Marian, in *No Name* both elements belong to Magdalen, with Norah possessing only moral rectitude.

Lady Isabel Carlyle, suffering heroine of Mrs Henry Wood's *East Lynne*, is yet another epitome of the ideal:

> Who – what – was it? Mr Carlyle looked, not quite sure whether it was a human being: he almost thought it more like an angel.
> A light, graceful, girlish form, a face of surpassing beauty, beauty that is rarely seen, save from the imagination of a painter, dark shining curls falling on her neck and shoulders smooth as a child's, fair delicate arms decorated with pearls, and a flowing dress of costly white lace. . . . Generous and benevolent was she; timid and sensitive to a degree; gentle and considerate to all. (ch. 1, 'The Lady Isabel', pp. 7–9)

Unlike Lady Audley's, her apparent benevolence is not a front for darker designs: Lady Isabel is more sinned against that sinning. Her fault is to allow herself to be seduced, but

> the seduction . . . scandalous as it might appear in potential, is never permitted to become anything more that an object lesson for erring wives. . . . the emphasis . . . falls on the punishment, on the exquisite agony of the penitent adulteress, rather than on the original temptation.[20]

The narrative and moral significances of the offences of Lady Audley and of Lady Isabel Carlyle are strongly divergent. Both are sexual in nature, but while adultery is a sin, bigamy is a legally punishable crime. Paradoxically, as Mrs Oliphant noted, bigamy also keeps sexual desire within societal moral control – it is sanctioned, if illegitimately:

> [Braddon] has brought in the reign of bigamy as an interesting and fashionable crime, which no doubt shows a certain deference to the British relish for law and order. It goes against the seventh commandment, no doubt, but it does it in a legitimate sort of way, and is an invention which could only have been possible to an Englishwoman knowing the attraction of impropriety, and yet loving the shelter of the law.[21]

In the novels of Braddon, bigamy has the effect of displacing sexual desire, and replacing it with the concerns of material wealth and social position. Even the sensual Aurora Floyd only marries originally from motives of lust – her subsequent, bigamous, marriage to a Tory squire is much more sensibly conceived. Adultery, as embraced by Mrs Henry Wood, has none of the ambivalent status of bigamy. It is an act motivated by lust, and, as such, is finally expiable only by the heroine's death. While adultery besmirches the chastity of the individual woman, bigamy casts doubt on the security of the institution of marriage, and questions its absolute centrality in the bourgeois novel. As Braddon remarks, having married off both her heroines half-way through *Aurora Floyd*, the convention of ending a novel with a marriage is curious:

> Now my two heroines being married, the reader versed in the physiology of novel writing may conclude that my story is done, that the green curtain is ready to fall upon the last act of the play . . . Yet, after all, does the business of the real-life drama always end upon the altar steps? Must the play needs be over when the hero and heroine have signed their names in the register? Does man cease to

be, to do, and to suffer, when he gets married? And is it necessary that the novelist, after devoting three volumes to the description of a courtship of six weeks' duration, should reserve for himself only half a page in which to tell us the events of two-thirds of a life-time? (p. 137)

That all-embracing 'man' contains a much more significant 'woman'. In refusing to see the wedding as the end of a woman's story, sensation fiction inevitably opens up a vast new arena of possibilities for female identity and action. Bigamy seems a small price to pay.

The femme fatale

The sensation novel represents a significant exception to the rule of covertly encoded Victorian sexuality examined in the previous three chapters. In many of these texts women are actively desiring beings, happy to express their passions openly, and – most significantly – gaining contented and successful futures as a result. Braddon's *Aurora Floyd* is perhaps the clearest example of this phenomenon. The eponymous heroine is wild as a child in the manner familiar from Catherine Earnshaw, and from Alcott's Jo March and Susan Coolidge's Katy:

> The truth of the matter is, that before Miss Floyd emerged from the nursery she evinced a very decided tendency to becomes what is called 'fast'. At six years of age she rejected a doll, and asked for a rocking horse. At ten she could converse fluently upon the subject of pointers, setters, fox-hounds, harriers and beagles. (p. 18)

Unlike those other heroines, however, there is no process of taming for her to undergo. Although Braddon ends the novel with a subdued Aurora, the change is minimal – she is 'a little changed, a shade less defiantly bright, perhaps' (p. 384). In effect, all that she has been required to forfeit in exculpation of her bigamous crime is the full passion of her interest in horse-flesh. Her adolescent preoccupation with horses and the race-track – perhaps the motive force behind her attraction to her father's groom – is replaced by her passionate love for her husband (we have here maybe the earliest example of the theme of mature female sexuality replacing adolescent horse-mania, familiar from a thousand twentieth-century girls' pony-stories). Unlike Jo March, Aurora is not required to temper her violent passions or her physical exuberance: it is precisely these qualities that attract her many admirers, as even the upright Talbot Bulstrode is forced to admit:

I cannot help admiring this extraordinary girl. She is like Mrs Nisbett in her zenith of fame and beauty; she is like Cleopatra sailing down the Cydnus; she is like Nell Gwynne selling oranges . . . She is like everything that is beautiful and strange, and wicked and unwomanly, and bewitching; and she is just the sort of creature that many a fool would fall in love with. (p. 40)

His judgement is all the more telling, as the novel entirely refutes his claim that Aurora is wicked and unwomanly – we recognize these assertions as functions of his fear of her power and attraction.

The youthful indiscretion of Aurora's first marriage, to her father's groom, is represented in precisely those terms familiar from the literature of guidance for the parents of young girls, examined in Chapter 1: the attraction arises from 'the wicked madness of her youth' (p. 273), and the marriage is contracted when Aurora – removed from under her father's watchful eye – runs away from one of the boarding schools that figured so prominently in the prurient imaginings of the moral authorities. Aurora's feelings for the groom, James Conyers, are described in terms that allow no uncertainty about her lust. Conyers is introduced to us through a lingering textual perusal that reveals him as physical temptation personified:

He is wonderfully handsome . . . the very perfection of physical beauty; faultless in proportion, as if each line in his face and form have been measured by the sculptor's rule, and carved by the sculptor's chisel. He is a man about whose beauty there can be no dispute, whose perfection servant-maids and duchesses must alike confess . . . yet it is rather a sensual type of beauty, this splendour of form and colour, unallied to any intellectual grace. (pp. 151–2)

Aurora is straightforward about the grounds of her attraction to him: 'I married him because he had dark-blue eyes, and long eyelashes, and white teeth, and brown hair' (p. 296), and acknowledges this as a mistake. In textual terms, however, this desire is not culpable because it is physical, but because it is *only* physical; because she had 'no romantic overwhelming love for this man' (p. 295). The model of the process of female maturation here, unlike in the surveillance manuals, is that mere lust is superseded by a capacity for eroticised love, rather than by an utter absence of physical desire.

Braddon is not so naive as to assume that such a radically new woman would have an easy passage in Victorian society. The pitfalls – familiar to the twentieth-century reader – of a declared, active sexual identity for a woman are interestingly represented in the pornographic fantasy of

Aurora indulged in by the malevolent hunch-backed 'idiot' Steeve Hargreaves (Steeve is perhaps justly malevolent, as Aurora had previously horse-whipped him for maltreating her dog):

> 'Shall I tell you what it is I am afraid of ?' said Steeve Hargreaves, hissing the words through his closed teeth in that unpleasant whisper peculiar to him.
> 'It isn't Mrs Mellish. It's myself. It's *this.*' – he grasped something in the loose pocket of his trousers as he spoke, – 'it's this. I'm afraid to trust myself a-nigh her, for fear I should spring upon her, and cut her thro-at from ear to ear. I've seen her in my dreams sometimes, with her beautiful white thro-at laid open, and streaming oceans of blood; but, for all that, she's always had the broken whip in her hand, and she's always laughed at me. I've had many a dream about her; but I've never seen her dead or quiet; and I've never seen her without the whip.' (p. 161)

It is Aurora's physical strength and powerful character, as well as the aggressive sexuality represented by her 'beautiful thro-at' that elicit Steeve's desire to attack her with his knife-phallus. No such vengeful erotic fantasies are harboured in these texts about the physically passive, demure Lucys (even Lady Audley attracts the sympathy of the husband she tries to murder, and the man who establishes her guilt): there are heavy costs attached to the extension of women's identity.

Another *femme fatale* is Magdalen Vanstone, protagonist of *No Name*. Exuberant and impulsive, Magdalen takes the initiative in her youthful romance with the languid and inept Frank Clare. When her governess surprises them in the summer house, it is clearly Magdalen who is making all the running:

> She stepped round to the entrance; looked in; and discovered Magdalen and Frank seated close together. To Miss Garth's horror, Magdalen's arm was unmistakably round Frank's neck; and worse still, the position of her face at the moment of discovery, showed beyond all doubt, that she had just been offering to the victim of Chinese commerce, the first and foremost of all the consolations which a woman can bestow on a man. In plainer words, she had just given Frank a kiss. (p. 57)

This reversal of the traditional roles of seducer and seduced had been anticipated by Miss Garth's estimation of Magdalen's character:

She is resolute and impetuous, clever and domineering; she is not one of those model women who want a man to look up to and protect them – her beau-ideal (though she may not think it herself) is a man she can henpeck. (p. 52)

Worse is to come, as Magdalen embarks on a plan to restore her and her sister's lost fortunes, by using her sexuality to ensnare the heir to the fortune – a cousin they have never met – into a loveless marriage. Such behaviour was doubly shocking for a contemporary reader, in that the novel triumphantly vindicates Magdalen, restoring the fortune through her sister's properly loving marriage to another cousin, and rewarding Magdalen with marriage to the son of her father's benefactor, a sea captain worthy of her adventurous nature.

Magdalen's behaviour is yoked together with Aurora's for specific disapproval by a contemporary reviewer:

In the sensation novel, even the heroine, without ceasing to be heroine, is permitted to indulge in such indiscretions as eloping with horse trainers or fleecing near relatives under false pretences, while the blame ultimately rests with vague inner compulsions, accidental rather than essential in relation to character.[22]

Although she does not cease to be the heroine, the *femme fatale* extends the diameters of that role, showing vulnerability, rage, violence, lust and vengeance as part of the range of female emotions. Despite this, it is notable that the only real sexual falls occurring in these novels are those of the demure ideal: the bigamists and adulteresses are Lady Audley and Lady Isabel Carlyle, not Aurora Floyd and Magdalen Vanstone. The exuberant, passionate woman, these novels assert, is *less* likely to allow herself to be seduced than her frustrated and supposedly ignorant counterpart. Such an assertion represents a direct contestation of the model of female sexual anesthesia insisted upon by many contemporary medical authorities and sociologists.[23] Even those such as W. R. Greg, who acknowledged that 'normal' women could experience sexual desire, contended that, unlike men, they experienced it only after the excitation of the first sexual experience – hence the catalytic effect of seduction in the creation of prostitutes.[24] By showing their virginal heroines experiencing an open, guilt-free and largely unpunished sexual desire, the sensation novelists offer a strong rebuttal to this still-powerful official proscription of female sexuality. Although I use the term *femme fatale* to denote these desiring women, they offer a very different image of female desire to that explored in the previous chapter's discussion of Decadence. Their sexuality does not induce in them states of trance or visionary power, and their sexual attractions, although compelling to men, are not fundamentally destructive. Most importantly, their power to attract is in their own control. It is possible to illustrate this control by considering the development of Magdalen Vanstone's awareness of her attraction, and the ways in which she makes use of it.

Our first introduction to Magdalen makes clear her sensuality, as, of course, does the marked symbolism of her name. She is compared with her sister, and found less perfect in features, but far superior in physical health and animal spirits:

> The girl's exuberant vitality asserted itself all over her, from head to foot. Her figure – taller than her sister's, taller than the average of woman's height; instinct with such a seductive, serpentine suppleness, so lightly and playfully graceful, that its movements suggested, not unnaturally, the movements of a young cat – her figure was so perfectly developed already that no one who saw her could have supposed that she was only eighteen. She bloomed in the full physical maturity of twenty years or more – bloomed naturally and irresistibly, in right of her matchless health and strength. (p. 6)

Her character matches her physique: 'how I do like pleasure!', she declares, prompting Miss Garth to quote Pope's dictum that every woman is at heart a rake. Magdalen is to become more of a rake than any one could foresee; the classic picaresque scamp, plotting her way to fortune. Although her sensuality and sexual attractiveness aid her in her stratagems, there is no implication that it is her libidinous nature that prompts her to her crimes. Magdalen's sensuality is enjoyed by her – and by the text – for its own sake. We are witness, for instance, to her pleasure in having her hair brushed for hours by her maid, when she is again compared to a cat, purring at the sensation. Where another novelist would employ such an image as symbolic of the heroine's vanity or as a presage of her fall, Collins leaves Magdalen's pleasure as just pleasure.

Magdalen's physical attractiveness moves men without her conscious volition throughout the novel. Her eventual husband, Captain Kirke, is overwhelmed when he sees her in the street, and continues to brood about her for over a year, despite the scowl with which she answers his interested glance. Admiral Bartram, into whose service she enters disguised as a parlour-maid in order to discover the 'Secret Trust' that alters Noel Vanstone's will, favours her for her looks, and his drunken manservant allows her to escape when he discovers her reading the Trust because of his profound admiration for her straight womanly figure – particularly her waist! None of these incidents reflect badly on Magdalen: it is only at the moment that she first consciously decides to use her sexuality to entrap her

feeble cousin Noel Vanstone that we – and Magdalen herself – doubt the
propriety of her conduct:

> What new means could she discover, which would lead her secretly
> to her end . . . ?
>
> She was seated before the looking-glass, mechanically combing
> out her hair, while that all-important consideration occupied her
> mind. The agitation of the moment had raised a feverish colour in
> her cheeks, and had brightened the light in her large grey eyes. She
> was conscious of looking her best; conscious of how her beauty
> gained by contrast, after the removal of the disguise. Her lovely light
> brown hair, looked thicker and softer now than ever, now that it had
> escaped from its imprisonment under the grey wig. She twisted it
> this way and that, with quick dexterous fingers; she laid it in masses
> on her shoulders; she threw it back from them in a heap, and turned
> sideways to see how it fell – to see her back and shoulders, freed from
> the artificial deformities of the padded cloak. After a moment, she
> faced the looking-glass once more; plunged both hands deep in her
> hair; and, resting her elbows on the table, looked closer and closer at
> the reflection of herself, until her breath began to dim the glass. 'I can
> twist any man alive around my finger', she thought, with a smile of
> superb triumph, 'as long as I keep my looks! If that contemptible
> wretch saw me now—' She shrank from following that thought to
> its end, with a sudden horror of herself: she drew back from the
> glass, shuddering, and put her hands over her face. (pp. 222–3)

The text creates a sense of ambivalence about Magdalen's self-approval,
which is located precisely around her consciousness of her powers. Such a
lack of modesty is, of course, profoundly antithetical to the behaviour
expected of the well-brought up middle-class girl; however, the real
turning-point in the reader's sympathy for Magdalen comes only with the
birth of her notion to sell herself to Noel Vanstone in marriage. It is this
idea that repulses Magdalen herself; and in the rest of the novel it is her
intermittent bursts of self-loathing and doubt as she pursues this plan that
retain the reader's identification. Magdalen is notably absent from the
'stage' during the section of the book between her marriage and her
husband's death. We are offered a strong hint that the union has remained
unconsummated when Noel Vanstone reveals to his housekeeper that he
hasn't seen Magdalen's neck closely enough to determine whether or not
she has two identifying moles. Magdalen is finally redeemed by the love of
the worthy Captain Kirke, and this time the courtship is accompanied by
all the necessary shyness and mutual misunderstandings – she has no
unfeminine certainty of her power to attract the man she truly loves.

Despite this requisite closure, Magdalen remains a heroine who is both sensual and assertively attractive, and one who is finally unpunished for these transgressions.

The protagonist

> When women are thus put forward to lead the action of a plot, they must be urged into a false position. To get vigorous action they are described as rushing into crime, and doing masculine deeds. Thus they come forward in the worst light, and the novelist finds that to make an effect he has to give up his heroine to bigamy, to murder, to child-bearing by stealth in the Tyrol, and to all sorts of adventures which can only signify her fall. . . . It is not wrong to make a sensation; but if the novelist depends for his sensation upon the action of a woman the chances are that he will attain his end by unnatural means.[25]

A notable feature of the sensation genre is the tendency for female protagonists to usurp the hero's role as the central instigator of the action. Although this tendency exists in other Victorian novels – Margaret Hale and Aurora Leigh are notable examples – the usurpation is seldom as complete as it is in the case of Magdalen Vanstone, whose exploits include running away from home, working as an actress, appearing in disguise as her governess, taking a job as a parlour-maid, marrying under a false name, and setting up in partnership to deceive with a disreputable rogue. Perhaps to allow Magdalen a clear stage, Frank Clare, the ostensible hero of the early part of the book is feeble and effeminate. Incapable of earning his own living, he is continually throwing himself on the mercy of his friends for financial support. His role as dependent child is a displaced representation of the conventional state of the Victorian female – revealed in its parasitic elements by the transformation of gender roles. Magdalen, in contrast, refuses to accept the dependent situation thrust on her by circumstance, and ventures out into the world to regain her rights by trickery, like the ubiquitous fairy-tale hero: a Tom Thumb or Puss in Boots. Her success is as much a result of her courage and ingenuity as it is of her sexual attractiveness.

Few other sensation heroines combine the roles of protagonist and *femme fatale* as centrally as Magdalen, but virtually every major example of the genre features a woman engaged in the apparently male activities of adventure or detective investigation. Marian Halcombe joins with Walter Hartright, the hero of *The Woman in White* to investigate the plots of Count Fosco and Sir Percival Glyde against Laura Fairlie. Her activities, as we saw in Chapter 2, involve her donning a modified form of female dress; the heroine-protagonist is not aping masculine behaviour in her activities: she brings her specifically feminine skills, ranging from dissimulation to the power of sexual attraction, to her tasks. The clearest indication of Marian's sterling qualities is provided by the villainous Count Fosco's surpassing admiration for her:

> Can you look at Miss Halcombe and not see that she has the foresight and resolution of a man? With that woman for my friend I would snap these fingers of mine at the world. With that woman as my enemy, I, with all my brains and experience – I, Fosco, cunning as the devil himself, as you have told me a hundred times – I walk, in your English phrase, upon egg-shells! And this grand creature . . . who stands in the strength of her love and her courage, firm as a rock, between us two and that poor, flimsy, pretty blonde wife of yours – this magnificent woman, whom I admire with all my soul, though I oppose her in your interests and mine, you drive to extremities as though she was no sharper and bolder than the rest of her sex. (pp. 346–7)

As is suggested by her masculine facial features and feminine bodily curves, Marian's strengths are hybrid: male 'foresight and resolution', female 'love and courage' – the latter to resist and endure.

Another detective female appears in *Lady Audley's Secret*. Clara Talboys, sister of the missing man, inspires Robert Audley to act on his suspicions, and insists on regular bulletins about his progress. Although, in the event, she takes little active part in the investigation, it is her determination to act that causes Robert to do so in her place:

> I myself will follow up the clue to this mystery; I will find this woman – yes, though you refuse to tell me in what part of England my brother disappeared. I will travel from one end of the world to the other to find the secret of his fate, if you refuse to find it for me. I am of age; my own mistress; rich, for I have money left me by one of my aunts; I shall be able to employ those who will help me in my search . . . Choose between the two alternatives, Mr Audley. Shall you or I find my brother's murderer? (p. 215)

As with Marian, the description of Clara – despite her possession of a beauty Marian lacks – is couched in terms of a resemblance to a man (in this case, her brother). There are no elements in this description of Robert's first glimpse of her that could not equally be applied to a man. He first likes her for her character, and then, later, loves her for her beauty:

Robert Audley now saw her face clearly for the first time, and he saw that she was very handsome. She had brown eyes, like George's, a pale complexion, . . . regular features, and a mobility of expression which bore record of every change of feeling. (p. 212)

Clara ultimately provides the romantic interest of the novel, as her spirit and courage attract the lethargic Robert sufficiently for him to settle down to a career, and to propose to her. This romance is peripheral, however, to the main story of the uncovering of Lady Audley's crimes and secret. Lady Audley is the protagonist, in a sense, of her own novel, but the exigencies of plot mean that her actions are revealed to us retrospectively, while the less interesting Robert occupies the central position as the reader's guide. The same displacement occurs in the case of Aurora Floyd as a result of the necessity of some, at least, of her actions and motivations being opaque to us.

Sensation fiction allows women greater potential for action precisely because it shows those women as complexly motivated and flawed. M. E. Braddon points this out, in defending her use of Aurora Floyd as heroine:

Her own hands had sown the dragon's teeth, from whose evil seed had sprung up armed men, strong enough to rend and devour her. But then, if she had been faultless, she could not have been the heroine of this story; for has not some wise man of old remarked, that the perfect women are those who leave no histories behind them, but who go through life upon such a tranquil course of quiet well-doing as leave no footprints on the sands of time; only mute records hidden here and there, deep in the grateful hearts of those who have been blest by them. (p. 330)

The intense, richly plotted stories of sensationalism demand equivocal, flawed women to enact them; a fact which moves its female characters outside the narrow confines of the domestic sphere, into a more dangerous, morally fluid public realm.

The governess

There is, of course, a woman who frequently ventures into this hostile public realm in the conventional nineteenth-century novel: she is the governess. Her treatment in the sensation novel is another telling example of the genre's contestation of the values and pieties of the realist novel.

The model of all governesses in nineteenth-century fiction is Jane Eyre.

Jane's dispossession and subsequent search for a home develops the tropes of liminality, exile and final recognition that invariably characterise the governess's progress in realist fiction. This model is effectively parodied in the person of Lucy Graham, soon to be Lady Audley, whom we first encounter as a governess:

> She had come into the neighbourhood as a governess in the family of a surgeon in the village near Audley Court. No one knew anything of her except that she came in answer to an advertisement which Mr Dawson, the surgeon, had inserted in the *Times*. She came from London; and the only reference she gave was to a lady at a school at Brompton, where she had once been a teacher. But this reference was so satisfactory that none other was needed, and Miss Lucy Graham was received by the surgeon as the instructress of his daughters. (pp. 5–6)

Even at the start of the novel, there is a covert threat to middle-class security represented by this utterly unknown quantity, summed up in the bald statement that 'no one knew anything of her'. The governess is threatening first because she is *déclassée*, and therefore represents the ever-present possibility of a loss of social status; and second, because she is an outsider established at the heart of the family: she carries all the potential for intrigue and disruption that belongs to the servants in the bourgeois imagination, but she has class and education, and therefore a right to be treated on more equal terms by her employers. Helena Michie interestingly notes that the governess is the heroine's alter ego in many novels of the period:

> Governesses and young ladies are linked in Victorian fiction by the possibility of an alternative narrative; every leisure-class heroine, given the possibility of financial disaster, is a possible governess. The novels of the period are, in fact, filled with heroines on the verge of becoming governesses who are saved at the last minute by marriage. Because the distinctions between governess and young lady are so fuzzy, the fall into governessing so eminently possible, the governess becomes the heroine's shadow-double, the figure in muted grey or brown who follows the gaily dressed heroine back and forth from church visits to the poor and who is always one step behind her in the progress through the novel.[26]

While in *Jane Eyre* we witness the experience of social exclusion from the outcast's viewpoint, in *Lady Audley's Secret* the unknown governess lives up to and beyond her perceived threat. She is responsible for the utter collapse of the aristocratic house into which she worms her way: Audley Court is closed up at the end of the novel, her husband a recluse. In Braddon's other major work, also, the ex-governess is an unpleasant character, resentful of her kind mistress and an inept schemer against her. John Mellish's denunciation of Mrs Powell exposes the envious hatred that might reasonably be expected to lie behind the meekness of the conventional nineteenth-century governess: 'You don't like my wife; you grudge her her youth and her beauty, and my foolish love for her; and you've watched, and listened, and plotted – in a lady-like way of course – to do her some evil' (*Aurora Floyd*, p. 287). It is Mrs Powell's anxiety to remain lady-like that limits her power to do evil – she is largely a pathetic figure. Patricia Thomson has argued that it is the Victorian governess's insistence on her status as a lady that is the determining element of her existence:

> No more adequate summing up of a survey of the Victorian governess could be found than those words . . . 'A governess is a lady'. They explain her reluctance to break the delicate, silver, slightly rusted chains that bound her to her past and forge herself with strong, iron ones to the future. They account for much of her unhappiness but also for her exasperating complacency. They set her irrevocably apart from the feminists who were content to forget their claims as ladies in furthering their rights as women. They are, at once, her epitaph and her extenuation.[27]

Of course the resentful dislike Mrs Powell experiences is familiar to us from another source: the Brontës' own accounts of their employment as governesses. Violently destructive impulses in *Jane Eyre* – in many ways actually a forerunner of the sensation novel – are enacted not by the virtuous Jane, but by her murderous alter ego Bertha Mason; once again the sensation novel is able to articulate overtly those impulses that are only covertly represented in other literary forms.

Governesses, in fact, throng sensation novels, as images of Brontësque dispossession as well as threats to the security of the domestic hearth.[28] In *No Name* both Norah, the good sister, and the girls' protectoress Miss Garth are governesses. Norah's first experience is classically unhappy: she is disregarded by the children and bullied by their grandmother. The shame of such an occupation for a middle-class woman is articulated in Magdalen's indignant outburst at witnessing the way her sister is treated: 'Norah made an object of public curiosity and amusement; Norah the hired victim of an old woman's insolence, and a child's ill-temper' (p. 199). In her next situation Norah attains the acme of the governess's lot; like Miss Garth before her, she finds a situation in which she is treated as one of the family, her dependent status tactfully ignored. Miss Garth, in fact, is explicitly disassociated from the common type of governess, 'This was evidently not one of the forlorn, persecuted, pitiably dependent order of governesses. Here was a woman who lived on ascertained and honourable terms with her employers' (p. 3).

The generally pathetic and degraded nature of the governess's dependent state is exacerbated in the case of Lady Isabel Carlyle, who returns disfigured and repentant from her adulterous liaison to pass the rest of her life, unknown, as her own children's governess. In this lowly disguise she is forced to witness her husband's marriage to her enemy, and endure the lingering death of her son. The liminal position of the governess, both within and without the family circle, intensifies her torment – she can constantly see her family and her ex-home and possessions, but has no real part of them.

In Henry James' *The Turn of the Screw* (1898)[29] the 'good' governess, gently-born but impoverished, is set against the 'bad' governess who threatens to undermine the home from within. James' novella is more a ghost story than a work of sensation, but it shares many techniques and preoccupations with the earlier sensation novels. The narrating governess's own story is filled with echoes of the Brontës' lives and works. She is the youngest of several daughters of a poor country parson, forced to work as a governess because of the family's indigent circumstances. Like Jane Eyre she falls in love with her rakish employer, but unlike Jane she does not marry him – in fact, she never again sees him after she accepts the job, although her subsequent actions are in part determined by her blind devotion to his wish not to be bothered with the details of his wards' lives.

The notion of the governess as a threatening force within the domestic sphere is worked out on several levels in the novella. Miss Jessell is a 'horror' independently of her ghostly status; first because of her debasing sexual liaison with her social inferior, the manservant Peter Quint, and second because she had made the children in her care privy to this association. The unspoken danger of the governess in the sensation novel is here made explicit: she is capable of corrupting the children she cares for. The idea of children as corruptible beings is one that runs counter to the dominant Victorian conception of the child as a source of salvation through innocence, but one which is at least covertly present in the pronouncements surrounding the dangers of puberty and the need to mount a surveillance over adolescents to prevent their indulgence in onanism.

A deeper level of the sense of the governess as dangerous lies precisely in the fear, paranoia and incompetence of the narrating governess. Her sense of her own incapacities, and her consequent complicity in the odd behaviour of her charges provides the opportunity for the horrific possession to run its course. Her incompetence is made doubly apparent because she is in the unusual position of educating a male child, who has been expelled from school under unspeakable circumstances, and whom she very quickly finds herself unable to match intellectually. The unnamed governess's relationship with her two charges is increasingly revealed as obsessional and possessive. Her passion for them is that of an overprotective mother, and takes the form of continual swoonings over their beauty and charm, and claspings of them to her bosom.

It is a part of the text's profound indeterminacy that we are unable finally to decide whether these effusions are a reasonable response to her terror for the children's souls, or a manifestation of her delusion. We increasingly doubt her judgement and her visions, and although she is apparently finally vindicated by Miles' acknowledgement of the existence of the ghost of Peter Quint, it is made clear by her triumphant cry – 'I have you, but he has lost you for ever!' (p. 160) – that one possession of the child has only been exchanged for another. Miles's death at that instant leaves in doubt even her final victory.

Unlike the earlier sensation novels, James's text leaves ultimately unanswered many of the questions it raises. The text's pervasive atmosphere of fear is constructed partly through the use of classically sensational devices for the acceleration of terror – the introduction of new doubts and uncertainties worse than those that proceeded them; carefully calculated turns of the screw – and partly through new techniques of purely psychological sensation – the increasingly vague use of personal pronouns, for instance, which places in question precisely who it is that fears who. Both governesses – the good and the bad – are ultimately disturbing figures in *The Turn of the Screw*: one because her illicit sexuality, excusable at least in a conventional sensation heroine, offers depths of corruption to her charges, and is sufficiently terrible to condemn her to the limbo status of a ghost after death; the other because her isolation, dispossession and fear make her as oppressive a force as the things from which she seeks to protect the children in her care.

More threatening even than the governess is the over-familiar servant of a lower class: a housekeeper or a lady's maid, privy to the secrets of the boudoir and the economics of the house. The villainous Mrs Lecount, who mounts guard over her feeble master in *No Name*, is nearly a match for the combined wits of Magdalen and Captain Wragge. She too is *déclassée*, but as a foreigner – widow of the late Professor Lecount, reptile specialist of Zurich – she has less right to be treated as a lady than would an impoverished indigenous female. Mrs Lecount is witch-like in her exertion of control over her master, and in her intuitive ability to see through the subterfuges of Magdalen and the Captain. She even possesses the requisite familiar – a toad inherited from her husband. Her greatest threat is in her ability to reverse the proscribed relation between master and servant: she manipulates her master, while he endeavours to extricate himself from her authority.

While Mrs Lecount's power stems from her superior intellect and will, the power of other servants is their knowledge, which gives them the ability to blackmail. Lady Audley's maid, another too-familiar servant, threatens her mistress with the revelation of her crime. Indeed, Lady Audley's fondness for associating with her maid is an early indication of her own threat to the social order. In *Aurora Floyd* Braddon articulates precisely the fear the hung around the figure of the servant in the bourgeois imagination:

> Your servants listen at your doors, and repeat your spiteful speeches in the kitchen, and watch you while they wait at table, and understand every sarcasm, every innuendo, every look, as well as those at whom the cruel glances and stinging words are aimed. They understand your sulky silence, your studied and over-acted politeness. The most polished form your hate and anger can take is as transparent to those house-hold spies as if you threw knives at each other, or pelted your enemy with the side-dishes and vegetables after the fashion of disputants in a pantomime. Nothing that is done in the parlour is lost upon those quiet, well-behaved watchers from the kitchen. (vol. I, ch. 16, p. 149)

The servants are not themselves the source of the primary threat, but are spies ever alert to the manifestations of enmity and violence that Braddon presents as the natural state of the domestic environment. In its treatment of servants, and of other groups – the disabled, the mentally subnormal – sensation fiction enacts the richest paranoias of the bourgeoisie. This element accompanies its radicalism on the question of women's identities quite unproblematically, for it is only the rights of bourgeois women that are at stake. Like most popular cultural forms, it reflects its readership's prejudices back on a magnified scale. Braddon, for example, warns quite seriously of the necessity to trust one's most instinctual prejudices, when she bolsters Aurora's repulsion from the idiot hunch-back Steeve Hargreaves with the injunction to the reader to avoid 'any creature who inspires you with this instinctive unreasoning abhorrence', because 'he is dangerous' (p. 115).

This magnification effect is a central feature of the sensation form, and applies not only to its expression of the middle-class paranoia about those outside its ranks, but even to the radical revisions of female roles thus far demonstrated. Just as Jane Eyre's sense of alienation undergoes fairground-mirror distortions to emerge as the bitter enmity of Mrs Powell and the destructive potential of Lady Audley, so we can recognize in the mad, bad heroines of the sensation novel echoes of the heroines of more conventional texts.

Realism in the distorting mirror of sensation

The resemblances we can trace between both the heroines and the ideas in the two forms are intriguing. The vain, manipulative Lady Audley has a distinct relationship to Eliot's spoilt Rosamund Vincy, with her ability to charm her husband with feminine wiles, and her approximation to the childlike ideal. Similarly, Clara Talboys, with her spiritual fervour and puritan garb is kin to Dorothea Brooke, who 'had the kind of beauty that is best set off by plain dress' (*Middlemarch*, p. 1):

> Clara Talboys was beautiful. Niobe's face, sublimated by sorrow, could scarcely have been more purely classical than hers. Even her dress, puritan in its grey simplicity, became her beauty better than a more beautiful dress would have become a less beautiful woman.
> (*Lady Audley's Secret*, p. 216)

Some such similarities can be traced to direct echoes, borrowings and influences – in both directions: Charles Reade nursed a probably paranoid conviction that George Eliot had plagarised his *Hard Cash* (1863) in *Felix Holt* (1866), because both novels contain trial scenes in which the heroines testify to support their beloveds.[30] Many of the similarities between Dickens' works and sensation novels can be traced to the formative influence of Dickens on the genre. Most markedly, later writers, notably Thomas Hardy, drew on the form for plot, character and philosophy. Hardy's first novel, *Desperate Remedies* (1871), was itself a sensation novel, and many of his later works take on new significance when viewed in the light of sensation conventions. In fact, Hardy could be said to re-naturalise those conventions in *Jude the Obscure* (1895) – marital disjunction, bigamy and child-murder are here no longer purely sensational phenomena, but are examined as arising from a social matrix. Arabella, in this novel, for example, can be plausibly read as a sensation villainess. She has marked similarities to Sibylla West, in Mrs Henry Wood's *Verner's Pride*; another sexually lax, unrepentant bigamist, who leaves a husband in Australia and conveniently forgets his existence, and who succeeds in manipulating the hero into marrying her twice.

Even such quirky texts as the *Alice* novels (1865 and 1872)[31] carry the mark of the sensation novel. The fluttery, gigantic Mrs Wragge, in thrall to her tiny husband in *No Name*, is the likely model for Carroll's White Queen: both are large, amiable and pathetic and both are entirely incapable of remaining tidy. Mrs Wragge's inability to remain 'up at heel' and symmetrical in her posture exasperates her husband beyond bearing throughout the novel, while Carroll's White Queen is equally timid and incapacitated by her dress: ' "Every single thing's crooked", Alice thought to herself, "and she's all over pins!" ' (p. 201). Tenniel's illustration of Alice 'a-dressing' the Queen could equally illustrate Magdalen's ministrations to Mrs Wragge, and the kindness and sympathy shown by the intelligent, active young woman to the less capable old woman has precisely the same emotional tone in each case. Although the White Queen is not as notably feeble-minded as Mrs Wragge, she does turn into a sheep – a rather precise emblem for Mrs Wragge's mental state. The trial scene at the end of *Wonderland*, with its innuendoes about sexual intrigue in the palace, revealed in the Knave's verse-letter, deals with sensation's favoured themes of sexual secrets and their investigation. Although the *Wonderland* trial, with its arbitrary secrets and summary justice effectively deconstructs the scenes of official closure that tie up the loose ends in both sensation and, later, detective fiction; with its atmosphere of amoral chaos lurking beneath the familiar furniture of Victorian bourgeois life it owes a clear debt to the sensation novel.

The spirit of sensation pervades the 1860s and 1870s like a heady scent, infusing the works of writers in all genres. Robert Browning's lengthy narrative poem *The Ring and the Book* (1868–9)[32] has frequently been read as a proto-detective story,[33] but might be more productively read as a response to the sensation phenomenon. Like many sensation novels, it centres on a crime: the brutal murder in early seventeenth-century Italy of a young woman and her adoptive parents by her cruel and vindictive husband. Like *East Lynne* the 'story' begins with an elopement – Pompilia escapes her husband in the company of a young priest – and ends with the heroine's death. Like the sensation novelists, Browning is interested in questions of guilt and innocence, the detection of evidence and uncovering of criminal responsiblity. Like *The Woman in White*, *The Ring and the Book* is narrated in turn by the participants in the action, but while the successive narrators in Collins' novel add to the on-going narrative, Browning's characters each re-tell the same events, over and over again, seeing them through the distorting lenses of their own perceptions. The result is a considerably more relativistic text, where doubt is cast on the processes of memory and the construction of coherent narratives, if not on the final guilt or innocence of the participants. Pompilia, it is clear from very early in the text, is the epitome of innocence. Her apparent elopement is undertaken only as a desperate measure to protect her unborn child from her violent husband; her developing love for the priest Caponsacchi is spiritual rather than fleshly, and remains unconsummated. Like Laura Fairlie, Pompilia is represented as a blank space onto which the fantasies of others can be inscribed. Where Laura, as we saw in Chapter 2, is pictured as a vague image, receding into the shadows and losing precision in the regressions of Hartright's memories of her; so, although hers is the name which imposes itself onto the page of text Caponsacchi reads (VI. 1025–6), the name and image that fills the minds of the avid gossips of Rome, Pompilia is ultimately lacking in subjectivity. She cannot control her own fate, because she cannot read or write (the source of the fundamental misunderstanding that allows her to be tricked and leads to her death). As the Pope – the ultimate moral judge in the poem – notes, she is the *object*, not the subject, of her own history (X. 1019–21). Browning's poem, like Collins' novel, foregrounds the blankness and victim status of its heroine to an extent that problematises the ideal that she represents. The fact, however, that her forgiveness and love are highlighted as the moral centre of the poem indicates that the self-sacrificing angel was not to be so lightly dismissed. Despite this adherence to the ideal, the socio-sexual politics of the poem are distinctly liberal. The fact that the ideal Pompilia is the illegitimate daughter of a prostitute is insisted upon as a refutation of the notion of illegitimacy as a moral slur on the child – precisely the same sense of a profound injustice that fuels Collins' defence of the illegitimate Vanstones in *No Name*.

Many such responses to sensationalism can be found throughout the literature of the 1860s and beyond. It is notable that a number of writers who were vociferous critics of the sensation phenomenon later made use of its devices and preoccupations themselves. This does not necessarily signal a change of opinion, or hypocrisy. Henry James had criticised sensation fiction for its lack of deep characterization and psychological insight. In *The Turn of the Screw*, as we have seen, he utilises sensation techniques to explore the notion of evil and corruption emanating from and infecting the domestic sphere. Taking off from the point at which sensation fiction stops, he uses the deep fears its mechanisms evoke to construct a literature of psychological realism.

George Eliot, whose dislike of sensationalism (and particularly the works of M. E. Braddon) was expressed in letters,[34] also made use of sensation techniques in some of her later fiction. *Felix Holt, The Radical* (1866), with its dramas of inheritance and illegitimacy and its employment of a ghostly atmosphere in connection with the aristocratic Transome family, is perhaps the most sensational, but in *Daniel Deronda* (1874–6) there is also, as Anthea Trodd suggests, a sustained tension between two readings of Gwendoline as a sensation heroine.[35] She sees herself as the Woman in White, victim of a Bluebeard-like threat from her husband

Grandcourt, but her fantasies of his dying, her strangling of her sister's canary, and her final claiming of responsibility for Grandcourt's mysterious death advance the opposite, Lady Audley, scenario. Mrs Oliphant, the most vociferous of the detractors of sensationalism incorporated sensation sub-plots into her 1862–3 serial of the rural Dissenting community of Carlingford, *Salem Chapel*[36] and *The Perpetual Curate* (1864). These sensational elements have been seen as unfortunate excursions away from domestic realism, undertaken merely to improve her sales,[37] but in both novels the sensationalism interestingly complicates the placid surface of the social comedies, hinting at darker realities beneath the surface.

It is a perhaps a key to resolving the paradox of realist writers' responses to sensation fiction to consider that the sensation plots they almost invariably adopt turn ultimately around the figure of the woman as victim. The terror we experience in reading *The Turn of the Screw* is that of the governess-narrator as she moves ever-deeper into her understanding of the corruption that assails her charges: the sexually voracious Miss Jessell is presented to us a besetting, inhuman force, not as the comprehensible but flawed being she would be in a conventional sensation novel. Browning's Pompilia is the passive, idealised victim of a corrupt husband in the Bluebeard mould. Eliot's Gwendoline, although she toys with fantasies of destruction and guilt, is ultimately persuaded by Daniel Deronda that she is in fact the victim that everybody else thinks her. As Anthea Trodd argues, her entertainment of the 'Lady Audley' role is a step in her moral development, rather than a genuine assignment of guilt.[38] Again, it is the Bluebeard plot, the Gothic inheritance transmitted through *The Woman in White*, that underpins the narrative. In Mrs Oliphant's *Salem Chapel* the three dangerous women who have haunted the latter half of the novel are explained away in much the same way that Mrs Radcliffe had ultimately accounted for and dismissed her supernatural happenings: Mrs Hilyard's attempt to murder her husband is explained by her desperation to keep her child; the mysterious 'Blue Veil' who has drifted, ghost-like, through the narrative is revealed as a backward and terrified adolescent, and the hero Vincent's own sister, in a delirious trance and suspected of the attack on Mr Hilyard, is revealed as entirely innocent.[39] The potential female aggressors are all transmuted into victims, and the domestic scene returns to tranquility.

On this evidence, the fundamental problem realist novelists had with sensation fiction was not, as they claimed, its lack of realistic characters, or its inflated emotions and plot-driven narratives. Rather, it was the fact that it carried their own extension of the feminine role far beyond what they had considered as its logical limit. While Eliot's rebellious heroines must ultimately conform in marriage or die (as Maggie Tulliver's fate graphically illustrates), Braddon's and Collins' prosper in their flouting of the conventions. While active female sexuality is only covert even in the self-consciously radical New Woman literature, sensation heroines habitually flaunt their sexual desires and powers, without forfeiting respect or femininity. The tentative moves 'serious' women novelists in particular were making towards more productive representations of women were shamelessly mocked by these fantastic hoydens, who could suddenly have, and do, it all. The heroine of the sensation novel does not just win herself a larger arena in which to exist within the framework of bourgeois society; like Alice, she tosses the whole framework sky-high, and thus shuffles the deck.

5 Private 'I's and 'I'-lessness
Autobiographical constructions of the feminine self

To bring anything really to life in literature,
we can't be life-like: we have to be literature-like.
(Northrop Frye, *The Educated Imagination*)[1]

Decadent constructions of femininity often featured women with veiled, apparently vacant eyes, the sightless seers of prophesy, gazing beyond this world into others invisible to the naked eye, but in reality it seems that many Victorian women felt 'I'-less in quite a different sense. This chapter considers the ways in which femininity was constructed in Victorian autobiographies, and argues that the very prescriptions surrounding femininity resulted in self-portraits which were far more complex, sophisticated, innovative, and satisfactory than their masculine counterparts – the kinds of autobiographies for which the last century is renowned.[2]

For reasons which will become apparent as the chapter progresses, the Victorian 'autobiography' which epitomises the masculine form of the genre is also one which explodes its veracity and rationale. The incessantly expounded autobiography of *Hard Time*'s Josiah Bounderby of Coketown looks at the growing fashion for men to write the stories of their lives and challenges not only the kinds of things they say, but the ways in which they say them. Dickens' dissatisfaction with the masculine mode of autobiography is evident in the following extract from Chapter 4, called simply 'Mr. Bounderby', in which the occasion of Bounderby's tenth birthday is brought forward for the edification of Mrs Gradgrind.

I hadn't a shoe to my foot. As to a stocking, I didn't know such a thing by name. I passed the day in a ditch and the night in a pigsty.

That's the way I spent my tenth birthday. Not that a ditch was new
to me, for I was born in a ditch . . . I was born with inflammation of
the lungs, and of everything else, I believe, that was capable of
inflammation . . . For years, ma'am, I was one of the most miserable
little wretches ever seen. I was so sickly, that I was always moaning
and groaning. I was so ragged and dirty, that you wouldn't have
touched me with a pair of tongs . . . How I fought through it, *I* don't
know . . . I was determined, I suppose. I have been a determined
character in later life, and I suppose I was then. Here I am, Mrs.
Gradgrind, anyhow, and nobody to thank for my being here, but
myself.[3]

Bounderby's monologue is not only portentous, it turns out to be
manifestly false. Bounderby the self-made man is a self-created myth.
Written in 1854, *Hard Times* is rejecting a further elaboration of the dyadic
mentality, which supported the logic and necessity of certain kinds and
classes of men producing the stories of their lives, but discounted the
need for women's stories entirely. Moreover, with its insistent use of the
first-person pronoun, this extract clearly questions the relationship
between the 'I' who is the subject of Bounderby's narrative and the 'I' who
is relating the story. Dickens' challenge to the masculine autobiographical
'I' has two effects. First, it expresses dissatisfaction with the established
and acceptable models of autobiography available to men. Second, it
makes it possible to consider the possible advantages to the female
autobiographer of being encouraged to remove herself from the centre
of her own narrative and to find new forms by which to convey
her experiences. Once again, the division of experience into masculine/
feminine spheres is shown to be inadequate for both sexes, and the
alternative strategies it necessitated for women who chose to write about
themselves imbue their work with the complexity and vision which so
often result from Victorian attempts to represent femininity and female
experience.

'I'-lessness takes many forms in Victorian accounts of the feminine self.
These range from what feminists have traditionally regarded as negative
and repressive denials of the self resulting from the kind of patriarchy
bound up in industrial capitalism and imperialist enterprises, to more
recent affirmations of the collective nature of femininity in this period.[4]
Close reading of a range of autobiographical accounts of feminine selves,
including one written by a man, shows how this form of writing
encapsulates and anticipates debates which have dominated literary and
cultural theories of the self a century on. Among these are concerns about
the relationship between the self and language, the reflexivity and
revisability of the self, and the subjective nature of experience. Perhaps

most important of all, from a contemporary perspective, Victorian feminine autobiographies appear to acknowledge and embrace the fact that any account of the self must be fictional. Whether or not this understanding was conscious, it appears to have been widespread and to have freed writers from the need for (and impossibility of) historical accuracy. It also makes unnecessary the compulsion underlying masculine autobiography to locate and reveal a single, coherent, permanent 'true' self. Instead, feminine autobiography blends the real and the written, the factual and the psychological, the writer and fictive creations, relying on an alliance between text and reader to make and reveal the subject in the text.

The tendency to present the self in relation to and/or through others is characteristic of femininity and is often identified as contributing to the repression of women. In 'Reflecting Women' Patricia Meyer Spacks observes, 'women have traditionally evaluated themselves in terms of their value to others, seen themselves through others' eyes, often accepted as natural the limitations imposed on them by society'.[5] This is the most familiar sense of 'I'-lessness associated with Victorian constructions of femininity, and it is precisely this habit of negating the self against which Virginia Woolf so often railed. For instance, when describing her earliest attempts at writing 'Professions for Women' (1931), Woolf felt herself being prompted, guided and admonished by a voice she recognised as belonging to the Victorian 'Angel in the House':

> when I came to write I encountered her [the Angel in the House] with the very first words. . . . She slipped behind me and whispered: "My dear, you are a young woman. . . . Be sympathetic; be tender; flatter; deceive; use all the arts and wiles of your sex. Never let anybody guess that you have a mind of your own."[6]

The belief that there would be consequences for such an indelicacy as admitting to having a mind of one's own – of constructing the self as independent – was clearly a powerfully repressive force and one way in which Victorian women could be said to have been made 'I'-less. The ethos associated with the Angel of the House was that a woman shouldn't have ideas and opinions of her own but should reflect and echo those of her male relations. The fact that Woolf was, by 1931, able to talk about her experiences directly, in the first person, is an indicator of how far she was able to resist the coerciveness of her angelic forebears and on occasion to declare herself as an individual with a unique personal history and a clear sense of herself as separate from others. This perception of the self as unique is seminal to the writing of autobiography, according to Georges Gusdorf, whose 'Conditions and Limits of Autobiography' (1956) is widely recognised as the progenitor of study into autobiography as a literary genre. 'Autobiography,' he says, 'is not possible in a cultural landscape where consciousness of the self does not, properly speaking, exist.'[7] Gusdorf traces the rise of autobiographical writing to the rise in the early modern period of the sense of the self as separate from the community – the same process which led to the sense of the artist as an individual of heightened sensibility and thus to the decline of anonymous, communal and omniverous art forms.

Significantly, Gusdorf is talking specifically (though perhaps unintentionally) about autobiographies written by men and which form the paradigm for masculine forms of writing about the self. Much has been made of the fact that this seminal exercise set the pattern for discussions of autobiography: autobiography, like so much of the literary canon, was defined and evaluated according to male standards, interests and experiences.[8] However, it seems less important *who* wrote autobiographies than *how* and *why* they chose to write them, and this means looking beyond biological classifications to those based on gender. The benefits of this change in focus are that it then becomes possible to talk in more detail about the changes and shifts in the way writers choose to present themselves at different times and in different situations. Neither femininity nor masculinity is the exclusive property of a biological or social group, and though most people ultimately assume the gender identity associated with their sex (females/feminine; males/masculine), it has long been accepted that these identities are not natural; neither are they permanent. When writing about masculine and feminine autobiographies, therefore, I will be referring to the characteristics of each rather than to the sex of the writer. Having said that, in a discussion such as this it is convenient to write as if *most* men at this time wrote masculine autobiographies and *most* women adopted feminine ways of writing about the self as this makes it possible to highlight the differences between the autobiographical modes with the minimum of confusion.

When Gusdorf is talking about a cultural landscape in which consciousness of the self as separate from the community is possible, he is speaking in very broad terms. Until very recently only a minority of people could afford to isolate themselves from their cultural communities, and the way in which modern western society now both promotes an ideology of individualism and has architecturally and institutionally fostered the myth of individual, autonomous identity has often proved problematic. This is not the place to enter into debates about contemporary constructions of the individual, rather I want to show that the masculine modes of constructing the self which have long been regarded as the dominant form of autobiography – and especially

Victorian autobiography – ignore the fact that most members of Victorian society (notably the poor, the mass of the workers, and women) were not in a position to think of themselves as autonomous. The majority of the population were necessarily interdependent, relying on pooled earnings and living under conditions in which having a bed of one's own, never mind a room of one's own, was a luxury.[9] Masculine autobiography, then, is a minority form. In its emphasis on action, information, world events and goals, it is also emotionally and psychologically limited and thus, if the purpose of autobiography is to explain how the writer came to be the person he or she is, then it is autobiography *manqué*. Who we are has more to do with internal perceptions than external events.

The relationship between internal and external realities preoccupied Virginia Woolf throughout her literary career. While technically Woolf's work does not belong to the Victorian period, it is nonetheless useful as a starting point for this discussion because she is so clearly and consciously reacting to its forms. Thus the techniques she evolves for writing about the self provide some valuable insights for understanding earlier constructions of femininity. For instance, though Woolf often found it both necessary and expedient to refer to herself as 'I' (for instance, in lectures, diaries and letters), in the majority of her literary productions she constantly reminds the reader of the fictionality of any 'I' persona. More importantly for the concerns of this chapter, Woolf repeatedly shows femininity to be a collective condition rather than one which makes individuality pre-eminent. Woolf's women are famous for collecting, reflecting and absorbing others. While most of her texts rely on multiple images of and surrogates for the self (perhaps most radically in *Orlando* which is explicitly concerned with the changing nature of the self through time and the way in which the perceptions of the individual at any given moment are the result of historical precedent), the most obvious example of the communal nature of Woolf's construction of femininity is provided in the study devoted to exploring the relationship between women and fiction: *A Room of One's Own* (1929). Here Woolf underlines the fictionality and inadequacy of the relationship of the 'I' on the page and the 'I' of the writer and then introduces multiple personae who stand for the narrator at various moments in the text: 'Here then was I (call me Mary Beton, Mary Seton, Mary Carmichael or by any name you please . . .)'[10]

By identifying herself with women from the past, by attributing the work she did in preparation for the lectures which make up the volume to fictional characters, and by highlighting the ways in which women's traditions and values diverge from those of men, Woolf is identifying herself with a way of constructing the self which Gusdorf says is incapable of being autobiographical because it is essentially communal, relational and representative rather than individual, independent and unique.

However, to deny the autobiographical impetus of this feminine way of constructing the self is entirely to misunderstand what autobiography is and how it is achieved. Evidence that Gusdorf's definition is too limited is provided by many recent and innovative autobiographies by men and women alike, which have their antecedents in the kind of feminine fictions of the self Gusdorf ignores.[11]

Susan Stanford Friedman has argued that a more satisfactory way of reading the kind of autobiographies associated with women is through the understanding of the feminine self provided by the work of Sheila Rowbotham and Nancy Chodorow.[12] Chodorow's theories on the acquisition of gender identities are particularly germane to this discussion because they emphasize the learned nature of masculinity and the personal costs involved in becoming masculine. This is important, for if masculinity is both learned and difficult to attain, then anything which has the potential to challenge or undermine it is likely to be avoided or repressed. Briefly, Chodorow contends that masculinity as the 'normal' goal of the boy child is more problematic for him than is femininity for the girl. This is because although all 'normal' development entails learning to separate from the primary carer, masculinity exaggerates the need for and extent of the separation. It relies on the illusory idea that it is possible (and desirable) to be totally separate, autonomous, independent. But, she says, because patriarchal societies both value masculinity and expect boys to achieve it, efforts are continually made to coerce boys into accepting the need to become masculine and to help them achieve and sustain a masculine sexual identity. The key to this lies in boys' Oedipal attachments to their mothers. Accepting a masculine sexual identity means the child must recognise himself as different from the mother and so identify with the father, who is physically like him. This emphasis on difference means that the boy learns to see himself apart, and as an individual. Chodorow concludes that in male-dominated societies, 'masculinity and sexual difference are intertwined with issues of separation and individuation almost from the beginning of a boy's life'.[13] This separation is not natural, neither is it necessarily desirable on a number of grounds. While the ability to perceive the self as autonomous is important to the kind of social schema which measure success in terms of money, power and prestige, exactly how successful it is in terms of the individual's well being is debatable: if Chodorow is right, the acquisition of masculinity entails minimising the ability to form affective relationships, to nurture, and to see the self in relation to others. The effort required to achieve and sustain a masculine sexual identity causes masculinity itself to be rigidly defined, and in pursuit of it, Chodorow says, a boy 'represses those qualities he takes to be feminine within himself, and rejects and devalues women and whatever he considers to be feminine in the social world' (p. 181). Elsewhere (*Girls Only?*, 1990) I have looked at the particular social conditions in the second half of the last century which promoted aggressive notions of masculinity and the possible effects of this hardening of masculinity on both sexes. While the resulting need to recognise certain things as male and superior has for long been subject to attack in relation to what comprises the literary canon, much work still remains to be done on its effects on forms of autobiographical writing.

Studies such as those by Benstock, Jelinek, Olney, Spacks and Wilson have sought to show that there are two distinct traditions, male and female, for writing about the self.[14] It is widely agreed that from its inception (often regarded as St Augustine's *Confessions*, written around the year 400) masculine autobiography has emphasized individuality. As in the case of Bounderby's life-story, it takes the form of coherent, linear explorations of how the writer came to be the mature adult who perceives himself to be of sufficient interest for others to want to read about the events of his life. A good example drawn from real life is provided by the *Confessions* of Jean-Jacques Rousseau (begun in 1766, but not published until after his death in 1778). Rousseau describes his project thus:

> I have resolved on an enterprise which has no precedent, and which, once complete, will have no imitator. My purpose is to display to my kind a portrait in every way true to nature, and the man I shall portray will be myself.
>
> Simply myself. I know my own heart and understand my fellow man. But I am made unlike any one I have ever met; I will even venture to say that I am like no one in the whole world. . . . Let the last trump sound when it will, I shall come forward with this work in my hand to present myself before my Sovereign Judge, and proclaim aloud: 'Here is what I have done. . . . I have displayed myself as I was.'[15]

Like Bounderby, Rousseau admits to no difficulty in identifying the 'I' who writes with the 'I' who is the subject of the writing. His modality is confident and assertive. Although Rousseau opposed many of the tenets of the Enlightenment and philosophically valued feeling over rationality, he nonetheless contributes to the evolution of the masculine model for writing about the self which came to dominate Victorian letters.

Other characteristics of masculine autobiographies are that they tend to show their central characters in relation to major historical events (including the history of ideas), and to follow the pattern of the *bildungsroman*, moving from the protagonist's youth to his maturity, from inexperience to experience, and from naivety to worldly wisdom. The typical masculine autobiography ignores or makes insignificant gaps in the memory and, astonishing to post-Freudian readers, assumes that the writer is the ultimate authority on himself. As well, as has been clear from each of the above examples, the masculine mode of writing about the self adheres to a literary convention which always seeks to imply that the writer and the subject in the book are one and the same person. It displays little interest in the subjective nature of writing about the self and/or experiencing the world; rather, this kind of personal account presents itself as the chronicle of one man's life and, usually, as a paradigm for others. The orientation of such texts is celebratory: they tell 'the secret of my success', or, as Gusdorf puts it, 'the wonder that he feels before the mystery of his own destiny.'[16]

While necessarily generalisations to which many exceptions could be found, these observations about the kind of autobiographies usually written by men are nonetheless useful and valid comments about masculine autobiography in the last century. By contrast, it is much more difficult to characterize feminine autobiography. This is largely because it lacks the continual return to a single 'I' directly linked to the writer as verification of reality; neither is there a clear sense of the boundaries of the self whose life is ostensibly being recorded. Indeed, it was precisely the kind of solid, domineering 'I' of masculine writing generally which irritated the Woolf persona/e in *A Room of One's Own* when she returned to the 'delights' of reading a man's writing after her sojourn into fiction by women: 'Not but what this "I" was a most respectable "I"; honest and logical; hard as a nut, and polished for centuries by good teaching and good feeding; (p. 95), but it had a tendency to obscure the landscape behind it and to cast a straight dark shadow across the page. This is the shadow cast by the autonomous, independent, masculine self (man or woman), while the less solid and coherent selves constructed in feminine autobiographies are so fragmented, camouflaged, fleeting and circumlocutious that, vampire-like, they cast no shadows and reflect no single face. Look, for instance, at the 'I' which makes up the narrating persona in *The Diaries of Hannah Cullwick* (1854–73). Of the texts chosen for this discussion, this is the one which most closely approximates to the dominant masculine forms of autobiography. Significantly, it is also the only text not written by a member of the middle class, which makes it likely that its author would have had a very limited range of models in mind when beginning to write about her life and experiences. No doubt each of these factors contributes to the fact that Hannah's diaries are overtly based on the events of her daily life, and unlike many of the autobiographical works by women of the last century, present themselves as intending to be about herself. Nonetheless, the diaries reject many of the conventions associated with masculine autobiography. This fact has no doubt been made more clear by their recent compilation in book form (Virago, 1984), which makes it possible to read the individual entries as part of a single, continuous text.

Hannah Cullwick was a Victorian maidservant who was in the unusual position of having a long-standing relationship with a man (not her employer) far above her social station. There is much that was out of the ordinary in the relationship between Hannah and Arthur Munby, 'poet, barrister, social worker, man-about-town and friend of the literary and artistic greats of his time',[17] not least the fact that the two eventually married. Hannah's diaries, which were both initiated and terminated at Munby's request, reveal almost as much about the man for whom they were written as they do about Hannah. This is especially true when read together with Munby's own record of the period (see Derek Hudson's *Munby: Man of Two Worlds*, 1974). In order to understand the ways in which Hannah chose to write about herself, it is necessary to spend some time looking at the man for whom they were written and contemplating the nature of the relationship between Hannah and Munby.

Like many of his contemporaries and near contemporaries (think of Charles Dodgson, Ruskin, J. M. Barrie), Munby seems to have found it difficult to form 'normal' relationships with women of his own age and class. Where Dodgson, Ruskin and Barrie found companionship with the very young, Munby was attracted to labouring women. It is necessary here to say that as with Dodgson and Barrie there is no reason to think of the liaisons formed between Munby and the working women with whom he associated as exploitative or purely sexual. Indeed, apart from his relationship with Hannah, Munby seems to have contented himself with observing, meeting, photographing and occasionally helping the women he collected. On the evidence of his diaries, Munby does not seem to have been a man with a highly developed sexual drive. The pleasures he found in these women seem to have been largely vicarious – looking and occasionally making minimal and discreet contact. More than once Hannah slept at Munby's flat, and though he records being tempted by her presence, he did not take advantage of her vulnerability and adoration. Leonore Davidoff's work on 'Class and Gender in Victorian England' gives a possible insight into the nature of Munby's attraction to working women, and his particular interest in servants.[18] She suggests that the frequency with which middle-class Victorian men sought relation-ships/found sexual satisfaction with working-class women owed much to the upstairs/downstairs mentality of the period (another example of the dyadic model gone berserk) which meant that mothers (who ultimately embodied the kind of women these men should marry), frequently had very little actual contact with their children. Far from feeding, changing and generally becoming physically intimate with their offspring, bourgeois patterns of 'mothering' largely relied on servants being the primary caretakers. Many parents saw their children relatively infrequently and under what today would be considered formal conditions. Children were cleaned up and presented to parents whom they would find immaculately attired and coiffured, and often in company. The modern mother, whose own hair and clothes are likely to be encrusted with whatever her small children have eaten or exuded during the course of the day, may look with longing and disbelief at the elaborate hairstyles and clothing of Victorian mothers, but if Davidoff is right, the long-term emotional consequences of this kind of parenting cannot be underestimated. No doubt this problem was exacerbated for young boys, whose separation was very often intensified by long periods away at school. With this kind of domestic pattern, inevitably many boys learned to think of women of their own class as elusive ideals and paragons, to be seen but not touched. Not surprisingly, when these boys grew to be young men they found it difficult to transcend the barriers internalised in their childhood and consequently turned to those with whom they were familiar and intimate – servants, children, or other young men.

Arthur Munby seems to have been a product of precisely this kind of system and to have internalised its rules to such an extent that, like Dodgson and Barrie, he appears generally to have preferred voyeuristic rather than real relationships. Just as Dodgson collected young girls and, more specifically, photographs of young girls, Munby went far afield to take photographs of labouring women for his collection. Munby's interests were not confined to servants, but encompassed manual labourers and especially those such as colliery girls who did the dirtiest forms of work. While such women were collected, and to be fair, often assisted by Munby, the lasting attachment of his life was for the maidservant, Hannah Cullwick. In Munby Davidoff's theory seems to have found its exemplar, for as a child Munby was cared for by the family Nurse, Hannah Carter. The similarity in name and even initials may be coincidental, but seems significant. As Derek Hudson observes in his biography of Munby, 'That she inspired Munby's lasting interest in working women is clearly a possibility, but it cannot be proved, though he faithfully visited her in retirement.' (Interestingly, Munby's brother married the family governess.)[19]

Hudson is at pains to show that Munby's interest in the girls he encountered was essentially philanthropic and platonic, and underlines the discomfiture Munby experienced when, as so often, his motives were misconstrued. Hudson nonetheless finds himself frequently referring to Munby's favourite areas as 'hunting grounds', and in the diaries themselves it is clear that the feelings which drove Munby towards such girls were not purely altruistic. He talks of his 'craving', and 'disturbance of mind', in relation to these activities, and increasingly in his references to Hannah. In her discussion of Victorian women and work, Helena Michie suggests that working-class women were often associated with prostitution and thought to have greater sexual appetites than their middle-class counterparts[20] (similar myths about black, usually male, virility are familiar from our own time). As Mayhew's analysis of the casual streetwalker discussed in Chapter 2 shows, some working women did supplement their wages with occasional sessions on the street (though the fear of pregnancy and the possibility of losing a post were effective deterrents). But the eroticisation of the working woman's body seems to have more to do with the visibility of her body than with its sexual availability. At a time when most 'respectable' women covered their bodies effectively from head to toe and in many layers, the labouring woman's body came to the fore as she tucked up her skirts, rolled up her sleeves, or, in the case of women in the mines, often wore only the minimum of clothing. Not only was her body less clothed than her middle-class counterpart, but it was also more active, and whatever her actual health, the working woman was presumed to be more robust than the middle-class domestic angel.

As if to compensate for a life of sanitised relations, Munby fantasised about literally dirty women, and Hannah colluded in this by constructing an image of herself in her diaries which was intended to serve the image she believed her 'Massa', as she styled Munby, desired. That her diaries *did* please Munby is evident from the number of entries in which Hannah records that Munby has been cross with her for not sending them and has set ultimatums and deadlines for their appearance.

Knowing that Hannah's diaries were not written for her self but specifically for Munby's perusal and retention underlines the extent to which in writing them she has constructed a fictional, often objectified self which nonetheless has clearly been shaped by class-based expectations and understanding of social relations. It also changes radically the meaning of the endless lists she includes detailing how many shoes she has cleaned, how many knives, floors, steps, etc. Her entries convey simultaneously the monotony and ceaselessness of the Victorian servant's life and the repetition of incident, vocabulary and trope characteristic of pornography, as can be seen in the following extracts:

> The day was *very* hot & so I sweated more nor usual, & being look'd at too all the time by the ladies made me still hotter. I thought I would show them how Massa likes me to clean a grate & I ventured to rub the bars with my bare hands, & yet I was afear'd they may think it a dirty way. But, instead, the Miss Knight in bed watch'd me, & spoke quite pleasantly, & when she saw I wanted more wet

said, 'Come here, Hannah, I'll wet your hand for you out of my bottle.' I had taken care to get my arms black & I rubb'd them across my face, & having my striped apron on & frock pinn'd up, you may guess how I look'd as I crawl'd on my knees to & from the bedside & holding my hand up for the water. [Her] been so delicate, as white as a lily & her face too . . . standing out against my dirty black hands, and my *big* red & black arms, & my face red too & sweating till the drops tumbled off, or stood on little drops o' crystal against the greasy black.

I wish'd much that M. could see me. (p. 66)

Wednesday 14 October . . . I'd a capital chance to go up the chimney, so I lock'd up & waited till ½ past ten till the grate was cool enough & then I took the carpets up & got the tub o' water ready to wash me in. Moved the fender & swept ashes up. Stripp'd myself quite naked & put a pair of old boots on & tied an old duster over my hair & then I got up into the chimney with a brush. There was a lot o' soot & it was soft & warm. Before I swept I pull'd the duster over my eyes & mouth, & I sat on the beam that goes across the middle & cross'd my legs along it & was quite safe and comfortable & out o' sight. I swept lots o' soot down & it come all over me & I sat there for ten minutes or more, & when I'd swept all round & as far as I could reach I come down, & lay on the hearth in the soot a minute or two thinking, & I wish'd rather that Massa could see me. I black'd my face over & then got the looking glass & look'd at myself & I was certainly a fright and hideous all over, at least I should o' seem'd so to anybody but Massa. (p. 139)

Sunday 7 March Swept the passage & took the things out of the hole under the stairs – Mary uses it for her dustpans & brushes. It's a dark hole & about 2 yards long & very low. I crawl'd in on my hands & knees & lay curl'd up in the dirt for a minute or so & then I got out the handbrush & swept the walls down. The cobwebs and dust fell all over me & I had to poke my nose out o' the door to get breath, like a dog's out of a kennel. (p. 119)

These passages are clearly written not for herself, but for Munby, and emphasize moments and aspects of her work she feels will interest and excite him. The repeated references to the size and colour of her hands, the roughness of her work, the filth and near bestiality of her work all seem to be designed to cater for Munby's erotic tastes, and the sense that he was always the intended reader of the work – that they were written for an audience rather than as a personal record – is underlined in the less frequent entries in which Hannah *appears* to forget that he will be reading them. A good example of this is provided in an entry made during the period 1866–72:

> When once I went to Massa in my dirt with striped apron on & dirty frock on purpose that he may see *how* dirty I got, he was, I think, disgusted. My face was dirty (I'd been cleaning the scullery out) & my arms black'd & my *hands* look'd swell'd and red, & begrimed with dirt – *grener'd* as we say in Shropshire. That is, the cracks in our hands ingrain'd with black lead & that, so that even scrubbing will not fetch it out, & in cold frosty weather one *dare* not brush them. . . . Well, I was a little hurt & thought Massa was changed that evening that I went so dirty – after telling me to come in my dirt to his chambers – for he told me to take my thick apron off & to wash myself. It seems he began to think I *was too low* & degraded & that he really pitied me. I could hardly understand that in him, after he had learnt me to love the lowest work & to give up wanting to be higher, & never teaching me nothing, nor for years have I read any books & my only practice in writing has been my diary, & letters to M. & to my sisters. (p. 62)

It takes very little reading between the lines to see that Hannah here is using the convention that the diary is an essentially private form of communication with the self in order to let Munby know what she finds it difficult to say to his face. The resentment and criticism in this extract are very near the surface. That Hannah has understood Munby's reaction when reality impinged on fantasy is evident from his own account of a similar incident. Munby's rationalisation for why he behaved in this way reveals the tension he felt between sexual and emotional desire on the one hand and class on the other.

> *Wednesday, 29 February* (1860) . . . Came a note from Hannah, asking me to go and see her, the mistress being out and she all alone. I went up . . . and found her dirty and unkempt, as she had been all day, she said; and the poor child evidently thought I liked to see her so. I made her wash herself at the sink – her only toilette place! – . . . Most sad, to see her wearing out her youth in such sordid drudgery, her only haunts the kitchen the scullery the coal cellar! . . . seemed for the first time to see the change that five years of exposure and menial work have made in her. . . . And she was pleased with the change – *pleased* that she is now 'so much rougher and coarser' – because it

pleases me, she thinks. Truly, every smear and stain of coarseness on
her poor neglected face comes of love. (p. 52)

The palpable sense in Hannah's diaries of their being written for
scrutiny and with a particular reader in mind is not unusual for women's
diaries and journals of this period. Judy Simons's work on *The Diaries
and Journals of Literary Women* (1990) stresses that such works were
often public and interactive (of course, unlike Hannah's diaries, the
material Simons discusses was quintessentially middle-class in origin).
Often members of a family shared the responsibility for recording events
and/or wrote in each others' 'private' papers. (The diaries of Louisa
May Alcott were regularly read and written in by at least one of
her parents; similarly, Dorothy Wordsworth's diaries were written
for William to read and use.) As well, such works were frequently
scrutinised by mentor/authority-figures in a relationship, and even
read aloud as a form of entertainment.[21] Under such conditions, it seems
fair to assume that far from recording the thoughts, feelings and ambitions
which were too personal to bear public scrutiny, women's diaries were
actually used as places for constructing and presenting the self in ways
designed to appeal to specific readers. True, this sometimes involved
'confessing' thoughts or actions which might in the short term cause pain,
but explanation and repentance could accompany or follow such entries
and thus diaries could make representations or intercede on behalf of their
writers.

But diaries, journals, letters, and similar forms of writing which
women have traditionally chosen when writing about themselves do not
properly belong to the category of 'I'-less texts referred to at the
beginning of this chapter. While on the one hand they may often say more
about the people with whom the writer lives and circulates than they do
about her own thoughts and actions, in most cases they do nonetheless
presuppose that the 'I' used by the writer stands for the writer herself.
They tend not to problematise this relationship; neither do they present
language or the act of writing as inadequate. There are, of course, many
exceptions to this description of personal accounts kept by women of the
past, but in general it holds. A far more interesting, effective and
innovative aspect of Victorian constructions of the feminine self is found
in fictionalised autobiographies. While acknowledging that all fiction is to
some extent autobiographical, looking at the frequency with which
women have chosen, and continue to choose, to construct themselves as
fictional characters in novels, rather than through traditional first-person
autobiographies, produces some extremely interesting insights. It is in this
kind of fictionalised autobiography that the prevailing feeling of 'I'-
lessness is made apparent. Moreover, this appears to become a major

component of feminine autobiography at the same time that Gusdorf's male model was in its ascendancy.

Fictionalising the self

Chapter 3 explored briefly the relationship between Marian Evans and Maggie Tulliver, Charlotte Brontë and Jane Eyre, and Sarah Grand and Beth Caldwell. In each of these texts the writer chose to construct a fictional persona as a way of writing about the self. Similarly, Hannah Cullwick begins her diaries in precisely this way. The diaries begin with a resume of Hannah's early life:

> [Hannah's places] from her leaving the Charity school in Shifnal, which was at eight year old & after she'd done her yellow sampler, her mother meaning her to do a white one for framing at a better school, but what her never could afford. Instead o' that a friend of Mother's (Mrs. Phillips) took me to work at her house off & on (not hired) from 1841 to about 1843. (p. 35)

Though Hannah almost immediately reverts to writing about herself as 'I', both the attempt to avoid this and the way in which she shifts, as it seems, unconsciously to the first person while still appearing often to talk about herself in an objective and distanced style is significant, for it aligns her diaries with the fictionalised autobiographies of her literary contemporaries. At the same time it shows her experimenting with ways for writing about herself, and, through her lack of familiarity with literary models, fashioning her own style and conventions.

It is easy to say that middle–class women were attracted to fictional ways of writing about themselves because they were afraid of appearing unfeminine by treating themselves as worthy subjects for autobiography. However, the evidence of the works themselves suggests that the appeal of fiction as a way of constructing the feminine self is more complex. To begin with, the deliberate creation of a fictionalised other self is yet another indication of these writers' understanding that it is impossible to recreate the self on the page – that there is no single self to recreate – and that any written account on its own can only be partial, and therefore falsifies experience. Paradoxically, it also acknowledges the risks inherent in autobiography, and encourages the reader to be aware of the mechanisms of protection this risk necessitates. As Derrida has observed, 'There is no writing which does not devise some protection, *to protect oneself against itself*, against the writing by which the "subject" is himself threatened as he lets himself be written as he *exposes himself*.'[22] Thus, from the outset, fictionalised autobiography foregrounds the two key problems involved in any attempt to write about the self: the inadequacy of language to convey the self, and the fear of exposing too much. Returning to Chodorow's theories about masculinity, it becomes clear that such writing holds many risks for the male who is uncertain about but values his masculinity. It raises questions about identity and individuality. Fictional personae make the reader conscious of the fact that the writer and character are not synonymous and never can be; they also signal the need for disguise. The use of disguise is itself suggestive of the way the unconscious tells stories to the conscious mind, and indicates that a search for other mechanisms associated with the storytelling techniques of the unconscious (such things as displacement, projection, condensation, and verbal jokes) may be productive. As in dreams, their use may be understood to be an attempt on the part of the unconscious to subvert the autobiographical act – to unmake or deny the official self being constructed. They function as guardians of the private self, and once aware of this the reader is reminded that the autobiographer, like the patient in analysis, may be in pursuit of something s/he doesn't want to know. 'Just as the effort to remember conflicts with the impulse to repress, autobiographical writing generally proceeds from two apparently contradictory impulses: the impulse to preserve the past and the equally powerful urge to be rid of it.'[19]

The fictionalised autobiography, then, rejects the forms associated with masculine accounts of the self as false, and facilitates more searching exploration and revelation through the safety mechanisms associated with dreaming and fantasy. At the same time, this use of fiction makes a political statement about the role of women in Victorian society and the ways in which that society regarded attempts by women to construct independent identities as subversive. This kind of personal account not only points to what the psyche is trying to silence, it also highlights the ways in which women were being silenced by society, and the kinds of things they were not supposed to do, think or say. As a kind of corollary to this, fiction also enabled women to try out and present to the world different versions of the self – not just as deviants and transgressors, but also as paragons and victims. Moreover, the fact that until recently it has largely been women who have rejected conventional autobiographical forms suggests that the presuppositions behind them – coherence, progression, opportunity, success and power – are inappropriate for describing most women's lives, and that well before what has come to be called the 'Modernist' movement in literature, preoccupations with subjectivity, fragmentation, and the reflexive natures of time, memory and experience were dominating women's attempts to write about themselves. The fictionalised autobiographies of the last century show women perceiving themselves as split subjects more accustomed to experiencing the world than acting upon it. More importantly, as the following illustrations will show, the removal of the 'I' from the centre of the narrative process restructures the self which is feeling alienated and represents it as a member of a community, with a group identity. These fictionalised autobiographies are rarely celebrations of personal, public achievements, but works of healing, restoration and shared experience. Accordingly, they had much to offer not only women who were silenced, ignored and/or marginalised under the powerfully patriarchal structures of Victorian society, but, as became increasingly evident as the century came to its end, they offered valuable strategies to those men who were also damaged by the relentless classifying and compartmentalising which characterised their lives.

One of the most common ways in which the individual 'I' is put to one side in feminine forms of autobiography is through the textual device (well known through fairy tales) of splitting the subject. Of course in reality this splitting off of the persona in the story from the storyteller takes place as soon as language is used to describe experience, but it becomes most visible when a fictional persona is deliberately created. This is true even when, as often happens in contemporary autobiographical writing by women, the central character has the same name as the author (think of Jeanette Winterson's *Oranges are Not the Only Fruit* or BeBe Macabe's *Sweet Summer: Growing Up With and Without my Father*). As we saw in Chapter 3, *The Mill on the Floss* is particularly interesting for the way in which it portrays the narrating consciousness as split between and continually negotiating past and present selves. It doubly removes Maggie from Marian by having a narrating self and a childish self, referred to in the third person. The narrator thus both represents Marian and functions as a character in the fiction written by her professional self, George Eliot. This is paralleled in the text with Maggie being both the narrator's childish self and a character in the story continually being told and retold.

This kind of splitting and multiplying of the self is a fundamental characteristic of feminine autobiography and is an almost inevitable consequence of the fluid boundaries which result from an Oedipal phase the resolution of which is predominantly feminine.[24] It seems to be the only publicly-sanctioned paradigm for nineteenth-century femininity, in which the feminine self had to learn to construct itself through and in relation to others, and masculine attributes such as preoccupations with action, facts, rationality, and the presentation of the self as unified and in relation to external events, must be denied. Because of the limitations officially placed on Victorian women's ability to move and participate in the social world as a consequence of public adherence to the dyadic model, and their related understanding that to see themselves as apart and unique was to jeopardise their reputations and forever to diminish their social prospects, women were reluctant to make themselves the subject of autobiography or even to identify themselves too closely with their fictional characters. Indeed, it is necessary to ask whether women were always capable of seeing, or indeed wanted to see, themselves in other than collective terms. For this reason, the kind of single-centred mode characteristic of Victorian masculine autobiographies may have been rejected by women not simply because their lives didn't seem to them to be sufficiently significant, but because the form did not correspond to the ways in which women generally experienced life: as collective, affective and relational beings.

To read split subjects as simultaneously articulating the problems of existing in a world which increasingly celebrated the significance of the individual while belonging to a social group for whom individuality was suspect, and affirming the advantages and values of constructing the self as part of a group, means that it is necessary to understand the 'I'-less condition as having many positive connotations. This positive construction of the denial of self offers useful insights into a problem which has troubled feminists for decades – the ways in which women have continued to collude in the 'repression' of other women. If the denial of self is *valued*, for instance for its healthy ability to link the individual to her community, rather than feared as inevitably holding women back, then the ways in which we read femininity, and especially the relational aspects associated with Victorian constructions of femininity, need to be slightly recast. Constructing the self relationally does largely impede the exploitation and manipulation of others on which success in capitalist, patriarchal societies largely depends. However, there are social and psychological benefits to be gained from identifying the self with others; of recognising interdependence, and of belonging to a community rather than always trying to construct a vision of the self as unique and individual. That this collective mentality need not necessarily result in economic and cultural bankruptcy is in our own time being shown by cultures such as that of Japan which has a long history of privileging the interests of the group over those of the individual.

A good example of a text which fictionalises autobiographical material and relies on the process of showing the self as made up of and containing many selves is Louisa May Alcott's *Little Women* (1868). Although Alcott was American, her novel nonetheless reflected many of the experiences and preoccupations of girls growing up in Britain at the time. This is suggested by the instant and enduring success of her books in this country. (Alcott was certainly not the only American writer whose work struck a strong chord with British girls as the popularity of Susan Coolidge's 'Katy' stories (the first of which was published in 1870), and earlier works such as Elizabeth Wetherell's best-selling *The Wide, Wide World* (1850) prove.) G. Kitson–Clark observes that in fact,

> much of what we consider to be typically Victorian was shared by the United States, where, at least till after the Civil War, the ways of life and thought resembled those of this country much more closely than many people on either side of the Atlantic would have desired to believe.[25]

Alcott's novel has been read both as a reactionary treatise, which condemns the behaviour of the rebellious and dissatisfied Jo March for her aspirations and her desire to be a boy, and as a text which subverts the values and goals of Victorian femininity.[26] The repressive reading concentrates on the ways in which the text subtly undermines Jo's actions and ambitions. It suggests that her values are shown to be inferior to those of Marmee, that domestic, self-sacrificing paragon, and that no good can come of Jo's talents and energies until, like her mother, she finds a man able to help her to control herself. The crisis of the book comes in the conversation between Marmee and Jo following the episode in which Amy nearly drowns because Jo is so angry with her that she chooses not to look after the younger girl when they are out skating. Amy falls through some thin ice and has to be rescued by Laurie and Jo. Jo's great anger is the result of Amy's having burned a book on which she had been working for many weeks. Jo hopes that her writing will eventually allow her to become independent and even to assume the role of 'man of the house' by supporting her family. The near catastrophe with Amy serves to make Jo value family and relationships over imagination, independence and a career. It also elicits her mother's confession that she too was once an angry young woman. The chapter is called 'Jo Meets Apollyon', and according to the repressive reading, its significance is that from this moment on Jo gradually learns to identify herself with her mother (this is almost a *re-learning* of the feminine position). She begins to acquire the domestic skills and the self-control which win her father's approbation and, ultimately, a husband and a whole school full of boys to whom she becomes the ministering angel. Amy's burning of her manuscript prefigures the moment when, under the watchful eye of Professor Bhaer, Jo consigns all her 'little writings' to the flames of the domestic stove! There is a great deal of evidence for this reading, not least the clearly identifiable pattern by which each time Jo is about to have a moment of satisfaction from her literary successes the plot throws up a twist which causes her work to fade into the background.[27] It is a book which undoubtedly examines the consequences which must be faced by the girl who fights against becoming 'properly' feminised, and which shows as necessary and legitimate the processes by which women collude in repressing each other – especially through mother–daughter relationships. While placing at its centre a girl who challenges the necessity of becoming feminine, *Little Women* is certainly not a celebration of liberated, independent womanhood. However, neither is it simply a book which promotes the feminine ideal as role model. The complex interaction between femininity and creativity, between autonomy and family is closely linked to the autobiographical element in the book.

Louisa May Alcott was the second of four daughters (her sisters are supposed to have served as the models for Meg, Beth and Amy March) born to Amos Bronson and Abigail (Abba) May Alcott. Because of their father's many and wide-ranging ideals, the Alcotts' parents did not provide a typical model of family life for the girls. Bronson Alcott was interested in changing society. His experiments ranged from educational reforms based on his own theories of child development to establishing a utopian community, Fruitlands. While he generally succeeded in attracting followers and in getting projects off the ground, Alcott was never successful in his enterprises. The result was that his wife and children were constantly being uprooted, always existed on the poverty line, and were forced to take some control of their own lives. Abba eventually had to support the family, and watching her mother's efforts to earn enough to keep them alive and together while simultaneously trying to hold to an idea of the wife as the self-sacrificing domestic ideal clearly had a profound effect on the young Louisa. She decided to show the world that she at least could support herself, and once begun, maintained the role of family breadwinner to her death.[28]

In her introduction to Alcott's lesser-known, sensation stories, Elaine Showalter points out that in many ways the Alcott parents provided models which deviated significantly from traditional gender stereotypes. They thus provided a ready-made challenge to the dyadic model for their daughters. Bronson Alcott believed that men should help with child-rearing and certain kinds of domestic tasks (apparently he was a great baker of bread[29]), and Abba was always involved in supporting the family and managing the domestic income. While liking to be thought of as a 'man of genius' and thus necessarily seeing *himself* as an individual, Alcott also believed strongly in the virtues of shared, interdependent existence, as evidenced by his experiments in communal living. Alcott's lack of financial success and his frequent absences from home meant that his all-female family had to learn to look after themselves, but as they were for a long time unable to earn enough individually, they also needed to depend on each other for emotional and financial security. All of these elements find expression in *Little Women*.

Perhaps the most powerful and enigmatic aspect of the book is its ambivalence towards female creativity and the independence it might bring. As Showalter's study shows, the roots of this ambivalence are exposed in the diaries kept by Bronson Alcott and those of Louisa as a girl. On the one hand, her parents supported Louisa's aspirations. Bronson encouraged her to spend time reading and writing, and gave her the run of his study. Both parents promoted the value of story-telling. Yet Louisa's independence of mind and character disturbed her father. When she was only two he decided it was necessary to make her more docile, and so established a nursery routine and a whole way of life for the child designed to teach her the 'sweetness of self-denial'.[30] This struggle between artistic expression (which had the potential to lead to financial independence) and acceptable femininity plagued Louisa throughout her life, and shows just how pervasive and potentially destructive the dyadic mentality could be. Her later diaries record her ambivalence towards writing, which at times she regarded as analogous to witchcraft, the imagination acting as a witch's cauldron into which experiences were poured and mingled to make stories.[31] This image evokes many of the same images and so the ambivalence towards female sexuality explored in relation to Decadent painting, and it is useful to recall that for Louisa at least the 'dark' side of writing was firmly counterbalanced by its positive aspects: it was only through writing that she could obtain independence, and independence was her overriding concern. Alcott may have written stories which show the problems in store for the girl who fails to conform to the feminine ideal, but she also wrote sympathetically and in support of unmarried women and chose not to marry herself.

Although she chose independence and, like Jo March, often felt she was a man trapped in a woman's body,[32] Alcott essentially adhered to a feminine model of the self. This is particularly evident in her attitude to writing:

> 'Work and wait' became her motto. The best women artists, she tried to persuade herself, were those who were truly unselfish and ultimately womanly self-denial would bring its own reward in an enriched art. In numerous short stories . . . as well as in *Little Women*, Alcott represented suffering, dutifulness, and self-sacrifice as necessary steps toward female artistic success.[33]

Louisa May Alcott's ambivalent feelings towards both her creativity and her femininity mean that it is unsatisfactory to read *Little Women*, the text which deals most closely with the material of her childhood, as one which advocates, or at least acknowledges as inevitable, the repression of women. Neither does it present creativity and femininity as mutually exclusive. Another way of reading it, which is clearly connected to the autobiographical nature of the text, concentrates on identifying beneath the manifest plot, another which gives voice to the problems inherent in being creative, ambitious and female. While this reading acknowledges Jo's final acceptance of femininity, it emphasizes the *cost* of this process, and in doing so shows negative aspects of the feminine ideal – those aspects which lead to such repression of the self that frustration and illness seem inevitable. The book thus reminds readers that femininity is not a girl's *natural* destiny, but the product of socialisation. The book struggles to express the hope that femininity need not be sacrificed for creativity, and that masculine ways of constructing the self are not necessarily better than feminine. Indeed, it seems significant that none of Alcott's central male characters is thoroughly manly. Having said that, a happy balance between the two was difficult to find in real life, though Louisa May Alcott herself found one possible, though perhaps not enviable, compromise. Having finally achieved financial success and security, she found herself unmarried and yet in the traditional female roles of mother and nurse. Her sister May having died in childbirth, Louisa raised her niece while simultaneously nursing her father throughout his dotage.

When reading *Little Women* as an autobiographical text, it is useful to think of all the March females as aspects of one self: together they comprise the autobiographical persona for Louisa. At one level each of Jo's sisters can be seen to represent one of the personality traits which needs to be overcome if the self is to learn to forget itself and become the 'intensely sympathetic' 'immensely charming' and 'utterly unselfish' Angel in the House.[34] While the *particular* aspects of the self and the trials Jo undergoes on the way to becoming a 'little woman' are specifically Alcott's, the need to assemble fragments of past and present selves and to repress 'undesirable' personality traits as part of the rite of passage into womanhood were experiences shared by many women of her day. As Judy Simons writes,

> individual women's lives, perhaps more notably than men's, were subject to continual change, as differing ideologies of femininity were imposed upon them. The successive stages in their lives – as daughter, sweetheart, wife, mother, widow – were defined through the appropriation of certain codes of behaviour, each considered suitable for one of these roles.[35]

In order to excel in 'the difficult art of family life' and sacrifice herself daily'; in order not to have 'a mind or wish of her own'[36] the 'I' must be totally expunged. Moreover, while it is easy to make connections between the dreams and desires of Louisa and Jo and the ways in which each chapter in the book enacts the processes through which Bronson Alcott required his daughter to learn the 'sweetness of self-denial', by splitting the self into several selves and presenting each girl as both a type and an aspect of a greater character, Alcott succeeds in making the autobiographical element of the book transcend individual identity and become representative. Even Beth, ostensibly the acme of self-sacrificing Victorian womanhood, has an aspect of the self to overcome. Until she learns to venture beyond the home and to use her power for good she is unable completely to fulfil her true feminine function of ministering to and transforming others. As it transpires, even with the support of her exclusive domestic community she is unable to withstand the demands of the world, for the ever-virtuous Beth is the figure of femininity gone berserk. She embodies in every way the feminine ideal, and so highlights the consequences for individuals and society of the ideological separation of women and their own needs and desires. As for so many Victorian women (and indeed for anorexic young women today) Beth's determination to repress herself becomes obsessive and self-destructive. In her portrait of this March sister, Louisa May Alcott makes her strongest case against the prescriptions and prohibitions of Victorian femininity, and does so through showing that taken to its logical conclusion, the 'feminine ideal' was so embattled in the struggle to deny the self that it was incapable of serving others and became alienated from and unfit for the world. Thus, *Little Women* is simultaneously about the problems and failings of individuals and the need jointly to reject the feminine ideal and the separate spheres mentality imposed by society. It demands that public and private, official and unofficial, licit and illicit aspects of female experience be acknowledged and integrated.

In making her case for the recovery of those aspects of femininity which the dyadic model repressed, Alcott avoids elevating herself to the role of heroic archetype in the manner of the masculine mode of autobiography. Instead, the form she adopts in *Little Women* represents an attempt to break away from this dominant masculine model and to establish a new set of values. This is made clear largely through the character of Jo. Jo's problem is that at first she wants to act like a boy and that she fails to act collaboratively. She is too preoccupied with herself, and this is shown to be the greatest wrong of all. In this text exaggerated emphasis on the self over the community leads to a range of social problems. It is at the bottom of the tension between Laurie and his grandfather, and self-interest in its many forms is what each of the March girls has to overcome before she becomes a proper little woman. The book constantly explores the tension between the needs of the community and the individual's search for identity. As individuality is associated with masculinity, the book suggests that the problems of society (remember that the background to the novel is the American Civil War) are associated with the drive to construct the self as autonomous. By contrast, what is visible in the book is the power of collaboration and mutual dependence. Marmee and the girls are respected and effective agents in the town, relieving the distressed and maintaining the community so that life can go on when the war is over. Though the collective way of constructing the self is associated with and embodied in the women in this text, it is advocated for all. The only way to resolve the war is through reconstruction – the nation must become the greatest model of collective activity of them all. More important for the individual reader, however, is the way in which splitting out aspects of the self in this way facilitates the identification process initiated by fictionalizing the self in the first place. Readers are less impatient with and judgemental of fictional characters than they are with people, as they understand that the structure of the novel both requires them to wait and see what happens, and ultimately assures them of full understanding.[37] Dealing with separate aspects of character allows for a range of identifications, both positive and negative. As has been shown with the reading of fairy tales, the need to recognise and accept negative as well as positive aspects of the self as normal is important and therapeutic. Particularly for Victorian girls who were having to deal with the restrictions inherent in the dyadic model and its feminine ideal, it must have been deeply reassuring to read about the problems and anger of others. This process of identification – of saying 'I'm like that too' rather than 'I'm different' – is entirely feminine. Understanding this means that the overall lack of an 'I' in the text does not imply that there is no sense of self, but that the feminine self recognises itself by identifying with and acknowledging the presence of others. Finally, of course, this kind of splitting out of competing and often contradictory aspects of the self mirrors the experiences of being feminine and female in Victorian society as this always entailed juggling at least two equally demanding and often contradictory roles – idealised virgin and mother, for example.

Victorian men and feminine autobiography

But the need to write feeminine autobiography was not unique to Victorian women. As I have explored elsewhere (see *Girls Only?*, 1990), the second half of Victoria's reign witnessed a crisis in masculinity, a crisis which was exaggerated because of the official dyadic mentality. The primary concern of this book is with what happens to women who were expected to conform to the feminine ideal and with showing that in reality this ideal satisfied no one. Equally important, however, are the problems experienced by men attempting to conform to the manly ideal. With the increased insistence on adherence to more manly roles and behaviours occasioned by conspicuous failures in traditionally male arenas such as the military and government, men too became acutely conscious of the pressures and costs involved in living up to the ideal. Such pressure inevitably generated in some men a sense of unease about the official public self and the inner experiencing self, once again calling into question the value and validity of the dyadic model for both sexes. The conflict experienced by men is analogous to the divided identity previously described with reference to women, and it is not surprising, therefore, that at least some men also experienced difficulty in adopting the masculine model when attempting to write about themselves. If feminine auto-biography is about constructing the self in collective rather than individual ways, acknowledging the fragmented and protean nature of experience, and attempting to give expression to repressed aspects of the self as part of a process of healing and transfiguring an existing self-image, then *David Copperfield* is a feminine autobiography. In this fictionalised autobiography, Dickens carefully and deliberately interweaves aspects of his life with fictional events and characters,[38] and though he changed the names and circumstances of the people in his life who also feature in his novel, the disguises are often very thin. Indeed, at least one of his acquaintances, the woman on whom the character of the dwarfish Miss Mowcher is based, recognised herself immediately and wrote to complain that she had been unfairly and unkindly ridiculed (Dickens apologised and promised to make suitable adjustments as the character developed[39]). Dickens always admitted that David Copperfield was a version of his younger self, and the fact that David's initials are simply Dickens' own reversed underscores the fact that David is meant to be an image of Dickens.

In creating a fictional persona for himself, Dickens aligns himself with those women writers whose fictionalised autobiographies explore the tensions between the impulses to confess and to conceal, to explore and evade, to express what language is incapable of expressing, and principally to trace their origins and histories while maintaining they are not as they were. Many other similarities can also be found in the narrative methods used by Dickens and those adopted by women writers of feminine autobiography. For instance, *David Copperfield* is deeply concerned with the need to convey a sense of fragmentation. The proliferation of names by which David is known (which can usefully be compared to that other narrating orphan, *Bleak House*'s Esther Summerson) is symptomatic of his inability to identify with a single, coherent self. Of course, all autobiography is in some sense a quest for origins and an attempt to discover who you are through tracing what you have done and been, but in this novel Dickens also underlines the fact that any construction of the self is unstable as it must always incorporate how others perceive and know you. Thus, though the book purports to be about 'David Copperfield', the central character has many identities which are reflected in the many names by which he is known. He is variously Davy, David, Copperfield, Brooks of Sheffield, Towzer, Trot, Trotwood, Daisy and Doady. These different names do not reflect a simple progression from child to man, neither are they primarily based on class or gender relations (to Steerforth he is 'Daisy', to Agnes 'Trotwood', and to Peggoty he remains 'Davy'). Rather, they reflect degrees of intimacy and the extent to which past selves are acknowledged or denied in present relationships. Those who know and love him best (with the possible exception of the Micawbers) always call him by his first names: Davy, and Trot or Trotwood (the name which his Aunt Betsey Trotwood belatedly bestows on him when he arrives at her house and becomes her surrogate child). It is principally as Trotwood that he ends the book, and this familiar name, with its youthful associations, clearly links the narrating persona and the adult David at the end of the book with all the other characters he has been in the preceding 950 pages. This link between past and present selves and the recognition that one doesn't succeed the other but that they co-exist is emphasised throughout the text. Indeed, it is brought into play in the famous opening line: 'Whether I shall turn out to be the hero of my own life, or whether that station will be held by anyone else, these pages must show.' This beginning not only seeks to displace the narrating 'I' from the centre of the text (in truly feminine fashion) while simultaneously constructing a sense of multiple selves, it also establishes the need to go back into the past in order to understand the present, implies that the meaning of the past can only be found in the present, and underlines that this meaning is never fixed, but is constantly revised and revisable. Perhaps the strongest feeling about earlier selves which emerges in this text is that they continue to exist and perpetually to reenact the same scenes and roles: 'When I tread the old ground, I do not wonder that I seem to see and pity, going on before me, an innocent romantic boy, making his imaginative world out of such strange experiences and sordid things.' (p. 225). Shortly after this passage, the compassionate but detached, historical, stance of the adult narrator breaks down completely to be replaced by the painful emotional reaction of the experiencing child:

> No words can express the secret agony of my soul as I sunk into this companionship; the deep remembrance of the sense I had, of being utterly without hope now; of the shame I felt in my position; of the misery it was to my young heart to believe that day by day what I had learned, thought, and delighted in, and raised my fancy and emulation up by, would pass away from me, little by little, never to be brought back any more; cannot be written. (p. 210)

The emphasis here on the inadequacy of language to convey experience contrasted with the strong sense of the need to write about what has happened again associates *David Copperfield* with feminine forms of autobiography. As if to underline that at least one part of his task in writing is to acknowledge the feminine side of the successful man, Dickens begins the work with a noteworthy subtitle: 'The Personal History and Experience of David Copperfield the Younger'. In this heading he combines the masculine mode (history) with the feminine (experience), and indeed the two are carefully balanced and intertwined throughout. At this point it is fruitful to recall why David becomes 'Trotwood'. This is not only his aunt's name, but the name she intended to bestow on her great-niece when she first descended on the Copperfield household. Aunt Betsey clearly despises the kind of conventionally manly man (of whom her husband had been an extreme example) and is determined that the new member of the family be a girl. When told that Clara has given birth to a son she, 'said never a word, but . . . vanished like a discontented fairy' for, David observes, 'Betsey Trotwood Copperfield was for ever in the land of dreams and shadows, the tremendous region whence I had so lately travelled' (p. 60). For the purpose of this discussion, the significance of Betsey's decision to call David 'Trotwood' is that it signals her recognition of the feminine side to his nature. Trotwood is bookish, companionable, dependent and victimised. Moreover, he is an orphan, and Chapter 1 argues, this puts him squarely in the domain of the feminine. It is entirely appropriate, therefore, that the autobiography of David Copperfield takes a feminine form, and as the life-story of Charles Dickens the choice of form is equally apt. For all his exuberance and public success, Dickens was never able to free himself of the anxieties and insecurities resulting from the dramatic reversals and failures of his family's fortunes. His father's financial mismanagement meant that, like the Alcotts, they were generally beholden to somebody or other. Eventually their impecunious state resulted in Charles's brief sojourn in the infamous blacking factory. The deep sense of personal injury with which this episode left Dickens found expression in *David Copperfield*. When the Murdstones arrange for David to work in the Murdstone and Grimsby warehouse the mature narrating David observes,

I know enough of the world now, to have almost lost the capacity of being much surprised by anything; but it is matter of some surprise to me, even now, that I can have been so easily thrown away at such an early age. A child of excellent abilities, and with strong powers of observation, quick, eager, delicate, and soon hurt bodily or mentally, it seems wonderful to me that nobody should have made any sign on my behalf. But none was made; and I became, at ten years old, a little labouring hand. (p. 208)

The sense of being superfluous, powerless, and unappreciated permeates much of the first four books of *David Copperfield* and again suggests reasons for Dickens' gravitation towards feminine ways of rendering experience.

The ways in which this novel resembles those fictionalised auto-biographies by women already discussed are manifold. For instance, drawing on the established association between children, orphans and femininity, Dickens' fictionalised autobiography too constructs a split version of the self, but the split is subtly different from those previously considered. In this text, the most obvious division is between the feminine, inexperienced child and the masculine, worldly man. Drawing on Victorian (largely Romantic) myths of childhood, it presents this phase as not just formative, but inspirational; its vision both untainted and linked to the heroic past. Like Wordsworth, Dickens attempts to revive the child in himself and to draw on the feelings and understanding generated by this process rather than simply recording significant events. The feminine fictionalised autobiography is the form required for this endeavour as it depends upon speculation, interpretation, and associa-tion. It doesn't declare, 'This is what happened', rather, it says 'This is what it felt like', and asks, 'What does it mean?'.

Another way in which *David Copperfield* can be said to belong to the category of 'feminine autobiography' is in its recognition that the power of the past is not exclusively positive and visionary, but that it has also the power to damage and unmake the present. This attitude to personal history is vividly conveyed in one of the earliest examples of an autobiography written by a woman, *The Book of Margery Kempe* (1436), and continues to be a recurrent theme in contemporary feminine autobiographies such as Carolyn Steedman's *Landscape for a Good Woman* (1986). It is unmistakable in Dickens' novel. For instance, in Chapter 10, 'I become Neglected, and am Provided for' David writes,

I now approach a period of my life, which I can never lose the remembrance of, while I remember anything: and the recollection of which has often, without my invocation, come before me like a ghost, and haunted happier times. (p. 205)

This passage is followed a few pages later by that quoted above, in which the narrating David recalls the misery, shame and despair he felt at having been set to work in the warehouse. Both are taken, almost verbatim, from what remains of Dickens' only, abandoned, attempt at masculine autobiography:

> No words can express the secret agony of my soul as I sunk into this companionship; compared these every day associates with those of my happier childhood; and felt my early hopes of growing up to be a learned and distinguished man, crushed in my breast. The deep remembrance of the sense I had of being utterly neglected and hopeless; of the shame I felt in my position; of the misery it was to my young heart to believe that, day by day, what I learned, and thought, and delighted in, and raised my fancy and emulation up by, was passing away from me, never to be brought back any more; cannot be written. My whole nature was so penetrated with the grief and humiliation of such considerations, *that even now, famous and caressed and happy, I often forget in my dreams that I have a dear wife and children: even that I am a man: and wander desolately back to that time of my life.*[40] (my emphases)

The sense of personal crisis and deep, unhealed wounding is clear. It is significant that Dickens was unable to complete or to share his 'shameful' memories in a conventional autobiography (he destroyed much of it and entrusted only fragments to his close friend and biographer, John Forster,[41]) but required the disguises and evasions afforded by fiction-alised autobiography to unearth and explore them. In *A Healing Art: Regeneration Through Autobiography* (1990) Marilyn Chandler considers the therapeutic qualities of autobiographical writing for victims of crises. While Chandler is exclusively concerned with twentieth-century works and major catastrophes of this century, many of her observations are equally applicable to personal traumas from earlier periods. Of particular interest to a reading of *David Copperfield* is her suggestion that the individual often experiences crisis as a result of 'discrepancies between lived experience and the expectations fostered by institutions that provide us with identity'.[42] This is exactly the problem experienced by Dickens and which he sets out to resolve in *David Copperfield*. Both at home and in the world his earliest expectations of being the loved child and successful scholar were queered by subsequent experience. He focuses on the brief nadir in the blacking factory – his personal crisis of rejection by family and society – and through his fictionalised autobiography manages both to indite the system which allowed this to happen and to construct an alternative.

His alternative has two principal characteristics. First is the abandoned child's desire to recreate the nuclear family, a task of reconstruction which takes two forms in the novel: the replacement of lost parents with good surrogates (notably Aunt Betsey and Mr Dick), and the creation of his own family. While his first efforts to do this with Dora end disastrously, the book closes with a domestic epiphany provoked by his vision of Agnes, mother of his children. (Significantly, Dickens was himself unable to stay within the large replacement family he made with his wife; neither did he fit comfortably into the role of conventional patriarch.) The second characteristic is the feminine transformation of personal experience into shared experience. This is seen particularly in the beginning of the text, with its displacement of the self as hero, and the characterisation of Davy (born with a caul) as a mythical, portentous and archetypal being. But it is also true of the book as a whole. David's life history cannot be extracted from those with whom he is involved; the strands of the narrative are overlapping and mutually dependent, and the conclusion in fact spends more time exploring what happens to those whose lives have affected David than it does bringing his own up to date. The book thus makes it clear that Dickens is not interested in constructing his fictional self as independent, but can only perceive and present him in relation to others, including the others he has been.

Dickens' rejection of traditional masculine autobiography anticipates developments in our own century, which has witnessed the decline of the masculine autobiography as a literary genre; the most celebrated early example of this change is provided by James Joyce's *A Portrait of the Artist as a Young Man* (1914–15). A new schism has emerged between popular autobiography (usually about famous figures from the worlds of sport, entertainment, or politics) and 'serious' or 'literary' autobiographies. Popular texts about both male and female personalities continue to rely predominantly on the conventions associated with masculine auto- biographies. They are linear, coherent, authoritative and celebratory. Literary autobiographies, by contrast, are largely in the feminine mode. They eschew certainties, progression, and the celebration of individual deeds. These works are largely ahistorical in the sense that they rely at least as much on story as they do on history, yet they also recognise the influence of earlier stories and generations on the individuals the writers have become. Accordingly the multiple personae they create frequently include characters from the past and from fiction. (A prime example of this kind of text is Maxine Hong Kingston's *The Woman Warrior* (1976), but an interesting contemporary example by a man, which also plays with the tensions between masculinity and existing modes for writing about the self, is Peter Fuller's *Marches Past* (1986).) Unlike *David Copperfield* and the other Victorian examples of feminine autobiography discussed here, these contemporary works avoid closure and, perhaps because they are often explicit confessional, are frequently punitive and bleak in their forecasts of the future. It seems, then, that in literary/intellectual terms a revolution in the construction of the self and the status of feminine autobiography has taken place. Socially, however, the residual discourses and goals of masculinity continue to be more attractive and persuasive, perhaps suggesting that, particularly as life becomes more conspicuously fragmented and accelerated, the old myths of the unified and controlling self acquire the respectable patina provided by nostalgia. In truth, however, it may be more useful to re-examine the strengths which have been dismissed in Victorian feminine autobiography. Much can be learned from re-examining these models, which are also articulating a sense of anxiety about reconciling the capitalist rhetoric of the individual with the experience of being female in the early years of our modern society. The conclusion that the myth of individuality is a pernicious one, and the advocacy of traditional group values, behaviours and identities are at least worth reconsidering.

Thus, in feminine autobiography many of the concerns which have preoccupied us throughout this study come together. The strategies Victorian women adopted for writing about themselves not only challenged the dyadic mentality as it was advertised and perpetuated by men *and* women, but offered solutions for rejoining the divided aspects of the feminine self. In the process, they encouraged women not to abandon the valuable networks for supporting and spurring each other on (networks widely used by women writers as evidenced by their correspondence) which had sustained them for centuries. While many of the genres largely concerned with the experiences of Victorian women (for instance, sensation novels, orphan-stories, and those texts which have at their centre the spectre of the unfortunate prostitute) have now been superseded, feminine autobiography, undoubtedly because of the difficulties it presented to its authors, became a complex and innovative form which can be credited with giving birth to many of the best-known experiments in twentieth-century literature. That men are increasingly attracted to feminine forms of autobiography suggests that the public rhetoric of difference which underlay the dyadic mentality has been dismantled, and that it is being replaced by one which takes account of experience and acknowledges the unconscious. As in our own *fin de siècle* we seek greater commonality of experience between the sexes, the routing out of residual discourses and representations which continue to divide the world according to dyadic principles needs to be continued. Since, as feminine autobiography emphasizes, present selves are always at the mercy of past selves, a fundamental factor in successfully achieving a fairer society involves re-visiting representations of ourselves from the past. If, as we maintain, they prove to be more complex and less rigid than has been supposed, then the ways in which they interact with current constructions of gender relations will eventually be adjusted accordingly.

Victorian Heroines is an attempt to offer new readings of the powerful and pervasive Victorian images of women which have been so influential in shaping our understanding of both past and present.

Notes

Notes for Introduction

1. Lynda Nead, *Myths of Sexuality: Representations of Women in Victorian Britain* (Oxford: Basil Blackwell, 1988), p. 1.
2. See, for instance, Sandra M. Gilbert and Susan Gubar, *The Madwoman in the Attic: The Woman Writer and the Nineteenth-Century Literary Imagination* (London: Yale University Press, 1979); Bram Dijkstra, *Idols of Perversity: Fantasies of Feminine Evil in Fin-de-Siècle Culture* (Oxford: Oxford University Press, 1986); and Lynne Pearce, *Woman, Image, Text: Readings in Pre-Raphaelite Art and Literature* (Hemel Hempstead: Harvester Wheatsheaf, 1991).
3. Pearce, *Woman, Image, Text*, p. 2.
4. Dijkstra, *Idols of Perversity*, p. 145.
5. *ibid.*
6. Pearce, *Woman, Image, Text*, p. 21. While we agree with Pearce's use of 'heroine', there have been a number of recent studies of the heroines of Victorian fiction whose approaches differ from ours. Tess Cosslett, in *Woman to Woman: Female Friendship in Victorian Fiction* (Brighton: Harvester, 1988) explores the ways in which heroine identity in women-authored novels is altered and extended through the agency of the heroine's contrasting female friends. Susan Morgan's *Sisters in Time: Imagining Gender in Nineteenth-Century British Fiction* (Oxford: Oxford University Press, 1989) considers the 'heroic' model of character as she finds it manifested in the heroines of Scott, Austen, Gaskell, Eliot, Meredith and James, advancing the interesting argument that gender functions for these authors as a means of redeeming the century's sense of history.
7. W. E. Houghton, *The Victorian Frame of Mind 1830–1870* (New Haven: Yale University, Press, 1957), p. xv.

8. Michel Foucault, *The History of Sexuality*, vol. I, *An Introduction*, trans. Robert Hurley (Harmondsworth: Penguin Books, 1979); Stephen Marcus *The Other Victorians: A Study of Sexuality and Pornography in Mid-Nineteenth Century England* (London: Meridian, 1977).

9. See, for instance, Helena Michie, *The Flesh Made Word: Female Figures and Women's Bodies*, (Oxford: Oxford University Press, 1987), p. 5.

10. G. Kitson-Clark, *The Making of Victorian England* (London: Methuen, 1962), p. 28.

11. Houghton, *The Victorian Frame of Mind 1830–1870*, p. 1.

12. *ibid.*, p. 8.

13. *ibid.*, p. 10.

14. Walter Pater, Conclusion to *The Renaissance: Studies in Art and Poetry*, first published by Macmillan and Co., 1873 (London: Collins, 1961).

15. Catherine Belsey discusses this interestingly in the third chapter of *Critical Practice* (London: Methuen, 1980).

16. Houghton, *The Victorian Frame of Mind 1830–1870*, p. 366.

17. *ibid.*

18. See Nancy F. Cott, 'Passionlessness: An Interpretation of Victorian Sexual Ideology, 1790–1850', *Signs*, 4, 2 (1978), pp. 219–36.

Notes to Chapter 1

1. Charlotte Brontë, *Villette* first published 1853 (Harmondsworth: Penguin Books, 1985), Chapter 19, pp. 275–6. Throughout the text, when discussing nineteenth-century novels we refer wherever possible to a recent paperback edition. The editions used will be found at first citation in the endnotes, and subsequent references in the main text will be to page and chapter numbers in these editions. Page, rather than chapter, numbers are used wherever the textual discussion is detailed enough that the extra precision is thought to be desirable.

2. Diana Mosley's famous explanation of why her husband chose black shirts for his supporters – because they were easy to wash and didn't show the dirt – is a similar case of such a self-revealing displacement. Thanks are due to James Davidson for supplying this example.

3. William Cobbett, *Advice To Young Men and (Incidentally) To Young Women*, first published 1830 (London: Peter Davies Ltd, 1926), p. 96.

4. Françoise Basch, *Relative Creatures: Victorian Women in Society and the Novel 1837–1867*, trans. Anthony Rudolf (London: Allen Lane, 1974).

5. Patricia Thomson, *The Victorian Heroine: A Changing Ideal, 1837–1873* (London: Oxford University Press, 1956), pp. 120–44.

6. Peter Gay, *The Bourgeois Experience: Victoria to Freud*, vol. I, *The Education of the Senses* (Oxford: Oxford University Press, 1984), p. 466.

7. Stephen Marcus, *The Other Victorians: A Study of Sexuality and Pornography in Mid-Nineteenth Century England* (London: Meridian, 1977).

8. Walter E. Houghton, *The Victorian Frame of Mind 1830–1870* (New Haven: Yale University Press, 1957); Duncan Crow, *The Victorian Woman* (London: George Allen and Unwin, 1971).

9. Michel Foucault, *The History of Sexuality*, vol. I, *An Introduction*, trans. Robert Hurley (Harmondsworth: Penguin Books, 1979).

10. Nancy Armstrong, *Desire and Domestic Fiction* (New York: Oxford University Press, 1987), p. 11.

11. See, for example, Helena Michie, *The Flesh Made Word: Female Figures and Women's Bodies* (Oxford: Oxford University Press, 1987), p. 6, and Armstrong, *ibid.*, pp. 13–14, p. 22.

12. William Acton, *The Functions and Disorders of the Reproductive Organs in Childhood, Youth, Adult Age, and Advanced Life* (London: John Churchill, 1857).

13. Acton, cited in Lawrence Lerner, *Love and Marriage: Literature in its Social Context* (London: Arnold, 1979), p. 134.

14. Acton, cited in Lerner, *ibid.*, p. 134.

15. Marcus, *The Other Victorians*, p. 13.

16. See Armstrong, *Desire and Domestic Fiction*, throughout; Martha Vicinus, 'Sexuality and Power: A Review of Current Work in the History of Sexuality', *Feminist Studies*, 8, 1 (1982), pp. 133–56 (p. 135); Philippa Levine, *Victorian Feminism 1850–1900* (London: Hutchinson, 1987), pp. 129–30.

17. Nancy F. Cott, 'Passionlessness: An Interpretation of Victorian Sexual Ideology, 1790–1850', *Signs*, 4, 2 (1978), pp. 219–36.

18. Havelock Ellis, *Studies in the Psychology of Sex*, first published 1903; 2nd rev. edn, vol. III (Philadelphia: F. A. Davis Co., 1913), 193–944.

19. See, for example Basch, *Relative Creatures*, p. 271 and throughout.

20. Erna Olafson Hellerstein, Leslie Parker Hume and Karen M. Otten (eds.), *Victorian Women: A Documentary Account of Women's Lives in Nineteenth-Century England, France, and the United States*, (Stanford: Stanford University Press, 1981), p. 92.

21. Charles Dickens, *Little Dorrit*, first published 1855–7 (London: Oxford University Press, 1967), Book the Second, Ch. 5, 'Something Wrong Somewhere', p. 477.

22. M. M. Bakhtin, *The Dialogic Imagination*, ed. Michael Holquist, trans. Caryl Emerson and Michael Holquist (Austin: University of Texas Press, 1981).

23. George Eliot, *Middlemarch*, first published 1871–2 (Harmondsworth: Penguin Books, 1985), Ch. 30, pp. 320–1.
24. John R. Reed, *Victorian Conventions* (Ohio: Ohio University Press, 1975), p. 105.
25. See Leonore Davidoff's discussion of the underground theme of father–daughter incest in Victorian literature in 'Class and Gender in Victorian England', in Judith Newton, Mary Ryan and Judith Walkowitz (eds.), *Sex and Class in Women's History* (London: Routledge and Kegan Paul, 1983), p. 22.
26. Cobbett, *Advice to Young Men and (Incidentally) To Young Women*, p. 211.
27. Reed, *Victorian Conventions*, p. 78.
28. *ibid.*, p. 44.
29. Charles Dickens, *Great Expectations*, first published 1860–1 (London: Oxford University Press, 1975), Ch. 29, p. 222.
30. David Bevington, *Action is Eloquence* (London: Harvard University Press, 1984), p. 138.
31. Alfred Lord Tennyson, 'The Princess', in *Poems of Tennyson* (Oxford: Oxford University Press, 1911). For the purposes of this discussion I adopt the modern consensus that views the Victorian narrative poem as the equivalent of a novel in its use of conventions of narrative, structure and character. There are, needless to say, significant differences between the two forms – not least in the greater symbolic patterning of the narrative poem, but it is the *narrative* conventions that provide the common ground that makes them part of the same discourse.
32. Terry Eagleton, 'Tennyson: Politics and Sexuality in 'The Princess' and 'In Memoriam', in *1848: The Sociology of Literature* (papers from Essex University Sociology of Literature Conference, 1977), p. 99.
33. Tennyson, *Poems of Tennyson*, p. 283.
34. Mrs Linton, quoted in Crow, *The Victorian Woman*, p. 326.
35. Charlotte M. Yonge, *Womankind* (London: Walter Smith, 1881), p. 7.
36. Charlotte Brontë, *Shirley*, first published 1849 (Harmondsworth: Penguin Books, 1974), ch. 10, 'Old Maids', p. 190.
37. Nina Auerbach, *Romantic Imprisonment: Woman and Other Glorified Outcasts* (New York: Columbia University Press, 1985); Reed, *Victorian Conventions*. Both authors provide intelligent accounts of this convention, but each assumes that it represents the same thing to all writers, and, as a consequence, they overlook the particular appeal of orphans to women writers.
38. Ivy Pinchbeck and Margaret Hewitt, *Children in English Society*, vol. II (London: Routledge and Kegan Paul, 1973), p. 363.
39. Andrew Mearns, *The Bitter Cry of Outcast London* (Leicester: Leicester University Press, 1970; repr. of 1883 original), p. 63.

40. Florence Nightingale, 'Cassandra', reproduced in Ray Strachey's *The Cause: A Short History of the Women's Movement in Great Britain* (London: Virago, 1978), p. 397.
41. The accounts left by women such as Vera Brittain, Florence Nightingale, Beatrix Potter and Beatrice Webb provide ample evidence of this.
42. From Florence Nightingale's 'Cassandra', p. 412.
43. *ibid.*
44. *ibid.*
45. See particularly Gillian Beer, *Darwin's Plots* (London: Routledge and Kegan Paul, 1984).
46. Sandra M. Gilbert and Susan Gubar, *The Madwoman in the Attic* (London: Yale University Press, 1979), p. 57.
47. Southfield, quoted in Carol Dyhouse, 'The Condition of England 1860–1900', in Lawrence Lerner (ed.), *The Victorians: The Context of English Literature* (London: Methuen, 1978), p. 192.
48. J. S. Bratton, *The Impact of Victorian Children's Fiction* (London: Croom Helm, 1981), p. 148.
49. *ibid.*, p. 159.
50. L. T. Meade, *Polly: A New-Fashioned Girl* (London: Cassell and Co., Ltd, 1889), p. 4.
51. Crow, *The Victorian Woman* p. 196.
52. Dyhouse, 'The Condition of England 1860–1900', p. 132.
53. L. T. Meade, *The Rebellion of Lil Carrington* (London: Cassell and Co., Ltd, 1898), p. 45.

Notes to Chapter 2

1. For a fuller account of this campaign see Glen Petrie, *A Singular Iniquity: The Campaigns of Josephine Butler* (London: Macmillan, 1971); and E. M. Sigsworth and T. J. Wyke, 'A Study of Victorian Prostitution and Venereal Disease' in Martha Vicinus (ed.), *Suffer and Be Still* (London: Indiana University Press, 1973).
2. Elaine Showalter, *A Literature of Their Own: British Women Novelists from Bronte to Lessing* (London: Virago, 1977), p. 193.
3. *ibid*, pp. 183–5; Terry Lovell, *Consuming Fiction* (London: Verso, 1987), pp. 101–2.
4. Nina Auerbach, *Woman and the Demon: The Life of a Victorian Myth* (London: Harvard University Press, 1982), p. 11.
5. George Egerton, 'Gone Under', in *Discords*, first published 1894, reprinted, with *Keynotes* (London: Virago, 1983), p. 104.

6. Cf. Showalter's interesting account of this, *A Literature of Their Own*, pp. 196–7.
7. Grant Allen, *The Woman Who Did* (London: Lane, 1895), pp. 39–40.
8. Reviews quoted in the publisher's advertisement on the fly sheet of *The Woman Who Didn't*, by Victoria Crosse (London: Lane, 1895). Crosse's novel is a clear response to *The Woman Who Did*, which reverses its moral codes (the heroine refuses to elope with her 'one true love', although she dislikes her husband and disapproves of the social institution of marriage, because she feels herself bound by a sacred bond that is independent from the debased nature of marriage in her society) but presents a similarly principled and unlikely heroine.
9. Millicent Garrett Fawcett, 'Review of *The Woman Who Did*', *The Contemporary Review*, 67 (May 1895), p. 265.
10. Patricia Stubbs, *Women and Fiction: Feminism and the Novel, 1880–1920* (Brighton: Harvester, 1979), Gail Cunningham, *The New Woman and the Victorian Novel* (London: Macmillan, 1978), John Goode, 'Women and the Literary Text', in Juliet Mitchell and Ann Oakley (eds.), *The Rights and Wrongs of Women* (Harmondsworth: Penguin Books, 1976).
11. Lovell, *Consuming Fiction*, p. 111.
12. Thomas Hardy, *Jude the Obscure*, first published 1895 (Oxford: Oxford University Press, 1990), p. 223.
13. Stubbs, *Women and Fiction*, p. 64.
14. Michel Foucault, *The History of Sexuality*, vol. I, *An Introduction*, trans. Robert Hurley (Harmondsworth: Penguin Books, 1979), p. 3.
15. See Stubbs, *Women and Fiction*, p. 118, where she sees *The Woman Who Did* 'poor though the novel is', as an 'attempt to shift the terms of the feminist argument away from the "safe" issues of work and the vote and into the more explosive issues of sex, marriage and maternity.'
16. A great deal of work has been done on the representation of the prostitute in the nineteenth-century. Stephen Marcus's seminal work on *The Other Victorians: A Study of Sexuality and Pornography in Mid-Nineteenth Century England* (London: Meridian, 1977) established the terms for much later work, with its examination of the ways in which the discourse of pornography impinged on other, apparently sexually uninflected, canonical discourses. Lynda Nead, in *Myths of Sexuality: Representations of Women in Victorian Britain* (Oxford: Basil Blackwell, 1988), explores visual and other non-literary representations of women in Victorian England. Françoise Basch devotes an entire third of her *Relative Creatures: Victorian Women in Society and the Novel 1837–1867* (trans. Anthony Rudolf, London: Allan Lane, 1974) to fallen women, exploring nineteenth-century legal, journalistic and charitable accounts of prostitution and comparing these to the novelistic representation of 'vice' in the works of Dickens, Thackeray,

Elizabeth Gaskell and George Eliot. Helena Michie, in *The Flesh Made Word: Female Figures and Women's Bodies* (Oxford: Oxford University Press, 1987) considers the tropes employed in nineteenth-century descriptions of prostitutes' bodies. George Watt, in *The Fallen Woman in the Nineteenth-Century English Novel* (London: Croom Helm, 1984) considers the extent to which fictional representations of fallen women and prostitutes throughout the course of the century engaged with and influenced changing social attitudes to the phenomenon of prostitution and the extent to which they challenged the cultural dichotomy of the 'two women'.

17. W. R. Greg, *The Great Sin of the Great Cities*, (London, 1853), p. 11.
18. Henry Mayhew, *London Labour and the London Poor*, 4 vols, with introduction by John D. Rosenberg (New York: Dover Publications, 1968, vol. IV, p. 219).
19. William Acton, *Prostitution Considered in its Moral, Social and Sanitary Aspects*, first published 1857 (London: Cass, 1972; repr. of 2nd edn of 1870), p. ix.
20. Greg, *The Great Sin of the Great Cities*, pp. 12–13.
21. Elizabeth Barrett Browning, *Aurora Leigh*, first published 1857 (London: The Women's Press, 1982), Ninth Book, ll, 402–15.
22. As was demonstrated by the campaign against the Contagious Diseases Acts, middle-class women could legitimately drop their veil of ignorance when addressing the issue of fallen women.
23. Jeanne Fahnstock, 'The Heroine of Irregular Features: Physiognomy and Conventions of Heroine Description', *Victorian Studies*, 24, 3 (Spring 1981), pp. 326–50.
24. Wilkie Collins, *The Woman in White*, first published 1860 (Harmondsworth: Penguin Books, 1985), pp. 74–5.
25. Elizabeth Gaskell, *Mary Barton* first published in 1848 (Harmondsworth: Penguin Books, 1985).
26. Charlotte Brontë, *Villette*, first published 1853 (Harmondsworth: Penguin, 1985), p. 283.
27. T. J. Edelstein has a fascinating list of examples of this theme in 'They Sang "The Song of the Shirt": The Visual Iconology of the Seamstress', *Victorian Studies*, 23, 2 (Winter 1980), pp. 183–210.
28. Elizabeth Gaskell, *North and South*, first published 1855 (Harmondsworth: Penguin Books, 1986), p. 39.

Notes to Chapter 3

1. Griselda Pollock, *Vision and Difference: Feminity, Feminism and the History of Art* (London: Routledge, 1988); Laura Mulvey, *Visual and*

Other Pleasures (London: Macmillan, 1989), and 'Visual Pleasures and Narrative Cinema', *Screen*, 16, 3 (1975). My attention was directed to Pollock and Mulvey's work by Lynne Pearce's introduction to *Woman, Image, Text: Readings in Pre-Raphaelite Art and Literature* (Hemel Hempstead: Harvester Wheatsheaf, 1991).

2. Pearce, *ibid.*, p. 17.
3. Helena Michie, *The Flesh Made Word: Female Figures and Women's Bodies* (Oxford: Oxford University Press, 1987), p. 127.
4. Alfred Lord Tennyson, *The Princess*, in *Poems of Tennyson* (Oxford: Oxford University Press, 1911), Song IX.
5. Cited in Bram Dijkstra, *Idols of Perversity: Fantasies of Feminine Evil in Fin-de-Siècle Culture* (Oxford: Oxford University Press, 1986), p. 45.
6. A good survey of such works is provided in the opening section of Chapter 4.
7. Elizabeth Gaskell, *North and South*, first published 1855 (Harmondsworth: Penguin Books, 1986), p. 35.
8. For instance, R. K. R. Thornton in *The Decadent Dilemma* (London: Edward Arnold, 1983), p. 69, confines decadence to the years 1889–97.
9. Max Beerbohm, quoted in John M. Munroe, *The Decadent Poetry of the 1890s* (Beirut: American University of Beirut Press, 1970), p. 3.
10. *ibid.*
11. *ibid.*, p. 7.
12. Stephen Prickett, *Victorian Fantasy* (Brighton: Harvester, 1979); Sandra M. Gilbert and Susan Gubar, *The Madwoman in the Attic: The Woman Writer and the Nineteenth-Century Literary Imagination* (London: Yale University Press, 1979); and Gillian Beer, *Darwin's Plots* (London: Routledge and Kegan Paul, 1984).
13. The theme for the Great Exhibition of 1851, interestingly elaborated in J. G. Farrell's novel, *The Siege of Krishnapur* (Harmondsworth: Penguin Books, 1982).
14. R. K. R. Thornton, 'Decadence in Later-Nineteenth Century England', in Ian Fletcher (ed.), *Decadence and the 1890s* (London: Edward Arnold 1979), p. 15.
15. Cited in *ibid.*, p. 17.
16. Quoted in Bernard Bergonzi, *The Turn of a Century: Essays on Victorian and Modern English Literature* (London: Macmillan, 1973), p. 39.
17. See M. M. Bakhtin, *The Dialogic Imagination*, ed. Michael Holquist, trans. Caryl Emerson and Michael Holquist (Austin: University of Texas Press, 1981).
18. From Mikhail Bakhtin, *Problems of Dostoievski's Poetics* (1929), quoted

in J. A. Cuddon, *A Dictionary of Literary Terms*, 3rd edn, (Oxford: Basil Blackwell, 1991).

19. Thanks are due to the late Allon White for this summary of Bakhtin's theories which originated in his series of Modern European Mind lectures at the University of Sussex, 1983; 1985.

20. George Eliot, *Felix Holt, The Radical*, first published 1866 (London: Panther, 1965), p. 13.

21. Steven Marcus, *The Other Victorians: A Study of Sexuality and Pornography in Mid-Nineteenth Century England* (London: Meridian, 1977).

22. Helena Michie writes interestingly about the fragmentation and fetishisation of heroines' bodies in ch. 4 of *The Flesh Made Word: Female Figures and Women's Bodies* (Oxford: Oxford University Press, 1987).

23. *ibid.*, p. 103.

24. Prickett, *Victorian Fantasy*, p. 30.

25. Christopher Wood, *Olympian Dreamers: Victorian Classical Painters 1860–1914* (London: Constable, 1983), p. 246.

26. *ibid.*, p. 246.

27. *ibid.*, p. 150.

28. Walter Pater, *The Renaissance: Studies in Art and Poetry* (London: Collins, 1961), p. 123.

29. *ibid.*

30. Humphrey Carpenter, *Secret Gardens: A Study of the Golden Age of Children's Literature* (London: Allen and Unwin, 1985), p. 30.

31. *ibid.*, Ch. 1. See also Susan Chitty's biography, *The Beast and the Monk* (London: Hodder and Stoughton, 1974).

32. Teresa Brennan (ed.), *Between Feminism and Psychoanalysis* (London: Routledge, 1989), p. 11. Brennan's argument (based on Foucault) is that to maintain a separate identity it is necessary to define the self against another. This characteristically results in aggression towards the other who threatens separateness.

33. *ibid.*, pp. 1 and 9. See also Sander Gilman, *Difference and Pathology: Stereotypes of Sexuality, Race and Madness* (Ithaca, N.Y.: Cornell University Press, 1985).

34. George Eliot, *The Mill on the Floss* first published 1860 (London: Routledge, 1991), p. 3. See Elaine Showalter's introduction to Sarah Grand, *The Beth Book* (London: Virago, 1980).

35. A useful discussion of this and other metaphors for the female body is found in Avril Horner and Sue Zlosnik's *Landscapes of Desire: Metaphors in Modern Women's Fiction* (Hemel Hempstead: Harvester Wheatsheaf, 1990).

Notes to Chapter 4

1. M. E. Braddon, *Lady Audley's Secret*, first published 1862 (London: Tinsley Bros., 1863), p. 154.
2. Winifred Hughes, *The Maniac in the Cellar: Sensation Novels of the 1860s* (Princeton: Princeton University Press, 1980), p. 66.
3. Elaine Showalter, *A Literature of Their Own: British Women Novelists from Brontë to Lessing* (London: Virago, 1977), p. 162.
4. Henry James, 'Miss Braddon', *Notes and Reviews* (Cambridge, Mass.: Dunster House, 1921), pp. 115–16.
5. Mrs Henry Wood, *East Lynne*, first published 1861 (London: Dent, 1988), p. v.
6. Hughes, *The Maniac in the Cellar*, p. 112.
7. Louisa May Alcott, *Good Wives*, first published 1869 (London: Thomas W. Jacques Ltd, n.d.), ch. IV, 'Literary Lessons', p. 40.
8. Francis Paget, *Lucretia: or the Heroine of the Nineteenth Century* (London, 1868), p. 297; quoted in Showalter, *A Literature of Their Own*, p. 161.
9. Leslie Fiedler suggests that the potential for mass production and distribution of the novel in the machine age made the bestseller an embodiment of the collective unconscious: 'the machine' produced commodity novel is, therefore, dream-literature, as surely as any tale told over the tribal fire. Its success, too, depends on the degree to which it responds to the shared dreams, the myths which move its intended audience' ('The Death and Rebirth of the Novel', in John Halperin (ed.), *The Theory of the Novel* (New York: Oxford University Press, 1974), p. 191; cited in Showalter, *ibid.*, p. 159.
10. The other major formal influence Hughes finds for the genre is theatrical melodrama, from which derives the stereotypical encounter between evil villains and pure heroines. Given the fact, however – as Hughes herself notes – that such a schema and such characterizations are mocked and undermined by all the major examples of the sensation genre, it is clear that melodrama is more a source ironically departed from than a genuine model.
11. Thomas Boyle, *Black Swine in the Sewers of Hampstead: Beneath the Surface of Victorian Sensationalism* (London: Hodder and Stoughton, 1990).
12. Interspersed at intervals throughout the text is the story of Boyle as scholar–detective, investigating his subject in the libraries of the world – an account that effectively (if unintentionally) imitates the self-regarding naivity of the investigative accounts of the amateur detectives within the sensation novel.

13. For critical accounts working from a contention of the radical threat posed by the sensation novel to contemporary values see Anthea Trodd, *Domestic Crime in the Victorian Novel* (London: Macmillan, 1989); Showalter, *A Literature of Their Own*, ch. VI; Hughes, *The Maniac in the Cellar*.

14. [Oliphant], 'Novels', *Blackwood's Magazine*, CII (11 September 1867), p. 259; quoted in Hughes, *ibid.*, p. 28.

15. Anon., 'Past and Present Heroines of Fiction', *The Saturday Review* (28 July 1883).

16. [H. L. Mansell], 'Sensation Novels', *The Quarterly Review*, CXIII (April 1863), p. 486.

17. James, 'Miss Braddon', p. 113; in Hughes, *The Maniac in the Cellar*, p. 23.

18. M. E. Braddon, *Aurora Floyd*, first published 1863 (New York, 1890), p. 19.

19. Wilkie Collins, *No Name*, first published 1862 (Oxford: Oxford University Press, 1992; reprint of the edition of 1864), p. 4.

20. Hughes, *The Maniac in the Cellar*, p. 113.

21. [Oliphant], 'Novels' (1867), p. 263; quoted in Hughes, *ibid.*, p. 30.

22. 'Our Female Sensation Novelists', *Living Age* LXXVIII (August 22, 1863), p. 365; quoted in Hughes, *ibid.*, p. 59.

23. Cf. Peter Gay, *The Bourgeois Experience from Victoria to Freud*, vol. I, *The Education of the Senses* (Oxford: Oxford University Press, 1984), p. 153.

24. 'Women's desires scarcely ever lead to their fall . . . the desire scarcely exists in a definite and conscious form . . . till they have fallen' ([W. R. Greg], 'Art. VII–I. De la prostitution dans la ville de Paris, par Parent-Duchâtelet . . .', *Westminster Review*, III (June 1850), pp. 456–57; cited in Gay, *ibid.*, p. 155.

25. E. S. Dallas, *The Gay Science* (London: Chapman and Hall, 1866), vol. II, pp. 297, 298; quoted in Hughes, *The Maniac in the Cellar*, p. 44.

26. Helena Michie, *The Flesh Made Word: Female Figures and Women's Bodies* (Oxford: Oxford University Press, 1987), p. 46.

27. Patricia Thomson, *The Victorian Heroine: A Changing Ideal, 1837–1873* (London: Oxford University Press, 1956), p. 56.

28. Patricia Thomson suggests Becky Sharpe as the literary model for all 'bad' governesses (*ibid.*, p. 49).

29. Henry James, *The Turn of the Screw*, first published 1898 (London: Dent & Sons, 1967).

30. Charles Reade, 'Charles Reade's Opinions of Himself and His Opinion of George Eliot', *Bookman* XVIII (November 1903), reprinted from an article in *Once a Week* (1872).

31. Lewis Carroll, *Alice in Wonderland and Through the Looking-Glass*, first published 1865 and 1872, (London: Macmillan, 1968).

32. Robert Browning, *The Ring and the Book*, first published 1868–9 (Harmondsworth: Penguin Books, 1981).
33. See, for example, R. D. Altick and J. F. Loucks, *Browning's Roman Murder Story: A Reading of 'The Ring and the Book'* (Chicago: University of Chicago Press, 1968).
34. George Eliot, *Letters*, ed. G. Haight (London: Oxford University Press 1954–68), vol. IV, p. 310 and vol. VI, p. 345.
35. Trodd, *Domestic Crime*, pp. 123–9.
36. Mrs Oliphant, 'Chronicles of Carlingford: Salem Chapel', *Blackwood's Edinburgh Magazine* LXXXXI–LXXXXIII (1862–3), published in 2 vols as *Salem Chapel* (1863).
37. See R. C. Terry, *Victorian Popular Fiction, 1860–80* (London: Macmillan, 1983), pp. 81, 85.
38. Trodd, *Domestic Crime*, pp. 128–9.
39. This summary derives in part from Anthea Trodd's fuller account of the novel in *Domestic Crime* (pp. 116–20).

Notes to Chapter 5

1. My attention was directed to this quote by Susanna Egan in *Patterns of Experience in Autobiography* (London: University of North Carolina Press, 1984), p. 17.
2. For discussions of the rise of masculine autobiography see especially Estelle C. Jelinek (ed.), *Women's Autobiography: Essays in Criticism* (Bloomington: Indiana University Press, 1980) and G. P. Landow (ed.), *Approaches to Victorian Autobiography* (Athens, Ohio: Ohio University Press, 1979).
3. Charles Dickens, *Hard Times*, first published 1854, p. 13.
4. See especially Susan Stanford Friedman, 'Women's Autobiographical Selves: Theory and Practice', in Shari Benstock (ed.), *The Private Self*, (London: Routledge, 1988).
5. Patricia Meyer Spacks, 'Reflecting Women', in *Yale Review*, (63), 1973.
6. Moers, Ellen, *Literary Women*, (London: The Women's Press, 1978), p. 13.
7. Georges Gusdorf, 'Conditions and Limits of Autobiography' trans. James Olney in James Olney (ed.), *Autobiography: Essays Theoretical and Critical* (Princeton: Princeton University Press, 1980), p. 30.
8. See, for instance, Friedman, 'Women's Autobiographical Selves', Jelinek, *Women's Autobiography*; and Patricia Meyer Spacks, *The Female Imagination* (New York: Knopf, 1972), and 'Reflecting Women'.

9. A good discussion of the relationship between living conditions and working-class morality is provided in the early chapters of Françoise Barret-Ducrocq's *Love in the Time of Victoria*, trans. John Howe (London: Verso, 1991).

10. Virginia Woolf, *A Room of One's Own*, first published 1929 (London: Grafton Books, 1977), p. 6.

11. A discussion of three contemporary experiments in autobiographical form is provided by Laura Marcus in 'Enough About You, Let's Talk About Me: Recent Autobiographical Writing', *New Formations*, 1 (Spring 1987).

12. Friedman, 'Women's Autobiographical Selves', p. 35.

13. Nancy Chodorow, *The Reproduction of Mothering* (Berkley: University of California Press, 1978), p. 106.

14. Benstock, *The Private Self*; Jelinek, *Women's Autobiography*; Olney, *Autobiography*; Spacks, *The Female Imagination*, 'Reflecting Women'; Elizabeth Wilson, 'Tell It Like It Is: Women and Confessional Writing', in Susannah Redstone (ed.), *Sweet Dreams: Sexuality, Gender and Popular Fiction* (London: Lawrence and Wishart, 1988).

15. Jean-Jacques Rousseau, *Confessions*, first published 1781–8 (Harmondsworth: Penguin, 1953), quoted in Peter Abbs, *Autobiography in Education* (London: Heinemann, 1974), pp. 38–9.

16. Gusdorf, 'Conditions and Limits of Autobiography', p. 31.

17. Hannah Cullwick, *Diaries*, (ed. Liz Stanley, London: Virago, 1984), p. 2.

18. Leonore Davidoff, 'Class and Gender in Victorian England', in Judith Newton, Mary Ryan and Judith Walkowitz (eds.), *Sex and Class in Women's History* (London: Routledge and Kegan Paul, 1983).

19. Derek Hudson, *Munby: Man of Two Worlds* (London: Abacus, 1974), p. 8.

20. Helena Michie, *The Flesh Made Word: Female Figures and Women's Bodies* (Oxford: Oxford University Press, 1987).

21. Judy Simons, *Diaries and Journals of Literary Women from Fanny Burney to Virginia Woolf* (London: Macmillan, 1990), pp. 3–4. Beatrix Potter is an interesting exception to this communal tendency. She wrote her journal in an elaborate code which kept it entirely private and personal until deciphered and published by Leslie Linder in 1966.

22. Marilyn R. Chandler, *A Healing Art: Regeneration Through Autobiography* (London: Garland Publishing, 1990), p. 54.

23. *ibid.*, pp. 53–4.

24. See Ch. 8 in Chodorow, *The Reproduction of Mothering*.

25. G. Kitson-Clark, *The Making of Victorian England* (London: Methuen, 1965), pp. 29–30.

26. These arguments are rehearsed and an extensive bibliography provided by Ann B. Murphy in 'The Borders of Ethical, Erotic, and Artistic Possibilities in *Little Women*', *Signs*, 15, 3 (Spring 1990).
27. *ibid.*, p. 581.
28. Elaine Showalter, *Alternative Alcott: Louisa May Alcott* (New Brunswick: Rutgers University Press, 1988), p. xxii.
29. *ibid.*, p. xi.
30. See Showalter, *ibid.*, p. xii; also Marmee's advice to Jo in 'Jo Meets Apollyon' in *Little Women*.
31. Showalter, *ibid.*, p. xx.
32. *ibid.*, p. xx.
33. *ibid.*, p. xviii.
34. Moers, *Literary Women*, p. 13.
35. Simons, *Diaries and Journals of Literary Women from Fanny Burney to Virginia Woolf*, p. 14.
36. Moers *Literary Women*, p. 13.
37. Roy Pascal, *Design and Truth in Autobiography* (Cambridge, MA: Harvard University Press, 1960), p. 163.
38. See Trevor Blount's introduction to Charles Dickens, *David Copperfield* (Harmondsworth: Penguin Books, 1966), p. 22.
39. *ibid.*, p. 23.
40. Taken from the 1847 autobiographical fragment given to John Forster and used by him in writing *The Life of Charles Dickens* (1872–4); reproduced in Stephen Wall (ed.), *Charles Dickens: A Critical Anthology* (Harmondsworth: Penguin Books, 1970), p. 39.
41. See John Forster's *The Life of Charles Dickens*, 3 vols, first published 1872–4 (London: Dent, 1966, rev. edn).
42. Chandler, *A Healing Art*, p. 185.

Bibliography

'A Century of Feminine Fiction', (Anon.) in *All the Year Round* (December 1894).

Abbs, Peter, *Autobiography in Education* (London: Heinemann, 1974).

Acton, William, *Prostitution Considered in its Moral, Social and Sanitary Aspects*, first published 1857 (London: Cass, 1972; repr. of 2nd edn of 1870).

Acton, William, *The Functions and Disorders of the Reproductive Organs, in Childhood, Youth, Adult Age, and Advanced Life* (London: John Churchill, 1857).

Alcott, Louisa May, *Good Wives*, first published 1869 (London: Thomas W. Jacques Ltd, n.d.).

Alcott, Louisa May, *Little Women*, first published 1868 (London: Frederick Warne & Co., n.d.).

Alexander, Sally, 'Women, Class, and Sexual Difference in the 1830s and 1840s: Some Reflections on the Writing of a Feminist History', *History Workshop Journal*, 17 (Spring 1984).

Allen, Grant, *The Woman Who Did* (London: Lane, 1895).

Altick, R. D. and Loucks, J. F., *Browning's Roman Murder Story: A Reading of 'The Ring and the Book'* (Chicago: University of Chicago Press, 1968).

Armstrong, Nancy, *Desire and Domestic Fiction* (New York: Oxford University Press, 1987).

Auerbach, Nina, *Romantic Imprisonment: Woman and Other Glorified Outcasts* (New York: Columbia University Press, 1985).

Auerbach, Nina, *Woman and the Demon: The Life of a Victorian Myth* (London: Harvard University Press, 1982).

Bakhtin, M. M., *The Dialogic Imagination*, ed. Michael Holquist, trans. Caryl Emerson and Michael Holquist (Austin: University of Texas Press, 1981).

Barret-Ducrocq, Françoise, *Love in the Time of Victoria*, trans. John Howe (London: Verso, 1991).

Barrett Browning, Elizabeth, *Aurora Leigh*, first published 1857 (London: The Women's Press, 1982).

Basch, Françoise, *Relative Creatures: Victorian Women in Society and the Novel 1837–1867*, trans. Anthony Rudolf (London: Allen Lane, 1974).

Beer, Gillian, *Darwin's Plots* (London: Routledge and Kegan Paul, 1984).

Belsey, Catherine, *Critical Practice* (London: Methuen, 1980).

Benstock, Shari (ed.), *The Private Self: Theory and Practice of Women's Autobiographical Writings* (London: Routledge, 1988).

Bergonzi, Bernard, *The Turn of a Century: Essays on Victorian and Modern English Literature* (London: Macmillan, 1973).

Bevington, David, *Action is Eloquence* (London: Harvard University Press, 1984).

Blake, Andrew, *Reading Victorian Fiction: The Cultural Context and Ideological Content of the Nineteenth-Century Novel* (London: Macmillan, 1989).

Bloom, Clive, Brian Docherty, Jane Gibbs and Keith Shand, *Nineteenth Century Suspense: From Poe to Conan Doyle* (London: Macmillan, 1988).

Boyle, Thomas, *Black Swine in the Sewers of Hampstead: Beneath the Surface of Victorian Sensation* (London: Hodder and Stoughton, 1990).

Bradbury, Malcolm and MacFarlane, James, *Modernism* (Harmondsworth: Penguin Books, 1981).

Braddon, M. E., *Aurora Floyd*, first published 1863 (New York, 1890).

Braddon, M. E., *Lady Audley's Secret*, (London: Tinsley Bros., 1863).

Bratton, J. S., *The Impact of Victorian Children's Fiction* (London: Croom Helm, 1981).

Brennan, Teresa (ed.), *Between Feminism and Psychoanalysis* (London: Routledge, 1989).

Brennan, Teresa, *The Interpretation of the Flesh: Freud and Femininity* (London: Routledge, 1992)

Brontë, Charlotte, *Jane Eyre*, first published 1847 (Harmondsworth: Penguin Books, 1966).

Brontë, Charlotte, *Shirley*, first published 1849 (Harmondsworth: Penguin Books, 1974).

Brontë, Charlotte, *Villette*, first published 1853 (Harmondsworth: Penguin Books, 1985).

Brown, E. K. and Bailey, J. O. (eds.), *Victorian Poetry* (New York: State University of New York Press, 1962).

Browning, Robert, *The Ring and the Book*, first published 1868–9 (Harmondsworth: Penguin Books, 1981).

Burrow, J. W., 'The Sense of the Past', in Laurence Lerner (ed.), *The Victorians, the Context of English Literature* (London: Methuen, 1978).

Carpenter, Humphrey, *Secret Gardens: A Study of the Golden Age of Children's Literature* (London: Allen and Unwin, 1985).

Carpenter, Humphrey, and Prichard, Mari, *The Oxford Companion to Children's Literature* (London: Oxford University Press, 1984).

Carroll, Lewis, *Alice in Wonderland*, first published 1865 and *Through the Looking-Glass*, first published 1872 (London: Macmillan, 1968).

Chandler, Marilyn R., *A Healing Art: Regeneration Through Autobiography* (London: Garland Publishing, 1990).

Chitty, Susan, *The Beast and the Monk* (London: Hodder and Stoughton, 1974).

Chodorow, Nancy, *The Reproduction of Mothering* (Berkley: University of California Press, 1978).

Clarke, Norma, 'Feminism and the Popular Novel of the 1890s: A Brief Consideration of a Forgotten Feminist Novelist', *Feminist Review*, 20 (June 1985).

Cobbett, William, *Advice to Young Men and (Incidentally) to Young Women*, first published 1830 (London: Peter Davies Ltd, 1926).

Colby, Vineta, *Yesterday's Woman: Domestic Realism in the English Novel* (Princeton: Princeton University Press, 1974).

Collins, Wilkie, *Armadale*, first published 1866 (New York: Dover, 1977).

Collins, Wilkie, *No Name*, first published 1862 (Oxford: Oxford University Press, 1992; reprint of the edn of 1864).

Collins, Wilkie, *The Woman in White*, first published 1860 (Harmondsworth: Penguin Books, 1985).

Conrad, Peter, *The Victorian Treasure House* (London: Collins, 1973).

Coolidge, Susan, *What Katy Did*, first published 1872 (Harmondsworth: Puffin Books, 1985).

Cosslett, Tess, *Woman to Woman: Female Friendship in Victorian Fiction* (Brighton: Harvester, 1988).

Cott, Nancy F. 'Passionlessness: An Interpretation of Victorian Sexual Ideology, 1790–1850', *Signs*, 4, 2 (1978), pp. 219–36.

Croser, Rose Laub (ed.), *The Family: Its Structures and Functions* (New York: St Martin's Press, 1974).

Crosse, Victoria, *The Woman Who Didn't* (London: Lane, 1895).

Crow, Duncan, *The Victorian Woman* (London: George Allen and Unwin, 1971).

Cruse, Amy, *The Victorians and Their Books* (London: George Allen and Unwin, 1935).

Cuddon, J. A., *A Dictionary of Literary Terms*, 3rd edn (Oxford: Basil Blackwell, 1991).

Cunningham, Gail, *The New Woman and the Victorian Novel* (London: Macmillan, 1978)

Cunningham, Valentine, 'Soiled Fairy: *The Water-Babies* in its Time',

Essays in Criticism, **XXXV**, 2 (April 1985).

Dallas, E. S., *The Gay Science* (London: Chapman Hall, 1866).

Davidoff, Leonore, 'Class and Gender in Victorian England', in Judith Newton, Mary Ryan and Judith Walkowitz (eds), *Sex and Class in Women's History* (London: Routledge and Kegan Paul, 1983).

Denvir, Bernard, *The Early Nineteenth-Century: Art, Design, and Society 1789–1852* (London: Longman, 1984).

Dickens, Charles, *A Tale of Two Cities,* first published 1859. (Harmondsworth: Penguin Books, 1985).

Dickens, Charles, *Bleak House,* first published 1852–3 (Harmondsworth: Penguin Books, 1971).

Dickens, Charles, *David Copperfield,* first published 1849–50 (Harmondsworth: Penguin Books, 1966).

Dickens, Charles, *Dombey and Son,* first published 1848 (Harmondsworth: Penguin Books, 1985).

Dickens, Charles, *Great Expectations,* first published 1860–1 (London: Oxford University Press, 1965)

Dickens, Charles, *Hard Times,* first published 1854 (London: J. M. Dent, 1969).

Dickens, Charles, *Little Dorrit,* first published 1855–7 (London: Oxford University Press, 1967).

Dickens, Charles, *Oliver Twist,* first published 1837–9 (Harmondsworth: Penguin Books, 1985)

Dickens, Charles, *Nicholas Nickleby,* first published 1839 (Harmondsworth: Penguin Books, 1978).

Dijkstra, Bram, *Idols of Perversity: Fantasies of Feminine Evil in Fin-de-Siècle Culture* (Oxford: Oxford University Press, 1986).

Dodd, P. (ed.), *Modern Selves: Essays on British and American Autobiography* (London: Frank Cass, 1986).

Dowling, Linda, 'The Decadent and the New Woman in the 1890's', *Nineteenth-Century Fiction* 33, 4 (March 1979).

Dyhouse, Carol, 'The Condition of England 1860–1900', in Laurence Lerner (ed.), *The Victorians: The Context of English Literature* (London: Methuen, 1978).

Eagleton, Terry, 'Tennyson: Politics and Sexuality in *The Princess* and *In Memoriam*' in F. Barker *et al.* (eds), *1848: The Sociology of Literature* (papers from the Essex University Sociology of Literature Conference, 1977).

Edelstein, T. J., 'They Sang "The Song of the Shirt": The Visual Iconology of the Seamstress', *Victorian Studies*, 23, 2 (Winter 1980) pp. 183–210.

Egan, Susanna, *Patterns of Experience in Autobiography* (London: University of North Carolina Press, 1984).

Egerton, George, *Keynotes*, first published 1893, and *Discords*, first published 1894 (London: Virago, 1983).

Eliot, George, *Adam Bede*, first published 1859 (London: Collins, n.d.).

Eliot, George, *Daniel Deronda*, first published 1874–6 (Harmondsworth: Penguin Books, 1986).

Eliot, George, *Essays* (London: William Blackwood and Sons, n.d.).

Eliot, George, *Felix Holt, The Radical*, first published 1866 (London: Panther, 1965).

Eliot, George, *Letters*, ed. G. Haight (London: Oxford University Press, 1954–68).

Eliot, George, *Middlemarch*, first published 1871–72 (Harmondsworth; Penguin Books, 1985).

Eliot, George, *The Mill on the Floss*, first published 1860 (London: Routledge, 1991).

Ellis, Havelock, *Studies in the Psychology of Sex*, first published 1903, 2nd rev. edn (Philadelphia: F. A. Davis Co., 1913).

Engels, Frederick, *The Condition of the Working Classes in England*, first published 1845 (London: Allen and Unwin, 1920).

Fahnestock, Jeanne, 'The Heroine of Irregular Features: Physiognomy and Conventions of Heroine Description', *Victorian Studies*, 24, 3 (Spring 1981) pp. 326–50.

Farrell, J. G., *The Siege of Krishnapur*, (Harmondsworth: Penguin Books, 1982).

Fawcett, Millicent Garrett, 'Review of *The Woman Who Did*', *The Contemporary Review*, 67 (May 1895).

Fiedler, Leslie, 'The Death and Rebirth of the Novel' in John Halperin (ed.), *The Theory of the Novel* (New York: Oxford University Press, 1974).

Forster, John, *The Life of Charles Dickens*, 3 vols., first published 1872–4, rev. edn (London: Dent, 1966).

Foucault, Michel, *The History of Sexuality*, vol. I, *An Introduction*, trans. Robert Hurley (Harmondsworth: Penguin Books, 1979).

Friedman, Susan Stanford, 'Women's Autobiographical Selves: Theory and Practice', in Shari Benstock (ed.), *The Private Self* (London: Routledge, 1979).

Gaskell, Elizabeth, *Mary Barton*, first published 1848 (Harmondsworth: Penguin Books, 1985).

Gaskell, Elizabeth, *North and South*, first published 1855 (Harmondsworth: Penguin Books, 1986).

Gay, Peter, *The Bourgeois Experience from Victoria to Freud*, vol. I, *The Education of the Senses* (Oxford: Oxford University Press, 1984).

Gilbert, Sandra M. and Gubar, Susan, *The Madwoman in the Attic: The Woman Writer and the Nineteenth-Century Literary Imagination* (London: Yale University Press, 1979).

Gilman, Richard, *Decadence: The Strange Life of an Epiphet* (London: Secker and Warburg, 1979).

Gilman, Sander, L., *Difference and Pathology: Stereotypes of Sexuality, Race and Madness* (Ithaca, N.Y.: Cornell University Press, 1985).

Gissing, George, *The Odd Women*, first published 1893 (New York: W. W. Norton & Co., 1971).

Goode, John, *Thomas Hardy: The Offensive Truth* (Oxford, Basil Blackwell, 1985).

Goode, John, 'Woman and the Literary Text', in Juliet Mitchell and Ann Oakley (eds), *The Rights and Wrongs of Women* (Harmondsworth: Penguin Books, 1976).

Gorham, Deborah, *The Victorian Girl and the Feminine Ideal* (London: Croom Helm, 1982).

Grand, Sarah, *The Beth Book* (London: Virago, 1980).

Greg, W. R., 'Art. VII – I. De la prostitution dans la ville de Paris par Parent-Duchâtelet', *Westminster Review*, III (June 1850).

Greg, W. R., *The Great Sin of the Great Cities* (London, 1853).

Gusdorf, Georges, 'Conditions and Limits of Autobiography' trans. James Olney in James Olney (ed.), *Autobiography: Essays Theoretical and Critical* (Princeton, NJ: Princeton University Press, 1980).

Hardman, Malcolm, *Six Victorian Thinkers* (Manchester: Manchester University Press, 1991).

Hardy, Thomas, *Desperate Remedies*, first published 1871 (London: Harper, 1896).

Hardy, Thomas, *Jude the Obscure*, first published 1895 (Oxford: Oxford University Press, 1990).

Heath, Stephen, *The Sexual Fix* (London: Macmillan, 1982).

Heilbrun, Carolyn G., *Writing a Woman's Life* (London: The Women's Press, 1989).

Hellerstein, Erna Olafson, Hume, Leslie Parker and Otten, Karen M. (eds), *Victorian Women: A Documentary Account of Women's Lives in Nineteenth-Century England, France, and the United States* (Stanford: Stanford University Press, 1981).

Horner, Avril, and Zlosnick, Sue, *Landscapes of Desire: Metaphors in Modern Woman's Fiction* (Hemel Hempstead: Harvester, 1990).

Houghton, Walter, E., *The Victorian Frame of Mind 1830–1870* (New Haven and London: Yale University Press, 1957).

Hudson, Derek, *Munby: Man of Two Worlds* (London: Abacus Books, 1974).

Hughes, Winifred, *The Maniac in the Cellar: Sensation Novels of the 1860s* (Princeton: Princeton University Press, 1980).

Irwin, David, *English Neoclassical Art: Studies in Inspiration and Taste* (London: Faber and Faber, 1966).

Irwin, Michael, *Picturing: Description and Illusion in the Nineteenth Century Novel* (London: George Allen & Unwin, 1979).

Jackson, Holbrook, *The 1890s: A Review of Art and Ideas at the Close of the Nineteenth Century* (Brighton: Harvester Press, 1976).

James, Henry, 'Miss Braddon', in *Notes and Reviews* (Cambridge, Mass.: Dunster House, 1921).

James, Henry, *The Turn of the Screw*, first published 1898 (London: Dent & Sons, 1967).

Jelinek, Estelle C. (ed.), *Women's Autobiography: Essays in Criticism* (Bloomington: Indiana University Press, 1980).

Kempe, Margery, *The Book of Margery Kempe*, written in 1436.

Kingsley, Charles, *The Water-Babies: A Fairy Tale for a Land-Baby*, first published 1863 (London: Dean and Son, n.d.)

Kitson-Clark, G., *The Making of Victorian England* (London: Methuen, 1965)

Landow, G. P. (ed.), *Approaches to Victorian Autobiography* (Athens: Ohio University Press, 1979).

Lerner, Lawrence, *Love and Marriage: Literature and Its Social Context* (London: Arnold, 1979).

Lévi-Strauss, Claude, *Elementary Kinship Structures*, trans. J. H. Bell, J. R. von Sturmer and Rodney Needham (London: Eyre and Spottiswoode, 1964).

Levine, Phillipa, *Victorian Feminism 1850–1900* (London: Hutchinson, 1987).

Lewis, Henry, *The Monk* (London: Routledge, 1907).

Lovell, Terry, *Consuming Fiction* (London: Verso, 1987).

MacDonald, George, *The Princess and the Goblin*, first published 1870–71 (London: Blackie & Son, 1960)

Mahood, Linda, *The Magdalenes: Prostitution in the Nineteenth Century* (London: Routledge, 1990).

[Mansell, H. L.], 'Sensation Novels', *The Quarterly Review*, CXIII (April 1863).

Marcus, Laura, 'Enough About You, Let's Talk About Me: Recent Autobiographical Writing', *New Formations*, 1 (Spring 1987).

Marcus, Stephen, *The Other Victorians: A Study of Sexuality and Pornography in Mid-Nineteenth Century England* (London: Meridian, 1977).

Mayhew, Henry, *London Labour and the London Poor*, 4 vols, with introduction by John D. Rosenberg (New York: Doiver Publications, 1968).

Meade, L. T., *A Sister of the Red Cross: A Tale of the South African War* (London: Thomas Nelson and Sons, 1901).

Meade, L. T., *Polly: A New-Fashioned Girl* (London: Cassell and Co., Ltd, 1889).

Meade, L. T., *The Rebellion of Lil Carrington* (London: Cassell and Co., Ltd, 1898).

Mearns, Andrew, *The Bitter Cry of Outcast London* (Leicester: Leicester University Press, 1970; repr. of 1883 original).

Michie, Helena, *The Flesh Made Word: Female Figures and Women's Bodies* (Oxford: Oxford University Press, 1987).

Miller, Nancy K., *Getting Personal: Feminist Occasions and Other Autobiographical Acts* (London: Routledge, 1991).

Moers, Ellen, *Literary Women* (London: The Women's Press, 1978).

Morgan, Susan, *Sisters in Time: Imagining Gender in Nineteenth-Century British Fiction* (Oxford: Oxford University Press, 1989).

Morris, Virginia, *Double Jeopardy: Women Who Kill in Victorian Fiction* (Kentucky: The University Press of Kentucky, 1990).

Mulvey, Laura, *Visual and Other Pleasures* (London: Macmillan, 1989).

Mulvey, Laura, 'Visual Pleasures and Narrative Cinema', *Screen*, 16, 3 (1975).

Munroe, John M., *The Decadent Poetry of the 1890s* (Beirut: American University of Beirut Press, 1970).

Murphy, Ann B., 'The Borders of Ethical, Erotic and Artistic Possibilities in *Little Women*', *Signs*, 15, 3 (Spring 1990).

Nead, Lynda, *Myths of Sexuality: Representations of Women in Victorian Britain* (Oxford: Basil Blackwell, 1988).

Newton, Judith L., Ryan, Mary P. and Walkowitz, Judith R. (eds), *Sex and Class in Women's History* (London: Routledge and Kegan Paul Ltd, 1983).

Nightingale, Florence, 'Cassandra', in Ray Strachey, *The Cause: A Short History of the Women's Movement in Great Britain* (London: Virago, 1978).

Oliphant, Mrs, 'Chronicles of Carlingford: Salem Chapel', *Blackwood's Edinburgh Magazine*, LXXXXI–LXXXXIII (1862–1863).

[Oliphant, Mrs], 'Novels', *Blackwood's Magazine*, CII (11 September 1867).

Olney, James (ed.), *Autobiography: Essays Theoretical and Critical* (Princeton: Princeton University Press, 1980).

O'Neill, Philip, *Wilkie Collins: Women, Property & Propriety* (London: Macmillan, 1988).

'Our Female Sensation Novelists' (Anon.), *Living Age* LXXVIII (22 August 1863).

Paget, Francis, *Lucretia; or the Heroine of the Nineteenth Century* (London, 1868).

Pascal, Roy, *Design and Truth in Autobiography* (Cambridge, Mass.: Harvard University Press, 1960).

'Past and Present Heroines of Fiction' (Anon.), *The Saturday Review* (28 July 1883).

Pater, Walter, *The Renaissance: Studies in Art and Religion*, first published 1873 (London: Collins, 1961).

Pearce, Lynne, *Woman, Image, Text: Readings in Pre-Raphaelite Art and Literature* (Hemel Hempstead: Harvester Wheatsheaf, 1991)

Pearsall, Ronald, *The Worm in the Bud: The World of Victorian Sexuality* (Harmondsworth: Penguin Books, 1983).

Petrie, Glen, *A Singular Iniquity: The Campaigns of Josephine Butler* (London: Macmillan, 1971).

Phillips, Walter, *Dickens, Reade and Collins: Sensation Novelists* (New York: Russell & Russell, 1962).

Pierrot, Jean, *The Decadent Imagination 1880–1900* (London: University of Chicago Press, 1981).

Pinchbeck, Ivy and Hewitt, Margaret, *Children in English Society*, vol. II (London: Routledge and Kegan Paul, Ltd, 1973).

Pollock, Griselda, *Vision and Difference: Femininity, Feminism and the History of Art* (London: Routledge, 1988).

Prickett, Stephen, *Victorian Fantasy* (Brighton: Harvester, 1979).

Radcliffe, Mrs, *The Mysteries of Udolpho*, first published 1794 (London: Oxford University Press, 1980).

Reade, Charles, 'Charles Reade's Opinions of Himself and His Opinion of George Eliot', (Anon.), *Bookmen*, XVIII (November 1903).

Reade, Charles, *Griffith Gaunt*, first published 1866 (Boston, Mass. and New York: Colonial Press, 1895).

Reade, Charles, *Hard Cash*, first published 1863 (Boston, Mass. and New York: Colonial Press, 1895).

Reed, John R., *Victorian Conventions* (Ohio: Ohio University Press, 1975).

Reynolds, Kimberley, *Girls Only? Gender and Popular Children's Fiction in Britain, 1880–1910* (Hemel Hempstead: Harvester Wheatsheaf, 1990).

Rose, Jacqueline, *The Case of Peter Pan or the Impossibility of Children's Fiction* (London: Macmillan, 1984).

Rousseau, Jean-Jacques, *Confessions*, first published 1788, trans. J. M. Cohen (Harmondsworth: Penguin, 1953).

Showalter, Elaine, *A Literature of Their Own: British Women Novelists from Brontë to Lessing* (London: Virago, 1977).

Showalter, Elaine, *Alternative Alcott: Louisa May Alcott* (New Brunswick: Rutgers University Press, 1988).

Showalter, Elaine, *Sexual Anarchy: Gender and Culture at the Fin-de-Siècle* (London: Bloomsbury, 1991).

Showalter, Elaine, *The Female Malady: Women, Madness, and English Culture 1830–1980* (London: Virago, 1987).

Sigsworth, E. M. and Wyke, T. J., 'A Study of Victorian Prostitution and Venereal Disease', in Martha Vicinus (ed.), *Suffer and Be Still* (London: Indiana University Press, 1973).

Simons, Judy, *Diaries and Journals of Literary Women from Fanny Burney to Virginia Woolf* (London: Macmillan, 1990).

Spacks, Patricia Meyer, 'Reflecting Women', *Yale Review*, 63 (1973).

Spacks, Patricia Meyer, *The Female Imagination* (New York: Knopf, 1972).

Spacks, Patricia Meyer, 'Women's Stories, Women's Selves', *Hudson Review*, 30 (1977).

Stanton, Donna C., *The Female Autograph: Theory and Practice of Autobiography from the Tenth Century to the Twentieth Century* (Chicago: University of Chicago Press, 1987).

Stanford, Derek (ed.), *Writing of the 'Nineties* (London: J. M. Dent, 1971).

Stanley, Liz (ed.), *The Diaries of Hannah Cullwick, Victorian Maidservant* (London: Virago, 1984).

Steedman, Carolyn, *Landscape for a Good Woman* (London: Virago, 1986).

Steegman, John, *The Consort of Taste* (London: Sidgwick and Jackson, 1950).

Stretton, Hesba, *Little Meg's Children*, first published 1868, and *Alone in London*, first published 1869 (London: Religious Tract Society).

Stubbs, Patricia, *Women and Fiction: Feminism and the Novel 1880–1920* (Brighton: Harvester, 1979).

Tennyson, Alfred Lord, 'The Princess' in *Poems of Tennyson* (Oxford: Oxford University Press, 1911).

Terry, R. C., *Victorian Popular Fiction, 1860–80* (London: Macmillan, 1983).

Thackeray, William, *Vanity Fair*, first published 1847–8 (Harmondsworth: Penguin Books, 1985).

The Age of Neoclassicism, catalogue to exhibition (London: Arts Council of Great Britain, 1972).

Thomson, Patricia, *The Victorian Heroine: A Changing Ideal, 1837–1873* (London: Oxford University Press, 1956).

Thornton, R. K. R., 'Decadence in Later-Nineteenth Century England', in Ian Fletcher (ed.), *Decadence and the 1890s* (London: Edward Arnold, 1979).

Thornton, R. K. R., *The Decadent Dilemma* (London: Edward Arnold, 1983).

Trodd, Anthea, *Domestic Crime in the Victorian Novel* (London: Macmillan, 1989).

Vicinus, Martha, 'Sexuality and Power: A Review of Current Work in the History of Sexuality', *Feminist Studies*, 8, (1982), pp. 133–56.

Vicinus, Martha (ed.), *Suffer and Be Still: Women in the Victorian Age* (London: Indiana University Press, 1973).

Victorian High Renaissance, catalogue to exhibition (Minneapolis: Minneapolis Institute of Fine Arts, 1979).

Walkowitz, Judith, Prostitution and Victorian Society: Women, Class, and the State (Cambridge: Cambridge University Press, 1980).

Wall, Stephen (ed.), *Charles Dickens: A Critical Anthology* (Harmondsworth: Penguin Books, 1970).

Watt, George, *The Fallen Woman in the Nineteenth Century English Novel* (London: Croom Helm, 1984).

Weeks, Jeffrey, *Sex, Politics, and Society: The Regulation of Sexuality Since 1800* (London: Longman Group, 1981).

White, Allon, 'Bakhtin' in the series of Modern European Mind lectures, University of Sussex, 1983; 1985.

Williams, D. A., *The Monster in the Mirror: Studies in Nineteenth-Century Realism* (Oxford: Oxford University Press, 1978).

Williams, Merryn, *Women in the English Novel 1800–1900* (London: Macmillan, 1985).

Wilson, Elizabeth, 'Tell It Like It Is: Women and Confessional Writing', in Susannah Radstone (ed.), *Sweet Dreams: Sexuality, Gender and Popular Fiction* (London: Lawrence and Wishart, 1988).

Wood, Christopher, *Olympian Dreamers: Victorian Classical Painters 1860–1914* (London: Constable, 1983).

Wood, Christopher, *Victorian Panorama: Paintings of Victorian Life* (London: Faber, 1976).

Wood, Mrs Henry, *East Lynne*, first published 1861 (London: Dent, 1984).

Wood, Mrs Henry, *Verner's Pride* (London: Bentley, 1888).

Woolf, Virginia, *A Room of One's Own*, first published 1929 (London: Grafton Books, 1977).

Woolf, Virginia, *Orlando*, first published 1928, ed. Rachel Bowlby (Oxford University Press, 1992).

Yonge, Charlotte Mary, *Womankind* (London: Walter Smith, 1881).

Index